Projecting Urbanity

Projecting Urbanity

Architecture for and against the City

 Artifice

Table of Contents

6	1	*David Leatherbarrow* **Introduction** Architecture at the Threshold of Urbanity
32	2	*Tonkao Panin* **Within and Beyond Architectural Boundaries** Sitte and Wagner
60	3	*Esra Şahin Burat* **City as Compass and Calendar** Le Corbusier's Radiant City and the Apartment Building 24NC
92	4	*Juan Manuel Heredia* **Urban Topography and the Workers' City** Juan O'Gorman's Labor-Union Architecture for Mexico
118	5	*Daphna Half* **Assembling Differences** Tel Aviv Culture Complex by D. Karmi, Z. Rechter, Y. Rechter, and A. Karavan
148	6	*Stephen Anderson* **Of Architecture, Its Artifacts, and the City** Sverre Fehn's Norwegian Pavilion and the Structure of Urbanity
170	7	*Jin Baek* **The Terrain of Urban Institutions** H-Sang Seung's Gudeok Presbyterian Church
192	8	*David Leatherbarrow* **Architectural Depth as Urban Communication** Skirkanich Hall by Tod Williams Billie Tsien Architects
210	9	*Joseph Rykwert* **Conclusion** Projecting Urbanity
212		**Biographies**
214		**List of illustrations**
223		**Acknowledgments**

1

David Leatherbarrow

Introduction

Architecture at the Threshold of Urbanity

> The threshold is not… another thing with respect to the limit; it is, so to speak, the experience of the limit itself, the experience of being-*within* an *outside*. This *ek-stasis* is the gift that singularity gathers from the empty hands of humanity.
>
> —Giorgio Agamben, *The Coming Community*.[1]

Figure 1.1 | Robert Rauschenberg, *Watermark*, 1973.

[1] Agamben, Giorgio, *The Coming Community*, Michael Hardt trans., Minneapolis, MN: University of Minnesota Press, 1993, p. 67.

Introduction

The studies in modern architecture that make up this book describe and interpret the many and varied relationships between single works and their urban surroundings. A basic premise is that the increasingly rapid growth and morphological change of cities during the 20th and 21st centuries have required architects to reconceptualize one of their key tasks, imagining how a single work can have a projective role in urban transformation. Fitting in was not the issue—had it ever been?—for the so-called context was continually changing and polymorphic. Why conform to arrangements that will be gone tomorrow? Nor was free-standing independence the aim or concern, for dependencies always exist, even if autonomy in conception is believed to be necessary. Urbanity wasn't so much given to modern architecture as the condition it projected. An indicative location of architectural projection was what I describe in these introductory pages as the urban threshold, though that wasn't a term used by this book's protagonists. The account I'll provide will couple my understanding of thresholds with evidence from historical examples. I'll note along the way where the several topics I address are developed in the chapters that follow.

Among the many elements of architecture that articulate a work's place in the constructed climates we call cities, both thresholds and apertures play a unique role, in a sense, tragic. They break through the boundaries that define it, undoing all the great work the building's outer walls have done to secure spaces that want to exist on their own, apart from but in the midst of others with the same desire. Why put rooms and the object's separate standing at risk? The chief aim, I believe, is to give the work a communicative voice,[2] a way of entering the conversations that others are having—their agreements and disagreements about the roles they play in the vicinity—and of acting on the several stages of contemporary culture.[3]

I've introduced the word articulation with current usage in mind, but also with an eye on its Latin stem, *articulare*, which refers to processes of separation and joining, as in cutting meat into joints or pronouncing words distinctly, to form intelligible phrases and sentences. Opposite processes have opposite results, unarticulated or unstructured bodies in the first case and inarticulate or unclear expressions in the second. Interestingly, architectural works constructed without windows and doors that intend expression, most tombs for example, compensate for their absence with non-spatial and a-tectonic means, writing on walls or some other form of signposting. Thresholds and apertures, by contrast, are communicative even though they aren't associated with writing. A good comparison is with the expressions and speech habits that sustain oral cultures, as well as gestural forms of communication in cultures that have been deeply affected by the use of writing. The wonder is that spatial articulations at a building's limits restructure the contextual reciprocities that set the stage for the work itself, though in time and by implication primarily.

---

[2] The topic of architecture's communicative role is also addressed in Joseph Rykwert's Conclusion to this book, see Chapter 9.

[3] This study has benefited greatly from the account of "communicative space" in Vesely, Dalibor, *Architecture in the Age of Divided Representation*, Cambridge, MA: MIT Press, 2005.

What reciprocities? In urban architecture, boundaries are where insides meet outsides, buildings meet streets, and works of architecture meet those of urban design and city planning. Were there no limits, both sets of phenomena would lack definition. The result of that would be architecture everywhere and nowhere, not something one desires, and the opposite of what is studied in this book.

The last of the boundaries I've just listed, the one that hints at the definition of disciplines, would seem to distinguish designs for single projects from plans for more than a few. But that distinction, numerical in essence, is far too simple—simply wrong—for it is no less obvious that the design of buildings must take account of conditions outside the work itself, while plans for urban areas always use buildings as their construction materials (together with open spaces, infrastructure, and so on). In broad terms, these are the reciprocities I mentioned. What kinds of external conditions enter into the make-up of single works? There are many. Some are material, others are matters of principle. With respect to the latter, architectural design must take account of urban legislation, for example, laws that intend the common good. But laws retain relevance through revisions (or amendments), one after another, that address unprecedented problems of single cases, or, in architecture, individual works.

Although little misunderstanding results from speaking of a boundary or limit as a single thing, it is when built always two-sided and to all appearances two-part. When insides meet outsides the encounter isn't all that friendly. Standing back-to-back, one side seems wholly preoccupied with the rooms or settings it faces, while the other busies itself with the sidewalk and street, wind and sun, your interest and mine. Though equally insouciant, the two sides are inseparable. Mutuality is in effect when both play their parts in tectonic functions, each in its own way meeting the need to cover and protect the enclosed settings and keep the work standing as it is, ready for use.

Thus defined—two-faced but reliable—the limit's carefully constructed achievements are, as I've said, undone by an equally consequential element in urban architecture, the threshold. Self-defeating though the design practice may seem, boundaries in urban architecture are made to suffer breakthroughs as soon as they've been laid out, as if space were enclosed only to be opened. Boundaries tend toward linearity, thresholds expansion. Doors are typically found in there, but the real key is the doorway, the place of passage. Compared to the boundaries they cut, these places are ample in their depths and projections. Because they enjoy getting caught up in the wide dilations of the what's in front of and within the work, they are in principle unbounded, but not for that reason formless. The work's surroundings, I've said, are a constructed climate, in whose structures and seasons they participate. A threshold's near-side reach encounters limits within the interior configuration, and its far-side projection is absorbed into the still greater spread of the urban and natural surroundings.

Introduction

What, then, can be said about the threshold's limits? How are they defined, particularly in the craft of architectural design? Of course they're edged in the side-to-side direction by the endpoints that mark the break in the perimeter, traditionally framed in one way or another with door- or gate-posts, window casings, jambs, and so on. But the real question is about the limits in the opposite direction, passage inward toward the rooms, hall, or stair, or outward to the sidewalk, terrace, street, or park. Axial configurations make the prolongations obvious, but they also exist in other layout types: through the space under a cantilevered projection, across the parallel terrace, down the steps onto and along the sidewalk, and so on. In reverse, the space of the threshold prolongs itself into the lobby's full depth, past the reception desk on one side and elevators on the other, into the central court, and then through the doors to the main hall, and still further. Therefore, one shouldn't say thresholds, like walls, are two-sided, intra- and extramural, for they bypass that distinction. It would be better to described them as topographical, one of its articulations.

Perhaps a painting by Robert Rauschenberg, *Watermark* (1973), will serve as a preliminary indication of this type of configuration. Watermarks on paper remain, no matter what comes to be written on the page. **Figure 1.1 (see p. 6)** Rauschenberg addresses the matter of permanence paradoxically, through images of movement, change, or passage. First, there is the curtain that's been moved to the left side of what I take to be a red lintel, the right end of which caps a fragment of clapboard cladding and a window frame's shadow. One imagines the fabric is warm to the touch, possibly domestic, but here used theatrically, a one-sided *coulisse*, within which additional emblems of movement appear, a car tire at the center, and a racehorse in the right corner. Also on the right is a reproduction of Botticelli's *Primavera*, with the dancing graces of course, the seasons, and much more. Memorable to him, us too, the painting within the painting is approximately monumental, in the cultural not architectural sense, as if to say change is permanent, which is also what thresholds maintain. Most prominent, however, are the crowds, moving independently, but taped onto and into the same terrain. Aggregated not arranged, probably audible, they advance toward the comparatively quiet enclosure we occupy, on the nearside of the curtain. That's not all that bypasses the interior's limit, there's also the shadowless gray-blue sky that passes from the painting's upper limit to its base, through places we tend to think of as separate.

With this compressed topography before us, how are we to understand and describe a place, the threshold, that is neither within the enclosure, huddled up and kept secure, nor outside it, free-ranging and wind-swept? What can be said about the place *between* those two, breathing the second for the animation of the first? More particularly, how can such a place be made, without apparent limits in the cardinal (pivotal or hinge) direction?

Figure 1.2 | North Broad, Philadelphia, c. 2010.

Figure 1.3 | Ambrogio Lorenzetti, *Effects of Good Government in the City* (left) and *Effects of Good Government in the Country* (right), Siena, 1338–9; detail.

4 Already at the beginning of the 20th century the terrain of city margins had become ambiguous; see, for example Tonkao Panin's discussion of developments in turn-of-the-century Vienna, in Chapter 2.

5 Un-enclosing enclosure is tantamount to disclosure, in the sense of opening up to view or revealing, as I will explain below. On the ample literature in architecture and urban theory addressing what has since the 1990s come to be called *terrain vague*, see most recently Mariani, Manuela and Patrick Barrons, eds., *Terrain Vague Interstices at the Edge of the Pale*, New York: Routledge, 2013. A French film from the 1960s used the term for its title, but it gained currency in architecture and urbanism following a widely read essay of Ignasi de Sola-Morales. The interdependency of city and countryside is also addressed in many studies; on Siena, illustrated here, see, for example: Frugoni, Chiara, *A Distant City*, Princeton, NJ: Princeton University Press, 1991, 158ff and Braunfels, Wolfgang, *Mittelalterliche Stadtbaukunst in der Toskana*, Berlin: Gerbrüder Mann, 1988, pp. 20–6.

6 Van Eyck, Aldo, "Is Architecture Going to Reconcile Basic Values," first published 1959, *Collected Articles and Other Writings 1947–1998*, Amsterdam: Sun, 2008, p. 204.

7 A setting's capacity to receive "gifts" is elaborated by Esra Şahin Burat in her account of Le Corbusier's private apartment; see Chapter 3, pp. 68–9.

Agamben, in the epigraph above, sidesteps the designer's question by shifting from geometry to experience: the threshold is experienced as "being-*within* an *outside*." In this situation, the varying depth of which, I've said, always exceeds the thickness of a plot line, enclosed space both un-encloses itself and plays its part in another enclosure, the latter different in kind because it extends rather more indefinitely,[4] into what these days has come to be called *terrain vague*, an obvious characteristic of our continually expanding cities, but also, in an admittedly different sense, of traditional, compact cities, in which the urban core and extramural surrounds (*città* and *contado*) were interdependent, with the latter extending through and beyond cultivated fields, rivers, and mountains, into territories that were probably less vague than their modern counterparts, but were likewise without apparent ends.[5] The topic is obviously decisive in design but has broader implications. The philosopher suggests that what is at stake at the threshold is an individual's encounter with nothing less than humanity. **Figures 1.2 and 1.3**

Though I doubt Agamben was aware of a precedent for his thesis in modern architectural theory, Aldo van Eyck said much the same thing six decades earlier in a CIAM (Congrès Internationaux d'Architecture Moderne) lecture that addressed the experience of border crossing in buildings: "To establish 'the inbetween' is to reconcile conflicting polarities. Provide the place where they can interchange and you re-establish the original dual phenomena… Get what I mean: two worlds clashing, no transition. The individual on one side, the collective on the other."[6] Several interpretations of this "interchange" are examined in this book's studies in urban architecture, as established between all manner of "conflicting polarities," spatial and social, historical, and environmental.

In his several elaborations on the theme, Van Eyck may have overstated the symmetry of the situation with terms like "reciprocity," "twin," or "dual" phenomena, in a desire for equilibrium in cities and social life. If both in- and outside can be described as worlds, as he suggests, it might be better to see them as different in kind, the first locally enclosed, the second extended without perceptible limit, as I've said. I'm not against the better balance he envisaged but prefer the implied asymmetry of Agamben's *ek-static* doorway, where enclosed space opens its edge in order to accept or refuse whatever gifts come to pass, and thereby expose itself as wanting, while offering its own necessarily limited contributions.[7] Humanity's empty-handed donations—a corporate gesture rather than an object—commonly called given conditions in architecture, are not only welcomed but required by the individual work, even if those conditions make their own demands on it—legal demands, I've said, but also environmental forces, and others, more broadly cultural. Again, more than receiving happens at thresholds, also giving. On this point, Van Eyck was surely right. But implied in receptivity is something

Introduction

Figure 1.5 | Hand doorknocker, Tavira, Portugal, nd.

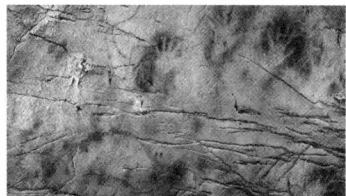

Figure 1.6 | Cave of Altamira Give, Santillana del Mar, Cantabria, Spain, 34,000 BC.

designers and owners tend to overlook or disavow, the enclosure's insufficiency or want of completeness, which is another theme this book's studies variously explore.[8] **Figure 1.4 (see p. 25)**

Humanity's empty hands at the doorway, a puzzling image, may point us toward an understanding of what architecture gives. Apart from being hard to understand—what gift can be given with empty hands?—the image may also seem ironic, perhaps tragic, unless one understands it as a readiness to receive. Humanity's hands aren't always full of resources, sometimes they're open to what a person or building has to give, or in the terms of design practice, what the work is able to project, involvement. At thresholds in Portuguese and Brazilian urban vernacular architecture one is commonly greeted by a hand-shaped door knocker, a welcoming and quietly communicative gesture, hand-to-hand, only graspable if the visitor's hand is empty. **Figure 1.5**

I understand the philosopher to have had human association in mind with his last phrase, insofar as hand gestures intend communication, thus social situations, together with their durable traces and prompts in cities and their architecture. The advent of association is certainly what Agamben's title, *The Coming Community*, encouragingly suggests, though he gives no assurances, still less a schedule, maybe just hope rendered apparent in thresholds thus defined. One must take care when interpreting hand gestures, for their meanings are no less nuanced than their movements are varied. And they can be equivocal. Yet, an empty or open hand is still a hand and never non-expressive, the most powerful if enigmatic traces of which may be those that inaugurated human art as we know it, the palm prints discovered in prehistoric caves, outlined on walls and low ceilings with blown or splashed pigment and called for that reason "negative." **Figure 1.6**

Though ambiguous today, they are thought to have been communicative, especially those with bent (not mutilated) fingers—more than a few in Altamira, Lascaux and Chauvet—understood by modern palaeontologists to be silent signs from one hunter to another. Tilted upwards, palms outward, they might say stop or enough; downwards they may ask what or why.[9]

To take the next step in my introduction of topics at issue in the urban architecture studied on these pages, I'd like to describe a not-so-well-known early modern example of equivalent articulation at an urban edge, a threshold that is both communicative and, like all good architecture, meant to be silently understood. My example is from the late 19th century, the period that early modern architecture sought to surpass, despite the cultural continuities it also relied upon.

An Urban Threshold

James Tissot's *Shop Girl* (c. 1885) shows that enclosures that are amply provisioned only come to life when they open themselves to street-side contributions that don't exactly promise, only propose, a public realm. We see several players on the stage: an urbane gentleman whose hat-shaded look seems to have solicited a shop-

---

[8] Both Leon Battista Alberti and Adolf Loos—two architects not studied at length in these pages—addressed *completeness* in their writings, the first positively, insofar as it characterized beautiful buildings ("nothing to be added or taken away") and the second negatively, as it was equivalent to finality ("now I know what it is like to go about one's life as a corpse").

[9] A gift could also be imagined. Isidore of Seville coupled *manus* (hand) with *munus* (gift): *Etymologies*, xi.1.61. On this topic more fully see: Barasch, Moshe, *Gestures of Despair*, New York: New York University Press, 1976. Le Corbusier's famous "open hand" is different yet again, more like Van Eyck's doorstep, an emblem of giving and receiving. See: Wogensky, André, *Le Corbusier's Hands*, Cambridge, MA: MIT Press, 2006. Two artists whose images of hands have occupied my attention are Rodin and Leonardo.

worker's awning-sheltered reply; a slightly more distant figure whose bonnet already displays a pricey bow, though her inclination suggests she fancies another; a street porter, nearly hidden by the window frame, waiting patiently (impatiently?) for the next arrival, beyond which a horse-drawn carriage has just entered the scene, while other shops across the street accommodate their business, and so on. The threshold opportunities we see from inside gather interest from some, not all outsiders who no doubt have their own concerns, which collectively contribute to the fund of possible communications. Though full of itself, the interior spends its days waiting and wanting. **Figures 1.7 (see p. 26) and 1.8 (see p. 27)**

Tissot's depiction is unique, but the situation it portrays had countless other articulations, each representing what might be called a cultural norm, lived and legible as a dimension of urbanity. One figure we don't see—it could be you, me, or anyone—is about to re-enter the street scene. Most on the outside, however, pass by, disinterested in what the interior has to offer, though they might take advantage of its external provisions, the awning of course, but also—let's imagine—the recessed entry when a cold wind blows, the shoveled walk after a snow, the mirroring glass, and so on. On the inside, there are also the unseen "donations" that play their parts: city water piped to a rear washroom sink we can easily imagine, also electricity or gas to the heating equipment and lights that enable afternoon and evening commerce, alley-access deliveries through the block interior to a service door, and so on. Without these and other gifts from the encompassing world, visible or not, from the street to the backyard, under the clouds but above the infrastructure, the shop Tissot portrays wouldn't be worth a visit, probably wouldn't even be there.

With this admittedly prosaic image of urban architecture in mind, freed, if possible, from its tokens of bourgeoise aspiration, I'd like to amplify my initial description of the thesis explored by the studies in this book: that built works are incomplete or wanting by definition, which is to say, not despite architectural intentions, nor through any fault in conception or execution, but by design. Why this proposition? Why stress deficiency and negativity when we know that rooms and buildings, especially well-designed ones, have so much to show and say? The projects examined in these chapters demonstrate that a work's partiality is a key factor in the emergence of urban reality, not only on the streets of Paris, but in cities throughout the world (in this book, Vienna, Mexico City, Tel Aviv, Brussels, Busan, and Philadelphia), from the early years of the 20th century (a couple of decades after Tissot composed this image) to the present.

The other edge-crossing element I mentioned, the window, may make the built work's incompleteness and outward reach clearer. In his celebrated study on bridges and doors from 1909, Georg Simmel gave the window less significance than the entry threshold because the passages it allows don't include a walk-through.[10] Obviously the comings and goings that windows permit

---

10 Simmel, Georg, "Bridge and Door," *Simmel on Culture*, David Frisby and Mike Featherstone eds., London: Sage, 1997, p. 173. Recently Agamben questioned what he describes as Simmel's mistaken conflation of the (panel) door and doorway (place of passage): Agamben, Giorgio, "Door and Threshold," *When the House Burns Down*, London: Seagull Books, 2022, p. 19.

Introduction

Figure 1.9 | Window onto the Campo, Siena, c. 1980.

are abbreviated when compared to doorway crossings (window walls and doors, like Tissot's, are special cases). But Simmel seems to have neglected something positive in the more limited place of passage: that windows plainly express what enclosed spaces require to make life on the inside what their occupants desire it to be, while showing the size and shape of their needs. It is not the desire that is necessarily positive, but the expression, insofar as it can indicate the unique requirements of the bedroom, dining room, or work room. Countless window paintings and photographs from past decades and centuries in cities throughout the world show personal and spatial longings that reveal what the setting needs from the outside to complete itself: fresh air, daylight, ample or elevated prospects, of course, but much, much more.[11] None of these in a general sense; rather, unfiltered light from the north in a painter's studio, for example, equally direct rays from the south in a workshop, ambient or indirect light in a reading room, clerestory light in a courtroom, and so on. Likewise, for air and views, in each case modulated to specific, if typified requirements, or, as Louis Kahn said, desires. Among the many poets who observed elbows resting on windowsills, Rainer Maria Rilke was impressively concise:

> She was in window mood that day:
> to live seemed no more than to stare.
> From a dizzy non-existence she could see
> a world coming to her completing heart.[12]

Like Van Eyck, he witnessed a meeting of worlds (in the completing heart), though here craving, not conflict, enlivens the correspondence. Nearside deficiency is also there, a "dizzy non-existence" (*d'inexistence ivre*) on the inside. Every building owes its identity half to its interiors and inhabitants, and half to the sky and street, and all that they embody and represent, arbitrated through apertures—rather like the law, I've said, architectural openings permit and forbid—according to the daily and seasonal cycles of everyday praxis and cultural experience. Again to repeat, an enclosure with neither openings nor needs is basically a tomb. Windows cut into walls, then, attest to the work's want of conditions it cannot supply on its own without which life on the inside would be terribly poor. Nor would we want these cuts to heal over. Because poverty of this kind is inescapable in architecture, it is also work-defining.[13] **Figure 1.9**

The words private and deprived are siblings.[14] Their extended family includes privilege and proper. These words, together with their offspring, express ideas and experiences of being on one's own. What might be the deprivation of private life and its spaces? In the middle of the 15th century, when the word deprived gained currency, it meant removed from office, rank, or position, which is to say de-vested or robbed of livelihood and the corresponding opportunities for commerce with others, ranging from professional collaborations to the many forms of political assembly in their

---

11 See: Delehanty, Suzanne, *The Window in Twentieth-Century Art*, Purchase, NY: Neuberger Museum, 1986; Gottlieb, Clara, *The Window in Art: From the Window of God to the Vanity of Man*, Norwalk, CT: Abaris, 1978, and the several essays on apertures in "Between Inside and Outside," *Daidalos Berlin Architectural Journal*, no. 13, September 15, 1984.

12 Rilke, Rainer Maria, "She Was in a Window Mood That Day", written 1924, "Window Poems XIII," *The Complete French Poems of Rainer Maria Rilke*, A. Poulin trans., Saint Paul, MN: Gray Wolf Press, 1979, p. 41. Emily Dickinson described the reciprocal desire: "Hunger is the way of people outside windows that entering takes away."

13 Putting poverty on show is, of course, a commonplace in several key chapters in architectural history, in those that tell the story of both western and eastern monasteries, for example. Cistercian architecture is a good case in point. See the discussion in Chapter 5 especially of Leatherbarrow, David and Richard Wesley, *Three Cultural Ecologies*, London: Routledge, 2018, pp. 101–14. See also: Aureli, Pier Vittorio, *Less is Enough*, Moscow: Strelka Press, 2013, and Agamben, Giorgio, *The Highest Poverty*, Stanford, CA: Stanford University Press, 2013.

14 Arendt, Hannah, *The Human Condition*, Chicago, IL: University of Chicago Press, 1958, p. 38.

various settings. With respect to some of these opportunities, today we might think that deprivations aren't so bad, or not always. It is not only agoraphobics that feel more time at home can be preferable. When social encounters or environmental conditions are expected to be disagreeable, in times of a public health crisis, for example, deprivation may feel like deliverance. Pascal famously coupled staying at home with happiness.[15] The preference became particularly strong in the modern period. Hannah Arendt observed that, "We no longer think primarily of deprivation when we use the word 'privacy'... [partly because of] the enormous enrichment of the private sphere through modern individualism."[16] A-political life was not, of course, something she endorsed, just the reverse. Her brief etymological note of the origins of the word idiocy (*idios* meant private or personal) made her thinking perfectly clear. Life on the private side of the inside-outside edge lacks what the street promises, for better or worse.

Figure 1.10 (see p. 28)

Because the chapters in this book endeavor to show the ways that some of the better examples of modern architecture have transcended their local concerns into the potentials of the urban environment, projecting urbanity I will say, the individual work's singularity requires a little more attention, particularly how a building's inborn need for involvement and gathering gifts from humanity's empty hands becomes apparent when what the urban environment had offered—places of shared interest, reciprocal action, non-violent conflict, and communication—are no longer given. Reciprocity seems to be what Tissot was wondering about. For many today, that wonder has become a worry. And the unease isn't recent. More than four decades ago, Richard Sennett published *The Fall of Public Man*. The problems he diagnosed, long in the making, have not gone away. A working premise of what I'll argue is that projects cannot progress in the absence of given conditions, even when they seem empty-handed, as they do so very often today.

But first, I'd like to note that although the reality of the current situation has its ironic dimensions, what modern and contemporary architects and their clients share most commonly is their commitment to the work's distinct individuality. When assumed to be the subject matter of architectural representation, authorship and ownership commonly subordinate purpose and place. Whatever one's views about this ranking, the accent on uniqueness or what is today often called "identity" is widely evident and impossible to ignore. Although the aim of this book is to discover and describe real potentials for shared sense within unenclosed spaces, it would be naive to pursue an inquiry into urban architecture without giving focused attention to the single work. Despite her great concern for the (public) "space of appearance," Hannah Arendt never renounced her commitment to singularity.[17] How that dimension of urban living arises, however, remains an open question.[18] Hence this book's focus on urban architecture, not infrastructure, neighborhoods, or entire settlements.

---

[15] Pascal, Blaise, *Pensées*, New York: Modern Library, 1941, p. 169: "When I have occasionally set myself to consider the different distractions of me, the pains and perils to which they expose themselves at court or in war, whence arise so many quarrels, passions, bold, and often bad ventures, etc, I have discovered that all the unhappiness of men arises from one single fact, that they cannot stay quietly in their own chamber."

[16] Arendt, *The Human Condition*, p. 38.

[17] Reiner Schürmann, in the Introduction to his collection of Arendt-inspired essays, describes her understanding that the singular was "*unhintergehbar*, impossible to subsume." See *The Public Realm: Essays on Discursive Types in Political Philosophy*, Reiner Schürmann ed., Albany, NY: State University of New York Press, 1989, p. 18.

[18] In architecture, the topic is introduced, but sketched only briefly in: Baudrillard, Jean and Jean Nouvel, *The Singular Objects of Architecture*, Minneapolis, MN: University of Minnesota Press, 2002.

Negative Potential[19]

The terrain of today's towns is not only often *vague*, it is frequently conflictual, and too often violent. One of the most striking consequences of the increasingly common hostility on city streets today is the resulting sense of shared suffering among its witnesses, after the fact. With no desire to condone malevolence, this observation suggests something potentially positive as its result: shared suffering among individuals who previously enjoyed neither kinship nor friendship. If the sharing not the suffering is thematized, the corresponding principle would be that one prompt for Agamben's "coming community" is force against some individual who would have been counted among its members. As I explore this a little further, I'll ask the reader to be patient with this indirect path toward urban potential, also my preliminary *via negativa*.

Force takes many forms in cities. The first division is between the behaviors of different individuals or groups and the powers at play in the environment, variously having their way without reason. Climate change seems to be intensifying the latter, and the reasons are becoming increasingly clear. The suffering someone I have in mind is no one special, anyone whomever who is no more or less distant to you or me than each of us is to countless others. In all cases, however, individual responses to whomever's suffering are urgently personal. Witnessing the event, or its consequences, each person silently says, "That could have been me." This leads to a second observation about urban violence and environmental force: everyone's sense of vulnerability is heightened by witnessing the other person's pain and suffering. Seeing what happened gives one a vivid sense of one's own exposure. One name for the place where citizens and buildings find themselves mutually exposed is the public realm.

The point this takes me toward is that singularity in our lives and our living spaces often finds its origin in sites of that kind. Individuality, I want to stress, is never an inherited condition or accomplished fact, it is always only a process, perforce incomplete, like every architectural project. Because we tend to privilege individuality and identity so very highly, we often think the reverse: that communicative space arises when individuals decide to come together. But an ancient and still persuasive premise, set down in the early days of democracy, maintains the opposite. "The state [the city-state] is by nature clearly prior to the family and to the individual, since *the whole is of necessity prior to the part*."[20] Below I'll say more about the interdependencies of wholes and parts, for they are key to architecture's projective role in urbanity. But for now, I want to observe that although each of us (and our buildings) has a singular voice—yours or mine is never the same as another's—speaking is always to someone else, in whose absence one generally stays silent.

Following what I've suggested about shared suffering and singularity, the third thesis I'd like to propose is perhaps even more challenging because it runs against the grain of current ideas

---

[19] When introducing this term, I have in the back of my mind John Keats' sense of "negative capability." In a famous letter to his brothers he wrote that the distinguishing characteristic of a figure like Shakespeare is: "Negative Capability, that is, when a man is capable of being in uncertainties, mysteries, doubts, without any irritable reaching after fact and reason..." See: Keats, John, *The Complete Poetical Works and Letters of John Keats*, Boston, MA: Houghton, Mifflin, 1899, p. 277.

[20] Aristotle, *Politics*, Book 1, 1253a, pp. 19-20, my italics.

Figure 1.11 | Uncontrolled burning, Detroit, nd.

Figure 1.12 | Controlled burning, Kansas, nd.

about identity and difference in both social life and architecture: newly discovered vulnerability ("it could have been me") includes a fresh understanding of mutuality, of oneself as another.[21] This is not an instance of empathy, for there is no "feeling the other's pain." Pain, when physical, is one thing individuals can never share; it is always one's own, rather like a voice, as I've described it.[22] But pain can be imagined. And it can be exposed, suggesting agency within vulnerability.[23] What's more, that sense of dependency can lead to recognition of interdependency, in architecture, this book argues, with streets and the wider environment, their explicit and implicit content, supplying not one but many buildings with what they lack and need, also with what they will choose to refuse. In architecture, a comparable sense of loss—loss of some dimension of urban reality in any of its forms, human or non-human, spatial or material—can lead to a corresponding realization of the support that works derive from something that no design can supply, the constructed climate's empty-handed donation.

In one of the scenes of a documentary film about the city of Detroit, *Burn* (2012),[24] an elderly woman asks a fireman if the raging blaze next door is likely to engulf her house. No direct reply is audible, only a sideways glance and an impatient hand gesture for her to move away, which sends her up the front porch steps, then indoors, presumably to collect the valuables she can carry, having realized that the fire's hunger won't be satisfied with what the adjoining house is serving up. Appetite suggests want. One imagines a comparable need may have quickened the evening's incendiary gestures, for "low-income" neighborhoods burned brightest, to everyone's amazement. The commonality of that attraction suggests that a discomforting contradiction cannot be avoided when speaking about a city's self-destruction: blazes that ruin also fascinate. Although it wasn't only wind-blown spray that wet the faces of the onlookers, they couldn't pull their eyes away. Compassion alternated with captivation. Fire can be concisely characterized by just this coupling; it injures and brings warmth. There are moral, approximately religious or mythical dimensions too; what spoils also purifies.[25] Again, these observations are not introduced in praise of Nero, or as an apology for something so devastating, only to indicate the duality, perhaps circularity of the topic. **Figures 1.11 and 1.12**

Agricultural fields are periodically set ablaze so that crops will later thrive. Controlled burning is also essential to the maintenance of a healthy forest. In remote antiquity, Cicero posited fire's role in the world's cyclical renewal. Centuries later, Paracelsus likewise accented its positive side; fire, he wrote, is an emblem of life. Closer to our field, Michelangelo saw it as an evidence of internal animation, hence his sense of the pyramidal (pyre-like) form of sculpture indicating how something as inert as stone could come to life.[26] Borromini's Oratory in Rome is decorated with hearts rimmed by flames. Despite the complementarity proposed by

---

21 A text by Paul Ricœur with this term as its title has been useful to me in formulating these comments: Ricœur, Paul, *Oneself as Another*, Chicago, IL: University of Chicago Press, 1992. I've read this book in dialogue with others that endeavor to indefinitely postpone reciprocity: Nancy, Jean-Luc, *Being Singular Plural*, Stanford, CA: Stanford University Press, 2000; Nancy, Jean-Luc, *The Inoperative Community*, Minneapolis, MN: Minnesota University Press, 1991, plus the text I cited at the outset, Agamben's *The Coming Community*.

22 A community can experience mental suffering—perhaps be generated by it—but physical pain is felt only by individuals. On this distinction, see: Buytendijk, F.J.J., "Personal Experience of Pain," *Pain*, London: Hutchinson, 1961, esp. pp. 1, ii.

23 See: Butler, Judith, *The Force of Non-Violence: an Ethico-Political Bind*, London: Verso Books, 2020, pp. 37–42. To exemplify her argument she cites the well-known and entirely persuasive cases of Martin Luther King, Jr. and Mahatma Gandhi.

24 *Burn*, directed by Brenna Sanchez and Tom Putnam, 2012.

25 On this last coupling, see: Douglas, Mary, *Purity and Danger: An Analysis of Concepts of Pollution and Taboo*, London: Routledge & Kegan Paul, 1966.

26 The thought here is that combustion combines opposites: earth and sky, or more locally wood and air.

these four and so many others, it is easier to see actual loss in Detroit more than potential gain, pain more than pleasure. But that positive potential, the renewal that could follow loss, is something to seek and expose because it can be seen to define, this book argues, the threshold of urban architecture.[27]

Strangers sometimes form communities when the loss they witness is not of a person or group, their freedoms or opportunities, but of something non-human, an animal or tree, for example, whose innocence can hardly be exceeded. Common suffering can also be felt when still other dimensions of the urban fabric are brought to an end, when air is polluted, or waters made to run dry. The latter miseries increasingly challenge contemporary cities. By extension, the same could be said for the loss of unclaimed spaces. Counter-intuitive though it may seem, communities and communicative spaces often find their origin in negation. This is to say, a sense of what exists no longer for something singular may be what is most decisive in the emergence of situations we think of as shared or properly urban. Proper here is the polar opposite of one of its cognate forms, property, and might be best thought of as what is improper, because of its sharp contrast to tacitly accepted norms. For this reason, institutions of commonality as inherited cannot be taken for granted as still-relevant. *Architecture for the city may be initially against it, particularly its atrophied forms.* Here, then, is my summary proposition: the experience and expression of lack and loss not only quicken communication and the formation of communicative space, they are often inaugural. This indirect proposition has a merit that is I think undeniable, it offers a sober approach to today's cities, where the loss of commonly desired goods is so plainly evident, while individuality and difference are valued so highly.

What Remains

After the embers of today's fires have died down, in Detroit and elsewhere, one's first thought is of recuperation, leading to restoration, rather like the reconstruction of Warsaw after the Second World War, which, one has to admit, was and remains impressive. Productive project-making is, nevertheless, something fundamentally different. The task of today's urban architecture, as it develops the premises of urbanity described in this book, is not the recovery or restoration of something that has been destroyed. Not only would that abbreviate understanding of what might well be better, but it could easily reinstitute the thinking that created the problems we now confront, which would double the disaster.

Let me, then, restate with sharper focus a question sketched out earlier: exactly what is it that's been lost or broken in today's cities and our lives within them? What urban condition typically sustains architecture's basic task of articulating/projecting communicative space?

Taking a long view, there would seem to be many losses. On the private end of the urban spectrum, one might say that we've lost

[27] For elaboration of this point, see Jin Baek's account of H-Sang Seung's Gudeok Presbyterian Church, Chapter 7, where the loss of home and town by refugees was formative in their sense of community.

Figure 1.13 | Abandoned house within cleared lots, Detroit, nd.

the bonding that is conventionally and conservatively associated with the so-called natural family, the one narrated in the Vitruvian myth of the origins of language, society, cities, and architecture. Likewise, there seems to be little evidence of the sense of common purpose that we assume existed among those who had a voice in the Greek polis. The same can be said for the proud citizenship that was thought to have existed among individuals in the Roman Republic, also the equality-before-God among members of a Christian community, as well as all the secular equivalents to that *ecclesia*—academic, artistic, or military communities, in colleges, colonies, and camps. Increasingly rare are bonds that are essentially organic, or experienced in intimate communications among members, resulting in equilibrium, sharing, and reciprocity among themselves, but a corresponding and dehumanizing exclusion of others.[28] Figure 1.13

As cities disintegrate, the individuality of buildings becomes increasingly apparent. Separate works are what we see when the urban fabric wears thin. Architectural objects are often the residue of urban dissolution. It is both ironic and unfortunate that the single work is commonly taken to be originary, when in fact it commonly results from the degradation and brutality I've characterized. Why then might the unique design be conceived in this way, as an original? Part of the story is surely the fact that the individual project is normally thought to result from the work of a single designer, whose creative role we'd rather not question.

But what if the whom- or whatever whose loss quickens communication has an analogue in the non-original, typical solution of a design topic, or more fundamentally in the typicality of a cultural pattern? Might this help us understand the advent of the singular work that both prompts and opens itself to urban potentials? This line of thinking would lead us to ask not only about what the work supplies but also what it lacks, not only its richness, also its poverty.[29] Just as loss of life can spark the formation of communities, the lack and work-defining requirements of built enclosures might be sufficiently combustible to ignite the emergence of communicative space or at least kindle a desire for it.

Again, this book's thesis: when openly exposed, lack and loss bring into view a desire for communication and sharing sense. To understand a work of architecture in this way means reversing our usual approach. We tend to think that commonality—more largely, urbanity—results from the engagements that follow the construction of a well-intentioned solution that has been fully worked out in its particularity and is thereby sovereign over the parts it organizes, prior to any voluntary associations. What if, instead, the real project, the reality of the project, is the realization of something singular by means of what is not? Singularity would then result from the *indetermination* of a basic idea into the powers and purposes of a place, responding to their conflicts and opportunities, as one work among others that have also opened themselves into what they lack, collective memory on

[28] In many instances, that rarity can be seen as positive or progressive. An especially useful critique of the idea of an "organic" community arising out of a politics and practice of exclusion was authored by a philosopher who suffered and then escaped the "communities" of national socialism: Plessner, Helmuth, *The Limits of Community*, Amherst, NY: Humanity Books, 1999.

[29] Opposed ideas of poverty in architecture, negative and positive meanings, are discussed by Juan Manuel Heredia in Chapter 4.

Introduction

the cognitive side and fresh air on the physical side, which none of them can supply on its own, but all want, and will variously internalize and modulate—you, in your office or apartment, me in mine, together with other things living on the same street, in the park, or the cemetery. Urban sense on this account would arise out of an understanding of shared finality. Similarly, streets would publicize interdependence. The single work wouldn't be realized as something complete in itself, even though it was probably conceptualized that way. Nor would it be something that would run smoothly on its own, like a well-oiled machine, high-performance or not.[30] What can be shared among communicative projects may not be a thing at all; rather, an element or elements of the world, variously rarefied or dense, received and projected. I believe that is what Agamben had in mind when characterizing the *ek-stasis* of a work or a person at its threshold.

Whole Parts

A term that I'd like to use to describe such a work is "whole part". I have in mind buildings that are designed to be internally coherent, but whose make-up anticipates interaction with external conditions that never asked for and remain indifferent to the project's interests, despite their roles as its necessary counterparts. In a single, admittedly contradictory phrase, the proposition is this: a well-designed architectural work is a whole that's partial. An important consequence of engaged autonomy is that single projects, through their disclosures and sufferings, can provide others that expose themselves similarly with the basis for unexpected, and unexpectedly relevant urban form. Urbanity, which is not something architects can design, is, nevertheless, what good architecture projects.

I should say that this proposal is accompanied by doubt that may well have been its origin, doubt about the under- and over-reach of today's designs for and in our cities: in the first instance, projects that submit to the expectations of comprehensive urban systems, such as infrastructure planning, landscape urbanism, and city-wide policy on energy use, zoning, historic preservation, and so on, and, in the second case, market-driven single ventures, no matter what style star-architects promote as the one for tomorrow, or developers seek to sell today. No less formative for this thesis is a concern about the spatial, environmental, and social injustices that fragment today's cultures and cities, the violence we lament so frequently, in architecture and outside it. Inwardly local interests are often those of discriminatory privilege, of wealth, race, or gender. Urban order that makes collective sense is today much more of a task than an inheritance, thus my accent on potentialities, even when negative, perhaps especially so. Although architecture plays a key role on the stage of city culture, the single building is just one among other performers. In fact, it is as I've said, precisely the work's singularity that the studies in the book reconsider and seek to redefine. My "whole part" thesis intends a restatement of

---

[30] On this point, Jean-Luc Nancy recommends "in-operativity." For an architectural extension of Nancy's arguments see: Goetz, Benoît, *La Dislocation: Architecture et philosophie*, Paris: Les Éditions de la Passion, 2001.

architecture's necessity but limited authority and responsibility, together with its corresponding need for lateral involvement and wide awareness, not as a matter of choice but of the project's interdependent independence.[31]

Despite decades of alternately progressive and reactionary claims about dramatic crises in contemporary urban culture, most cities show a significant measure of cultural continuity, no matter whether you consider places like Shanghai, Stockholm, or Santiago, or at least parts of them. No one would mistake any one of them for the others, despite their many changes. Detroit, I've stressed, is something of an exception, but indicative of something essential, perhaps because of its unusually dramatic history. We commonly think that our times are like none other and expect built works to be correspondingly unique. But when holding this expectation or making this claim we tacitly compare today's historical moment with those that came before, dragging the past back into the present, in order to provide a background of similarities for foregrounded differences, making the latter apparent by contrast. No specially trained skills are required to observe that the sizes of urban elements have changed, dramatically so in many locations. Buildings are much taller and infrastructure much bigger and brutally single-minded, while open spaces are more open and oddly peripheral, in the midst of ever-increasing density and expanse.

Yet, despite all the complaints along these lines, nonsense isn't the result; often, just the reverse. In any city's different localities, intelligible topography is still in evidence, though localized. Not despite radical changes, which could be overcome through the repetition or restoration of pre-modern typologies, nor thanks to them, in the form of big architecture, megastructures, or large-scale engineering and landscape projects, but because intelligent and creative architectural projects have contributed to both transformation and continuity. Over time, cities have the remarkable capacity to absorb interventions that initially opposed them, obtaining greater richness as the result. Scale and proportioning are at issue, but also disorientation and divergence from long-standing norms, together with the productive potential of unprecedented designs. Insofar as scale is a matter of relationships, the heart of the issue is difference, but the kind of separateness that sustains mutuality, when parts are seen as counterparts, not despite but because of dissimilarity.

As already suggested, whole parts possess internal economy or coherence, expressing the self-sameness that Alberti said would result in architectural beauty, an animating completeness—animal life was his model—that would be destroyed by any addition or subtraction.[32] It is a wonderful but unrealistic idea, because additions and alterations are inevitable in the lifespan of buildings, as recent writing on adaptive reuse, life-cycle planning, the use of *spolia*, and the unending need for maintenance regularly insist.[33] Insofar as a work's unity includes parts that require marginal or field engagements, wholeness is always only implied, sketched-out one

---

[31] Elaboration of this point can be found in Daphna Half's study of the Tel Aviv Culture Complex in Chapter 5.

[32] Here's the well-known definition to which I referred earlier: "Beauty is that reasoned harmony of all the parts within a body, so that nothing may be added, taken away, or altered, but for the worse." Alberti, Leon Battista, *On the Art of Building in Ten Books*, Book 6, Chapter 2, Cambridge, MA: MIT Press, 1988, p. 156.

[33] Relevant texts include: *Reuse Value: Spolia and Appropriation in Art and Architecture from Constantine to Sherrie Levine*, Richard Brilliant and Dale Kinney eds., Farnham, Surrey: Ashgate, 2011; Sample, Hilary, *Maintenance Architecture*, Cambridge, MA: MIT Press, 2016; and Kieran, Stephen and James Timberlake, *Loblolly House: Elements of a New Architecture*, New York: Princeton Architectural Press, 2008. My contribution to the topic has appeared as Leatherbarrow, David, *Building Time: Architecture, Event, and Experience*, London: Bloomsbury, 2020.

might say. What's more, a work's intrinsic externality allows it to recall or project complementary and contrasting forms, sometimes designed, other times not, alternately pre-existing and yet-to-come. I realize there is something unsettling here: an internal coherence that inclines the building away from itself, while diverging from configurations that had been till then familiar and well-managed. But thanks to this divergence, whole parts can suggest new forms of co-operation, because every discrete design, so conceived, is non-discrete in time, subjected—perhaps condemned—to eventual unfoldings that its author had not foreseen, including subsequent projects by others that discern then extend what was intended, or not.

I recognize the appeal of architectural autonomy. It allows one to grasp the solid, durable core of the discipline. The obvious way to avoid succumbing to time is not to enter it. But an architectural idea is not a household pet, even if types, strictly defined, typically reside in thought or books. What would a market be without traffic from elsewhere, deprived of pedestrians passing by, or the day's dull light? In itself architecture is rather poor. Poverty, I've said, is intrinsic to realized buildings and is therefore work-defining. Autonomy cannot be the last word in urban architecture, even if it must be spoken. **Figure 1.14 (see p. 30)**

Once a work's elements are quickened by ambient qualities, lateral contributions, and latent conditions, it shows itself to be whole in another, external sense: the condensation or epitome of the entire urban landscape as it cycles through time. Individual urban settings radiate or silently voice the culture and environment that both surround and infiltrate them. The difficult point is that the individuality they possess assumes a prior or native involvement with that same world, the one they provisionally renounced, and then after construction made public. Earlier I used the term "intrinsic externality" to describe this manner of definition.[34] Settings are exceeded by what they gather together and render legible. Though we tend to think of them as unified, they are more fundamentally unifying. Before there is a work of architecture there is an urban topography, as Aristotle said of the state or polis, even if it is buildings that largely compose it. Again, the work takes and makes its place in the city, while at the same time the building is (and buildings, yards, gardens, and streets are) precisely where the life of the city takes place. Actual architecture assumes involvement, rather like a person's civility assumes a city, or the memory of one.

Urban Architecture

The chapters that follow exemplify whole parts in various ways. Different times through the whole of the 20th century are studied, also different locations: in South Korea, Israel, Austria, France, Belgium, the United States, and Mexico. In the first chapter Tonkao Panin examines a number of projects in early 20th-century Vienna, focusing in particular on writings and works by Camillo Sitte and

[34] A parallel conception is Rainer Maria Rilke's sense of the *Weltinnenraum*.

Otto Wagner, in the much-debated urban "zone" of the famous Ringstrasse. What role might the individual building play in making sense of a space that is neither urban, in any traditional sense, or suburban, or rural? That study is followed by Esra Şahin Burat's reconsideration of Le Corbusier's Parisian apartment, a marvelous space in itself, but also one that was fully enmeshed in the wider urban area, as a matter of fact and intention, the latter set forth in *The Radiant City*. Urban architecture on the other side of the Atlantic comes into focus in the next chapter, with Juan Manuel Heredia's study of an oddly forgotten building by Juan O'Gorman in Mexico City, the home of the Mexican Cinema Workers Union, that not only served that institution's purposes but also crystallized the wider urban topography, a Labor City. The Post-War period provides the historical context of Daphna Half's close reading of the Tel Aviv Culture Complex by Dov Karmi, Zeev Rechter, and others, as well as the collective desire for a modern nation state and modern city. **Figure 1.15** The chapter that follows, by Stephen Anderson, discovers urban thinking and reality in the work of an architect who is rarely—if ever—thought to contribute to the urban dimension of architecture culture, Sverre Fehn. His Norwegian Pavilion of 1958 in the landscape of the Brussels Expo presents the key aspects of urban architecture, even though the density, heterogeneity, and permanence typically associated with city did not define its surroundings. A still more recent project, H-Sang Seung's Gudeok Presbyterian Church, built in 2008 in Busan, describes how the reinterpretation of two spatial topics, platform and tower, can structure an ensemble of settings that both concentrates and expands a single urban institution. Lastly, I consider a relatively recent building by Tod Williams and Billie Tsien, Skirkanich Hall, built on the campus of the University of Pennsylvania in Philadelphia, describing the ways that an infill project can not only recast the urban sense of the block that surrounds it, but also provide a model for projects by other architects that are yet to come.

Figure 1.15 | Dov Karmi and Zeev Rechter, Tel Aviv Culture Complex, Tel Aviv, 1951.

Seen together, these studies describe ways that cities have been transformed through the reinterpretation or deformation of spatial and cultural norms, architecture for and against the city. If still more projects were considered, the better examples of modern and contemporary architecture would indicate that whole parts can project urbanity in surprisingly productive/progressive ways. One hopes that the studies in this book will be sufficiently indicative to prompt more work along these lines. A courtyard on and as a street in Juan O'Gorman's work created a new space for collective assembly. A partially enclosed courtyard designed by H-Sang Seung became the epitome of the wider urban territory. An unprecedented combination of a garden, public square, and pedestrian route in the work of Karmi and Rechter has given the surrounding city a set of spaces that both opens an important cultural institution and infiltrates an urban landscape that is otherwise entirely pedestrian. A no less improbable conjunction was developed in the work of Otto Wagner: a public platform above cross-city infrastructure, alongside a ring road that proposed spatial definition in undefined terrain, without resorting to the kinds of urban enclosure that fill the pages of typology textbooks. Near and far were conjoined in Le Corbusier's project, such that a very small part implied connections to very remote places, not only in the project's immediate vicinity, but more distant locations, some at the eastern limit of Europe, others only imagined, but not for that reason any less compelling. That a landscape would seem to have no place in an institution's interior did not prevent Sverre Fehn from evoking wider territories, staging an experience that is essentially urban. And an improbably public space within a previously neglected block interior redefined the sense of the wider perimeter in the work of Williams and Tsien.

Neither professional intention nor public perception is accented in these studies; instead, different kinds of performance, hence my repeated allusions to stagecraft.[35] The concern is less what the work is (resulting from design, to be appreciated in experience) than what the work does, how it embodies and articulates culture, structures settings, and makes objects. Operations thus conceived are probably best thought of as events that sometimes conform to established and pre-conceived patterns, but generally not—and that's what makes unscripted performances memorable. Architectural enactment couples things and places, as they've been built, but also as they are animated by forces (sometimes violent) no one constructed, as they prevail in and around a given location. A building's wide horizon consists of a range of counterparts, the absence of any one of which noticeably impoverishes the work. Its dilations and prolongations, together with is acceptances and refusals, allows the single building to reward attention when it is given, but also recognize the fact that we normally expect it to play its part quietly, confidently assuming it will be silently understood.

---

[35] The theatricality of settings at different scales is elaborated by Stephen Anderson in his account of Sverre Fehn's domestic and urban spaces, see Chapter 6.

Figure 1.4 | Doorstep, from Aldo van Eyck, "The In-between Realm."

Figure 1.7 | James Tissot, *Shop Girl*, c. 1885.

Figure 1.8 | Streetside bar, Philadelphia, 2019.

Figure 1.10 | O'Donnell + Tuomey, Lyric Theater, Belfast, 2011; entry threshold.

Figure 1.14 | Italian market, Philadelphia, 2015.

Tonkao Panin

Within and Beyond Architectural Boundaries

Sitte and Wagner

As soon as several self-contained spatial bodies are placed together, architecture as the creatress of space comes back into its own by arranging these building elements into larger spatial enclosures and placing them in new organic relations—whether it be house facades along a street or groups of buildings around a square, perhaps with a central monument and vistas along the streets directed towards it. We consciously claim all of this, even the artistic layout of a city plan, explicitly for architecture as an art. Architecture, the art of building cities, stretches out its hand.

—**August Schmarsow**, *The Essence of Architectural Creation.*[1]

Figure 2.18 | Otto Wagner, Kaiser Franz Josef-Stadtmuseum, Vienna, 1910; scale model of two bays of Kaiser Franz Josef-Stadtmuseum on Karlsplatz.

1 Schmarsow, August, *Das Wesen der Architektonischen Schöpfung*, originally published 1893, Harry Mallgrave and Eleftherios Ekonomou trans., Santa Monica, CA: The Getty Center for the History of Art and the Humanities, 1994, pp. 294–5.

In *The Essence of Architectural Creation (Das Wesen der Architektonischen Schöpfung)*, August Schmarsow briefly alluded to architecture's double obligation: the practice of the art requires attention to both the single building and the urban ensemble, one art with two distinct commitments. On the one hand, architecture is essentially *bounded*. The walls of single works form limits that enclose inhabitable space. Penetrations and passages presuppose this most basic architectural premise. Building design is the creation of self-contained spatial bodies. But architecture also creates urban spaces, which are themselves sometimes bounded, rather like buildings and their rooms, but equally often *unbounded*, particularly when they serve infrastructural purposes, or when the vistas Schmarsow describes are not toward but away from monuments. He says that when self-contained spaces adjoin, they arrange still larger spaces. In principle, this is fine. It accords with the familiar line from Alberti: "The city is like some large house, and the house is in turn like some small city."[2] The parts of the smaller arrangement enclose, while those of the city-size pattern not only do that but also extend. Even if we agree that the two-part task of enclosure and extension defines the art of building cities, we cannot assume it is problem free. In point of fact, the two Viennese architects studied in this chapter, Camillo Sitte and Otto Wagner, struggled to fulfill this double task. Because the problem they addressed has not gone away, their work remains a testament to the topic, perhaps also a key to what's at stake with the resumption of this kind of work today and in the future.

In May 1889, an essay titled "The Art of Building Cities According to Artistic Principles" ("*Der Städtebau nach seinen künstlerischen Grundsätzen*")[3] was published in Vienna. The author, Camillo Sitte, analyzed the civic and artistic character of old European towns that had remained well-preserved from the pre-industrial age. Searching for hidden principles that might serve both historical understanding and contemporary practice, Sitte turned to ancient towns that hadn't been planned but developed incrementally. Studying and comparing spatial patterns from Roman times to the 19th century, Sitte believed that the three-dimensional relationships between spaces of public squares, plazas, and streets demonstrated inner structures or hidden patterns that allowed for seemingly natural transformations.

During the course of the 19th century, when the profession of city planning was established, architects and historians had widely expressed their ideas through essays and debates. Sitte's *Der Städtebau* was among them. His work was presented as a warning from a concerned but culturally sensitive citizen of Vienna about the problems of its recent development. Sitte's stance could be traced to his experience with traditional crafts and folk arts as he was professionally involved with those arts more than with architecture and city planning.[4] As director of the Vienna State School of Applied Art (Staatsgewerbeschule), he was engaged in teaching the technical as well as the artistic aspects of *Kunstgewerbe*

2   "*Civitas...maxima quaedum est domus et contra domus minima quaedam est civitas,*" Alberti, Leon Battista, *De re Aedificatoria*, Florence, c. 1452, *Leon Battista Alberti: On the Art of Building in Ten Books*, Joseph Rykwert, Neil Leach and Robert Tavernor trans., Cambridge, MA: MIT Press, 1988, p. 23.

3   Sitte, Camillo, *Der Städtebau nach seinen kunstlerischen Grundsätzen*, first published 1889. For the complete biography of Camillo Sitte see the work of his son Heinrich Sitte, "Camillo Sitte," *Neue Österreichische Biographie*, part I, vol. VI, 1929, pp. 132–49. See also Wurzer, Rudolf, *Camillo Sitte: Archive Catalogue*, Vienna: Technische Universität Wien. The majority of Sitte's biographical data from the *Archive Catalogue* is collected in Collins, George and Christiane Collins, *Camillo Sitte: The Birth of Modern City Planning*, New York: Dover Publications, 1986, pp. 411–18.

4   Schorske, Carl, *Fin-de-Siècle Vienna: Politics and Culture*, New York: Vintage Books, 1981, pp. 24–115.

(applied art). In general, he sought to extract principles from vernacular works that had been created anonymously rather than by masters. To some degree, this represented an indictment of contemporary educational paradigms. When considering the city, his fundamental complaints originated from the Vienna Ringstrasse project that had been developed mainly through two-dimensional plans. Sitte believed that a radically different approach was required. He urged the use of a city plan conceived in *Bebauungsplan* (three dimensions).[5] Sitte's advocacy of three-dimensional relationships between urban constructs was not reserved for architecture's exterior but included sequential relationships between a building's bounded interior and its extended surroundings as well. Yet, Sitte built very little during his lifetime. Though his ideas were hardly realized in his own designs, they had been unexpectedly manifested in the works of his opponent, Otto Wagner. To recover the starting point of their ideas—opposed and shared—we must turn to the Ringstrasse.

The Ringstrasse and Camillo Sitte

Old Vienna had not undergone any radical change in form from the 13th century to the second half of the 19th century, when the ambitious project of the Ringstrasse was launched. From the time it became a fortified capital of Babenbergs in 1135 until 1843, when Sitte was born, the town had roughly the same perimeter. The city's form survived without much change as it became one of the major European capitals and commercial centers late in the 18th century. Its medieval towers and walls had been replaced by a modern earthwork bastion and *glacis*, while the city's suburbs lay beyond the fortifications. By 1850, there were 34 suburbs beyond the *glacis*, which now covered a far greater area than the inner city itself. **Figure 2.1 (see p. 47)**

After the revolution of 1848, the emerging middle class sought control of the fortified area, which separated the medieval core from its fast-growing suburbs. The revolution politically redefined the place of the *glacis* in the life of the city. After centuries of direct imperial rule, the liberal bourgeois could now demand from the emperor the right to establish a self-governed municipality. New municipal statutes provided a political framework for allowing civilian claims to the old fortifications. The rapid growth of its population aggravated a long-standing problem of housing. The use of land along the *glacis* seemed ideal.[6]

As political and economic pressure mounted, Emperor Franz Joseph finally announced his intention to open the space for civilian use and established a City Expansion Commission to plan and execute its development.[7] On December 20, 1857, the emperor issued his famous memorandum ordering an ambitious town planning project that would follow the demolition of the fortifications enclosing the old city of Vienna. The *glacis* and bastion were to be replaced by an 18-meter wide, tree-lined boulevard, the much-celebrated Ringstrasse, with vast complexes of public buildings occupying

[5] Collins and Collins, *Camillo Sitte: The Birth of Modern City Planning*, p. 36.
[6] For accounts of political issues behind the development of the Ringstrasse, see Schorske, *Fin-de-Siècle Vienna*, pp. 24–115.
[7] Schorske, *Fin-de-Siècle Vienna*, pp. 24–115.

broad strips of land alongside it. Land around each of these new buildings would be sold to pay for the construction, creating an area for the development of new apartment buildings.[8]

First prize in the competition for planning the Ringstrasse was won by Ludwig von Förster. His motto clearly indicated his approach—"The straight line is the best" ("*Der gerade Weg ist der beste.*") Other awards went to Friedrich Stache and the team of Eduard van der Nüll and August von Siccardsburg. But the actual plan that was employed was produced by the new Building Department of the Ministry of Interior and approved by the Emperor in 1859.[9] From a town that had gradually been transformed within the physical structure of a medieval town, Vienna was to transform itself into a metropolitan *Großstadt*. It was the beginning of the Ringstrasse era. **Figure 2.2 (see p. 48)**

In the wake of the Ringstrasse development, Camillo Sitte had entered the atelier of the architect Heinrich von Ferstel, at the Technische Hochschule. It was his critical view towards Von Ferstel's practice that would later provide a platform for Sitte's theory. Between 1863 and 1868, he undertook research on the physiology of vision and space perception that led to his dissertation on perspective, which would also influence the ideas of *Der Städtebau*.[10] Having established himself as an architect, Sitte was called to organize in 1883 the new State School of Applied Arts, whose new building was underway on the Schwarzenberggasse, at the edge of the Ringstrasse. His first book, *Der Städtebau*, was formulated during his years at the school. Despite his criticism of the Ringstrasse, Sitte did not believe in the possibility of recovering or recreating the beauty of pre-industrial city space, having realistically assessed the scope of the spatial and social disruption brought on by the Industrial Revolution. The stages of the Ringstrasse project from 1858 to 1890 became the subject of Sitte's book, a study that was later received with much enthusiasm from the public.

As Carl Schorske stated in his extensive study of the Ringstrasse, although its scale and grandeur suggested the persistent power of the Baroque, the spatial conception that inspired its design was rather new. For the Baroque planners, "Space was organized to carry the viewer to a central focus: space served as a magnifying setting to the principal buildings which encompassed or dominated it." The Ringstrasse, by contrast, used buildings to magnify the horizontality of its space by organizing all the elements in relation to a central grand *corso*.[11] The lack of architectonic containment—boundedness—and visible destination was to become Sitte's principal concern. The Ringstrasse became an independent and dominating element in the vast complex enveloping the old city without any perceptible relationship to other spatial entities. The streets, coming from either the inner city or the suburbs, were disrupted by the Ringstrasse's circular flow.[12] The military strip of fortifications and *glacis* were now replaced by a strong traffic belt that was, unexpectedly but unambiguously, much more difficult to penetrate.

---

8 For full accounts of the development of Ringstrasse apartment buildings, see *Die Wiener Ringstrasse, Bild einer Epoch: die Erweiterung der inneren Stadt Wien unter Kaiser Franz Joseph*, 14 Banden, Vienna: Böhlau, 1969–81, vols 1–2.

9 Stache's project was presented in the booklet *Denkschrift zu den Plänen für die Erweiterung und Verschonerung Wiens*, Vienna, 1858.

10 Collins and Collins, *Camillo Sitte: The Birth of Modern City Planning*, p. 24.

11 Schorske, *Fin-de-Siècle Vienna*, p. 32.

12 Schorske, *Fin-de-Siècle Vienna*, p. 32.

Along with public spaces, such as parks and plazas, Viennese masters were summoned to contribute to the Ringstrasse development. A series of public building along the Ringstrasse included the Votive Church (1856-79) and the University of Vienna (1873-84) by Heinrich von Ferstel; the Rathaus by Friedrich Schmidt (1872-83); the Opera House by Eduard van der Nüll and August von Siccardburg (1861-69); the Parliament by Theophil Hansen (1874-83); the Hofburgtheater (1874-88); and the Art and Natural History Museums (1872-81) by Gottfried Semper and Carl von Hasenauer. The creation of the Ringstrasse and the development of its neighboring residential areas had given both physical form and identity to the new city life.[13]

In the late 1860s, another event in the work on the Ringstrasse took place, which was to have a decisive influence on Sitte. It was the calling of Gottfried Semper to Vienna to advise on the further development of the Hofburg area.[14] Semper planned to amend the way the Ringstrasse cut through the new Hofburg layout by breaking its flow with triumphal arches and removing the old Burgtor, thereby creating a bounded spatial entity. It was a solution that would shift the focus from a grand boulevard of traffic to an area of spatial containment and human activities, variously commercial, social, cultural, or recreational. The strong influence of Semper's planning idea on Sitte is evidenced in his repeated comments on Semper in *Der Städtebau*, as well as in numerous earlier essays on Semper's theory published in the *Neue Wiener Tagblatt* and the *Salzburger Gewerbeblatt* between 1887 and 1902. Sitte saw the failure to carry out Semper's plan as a significant loss for Vienna, and during the following decades preserved the hope that it would be completed eventually. In fact, he continued to remark about it in the later editions of *Der Städtebau*, long after it had been decided that Semper's plan would not be implemented.[15] Figure 2.3

The second phase of the Ringstrasse program began in 1892 when an international competition was held for various works. Joseph Stübben and Otto Wagner were the winners of the overall plan for Greater Vienna. By the turn of the century, a shift in the aesthetic dialogue in architecture was imminent. Organic lines and patterns seemed to have been transformed into straight lines, as can be seen in applied art, architectural design as well as city planning, as clearly shown in the initial Ringstrasse plan. The former style often came to be associated with romantic subjectivity, while the latter with radical objectivity.[16]

Otto Wagner and the Ringstrasse

During the 1890s, the first phase of the Ringstrasse was well underway. Its program largely ignored Sitte's warnings. After 1890, the major undertaking was shifted to the improvement of street connections through the inner city, the connection of the network of metropolitan railways, and the transformation of the Linienwall (outer defense of rampart and fosse erected in 1705) into a series of *Gürtelstrassen* (ring-boulevards).[17] While the second and third phases

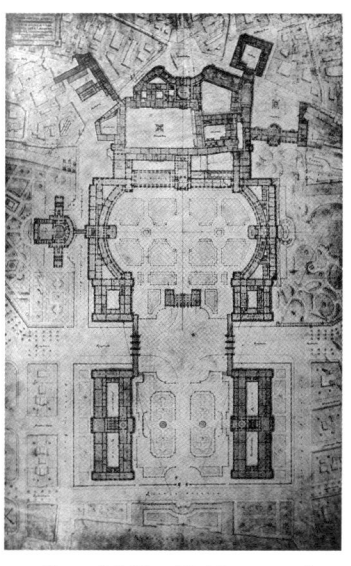

Figure 2.3 | Gottfried Semper and Carl von Hasenauer, Kaiserforum, Vienna, 1869; plan.

[13] See the discussion of each building in *Die Wiener Ringstrasse, Bild einer Epoch*, vols 2-4.
[14] Collins and Collins, *Camillo Sitte: The Birth of City Planning*, p. 56.
[15] Collins and Collins, *Camillo Sitte: The Birth of City Planning*, p. 56.
[16] See Sitte's introductory chapter of *Der Städtebau*, and Wagner, Otto, "The Development of the Great City," *Architectural Record*, 1911, pp. 485-500.
[17] *Die Wiener Ringstrasse, Bild Einer Epoch*, vols 1-2.

of the city transformation were underway, Otto Wagner became heavily involved and soon assumed a prominent role in the city planning of Vienna.

Sitte's senior by two years, Otto Wagner studied at the Polytechnic Institute in Vienna and proceeded to the Königliche Bauakademie in Berlin. In 1861, Wagner returned to Vienna where he attended the Academy of Fine Arts under the guidance of Eduard van der Nüll and August von Siccardsburg, whose "utilitarian principle" Wagner admired throughout his life.[18]

After working briefly in the studio of the Ringstrasse architect Ludwig von Förster, Wagner won the competition for the casino in the Wiener Stadtpark. This competition was the first of many that Wagner would win during his lifetime, accelerating his career and helping to establish him as the master architect of Vienna. His artistic reputation culminated with an appointment to the chair of the Academy in 1894, after the death of Karl von Hasenauer. By that time, Wagner had established himself as one of the most influential architects in Austria.[19]

Having joined the most prestigious art school in the Empire, Wagner felt obliged to define, establish, and defend the practice of his art, as well as to define his role as a teacher. In 1895, he published his book *Modern Architecture* (*Moderne Architektur*), which was reprinted in 1899, 1902, and 1914, the last reprint in his lifetime appearing under the title *Building-Art of Our Time* (*Baukunst unserer Zeit*). He began his chairmanship at the Academy while the second phase of the Viennese planning was underway. At the beginning of the second phase, an international competition was held for various works. Wagner, with Stübben, won the competition for the overall plan for Greater Vienna and was subsequently given the responsibility of designing the entire metropolitan railway system. Its stations, tunnels, and overpasses became the perfect illustration of his ideas, which were later summed up in a 1911 book on the metropolis, *Die Großstadt*. By that time, Wagner's idea for the Viennese plan was clearly formulated. Its departure from Sitte's views became plainly evident.

A common enemy doesn't always unite opponents. Although it was against the Ringstrasse ideology that both Camillo Sitte and Otto Wagner developed their ideas of urban life and form,[20] their views differed vastly. Using the Ringstrasse as a negative model, Sitte unleashed a biting critique of the modern city from the point of view of history, criticizing its inhumane configuration. Wagner launched his attack from the opposite direction, criticizing the obstruction of modernity behind the stylistic screens of history.[21] At first glance, Sitte and Wagner thus seemed to represent the unreconciled characters of the Ringstrasse legacy. Yet, when viewed more closely, both were united by their advocacy of contained urban space, composed by its enclosing architecture.[22] Under the influence of Gottfried Semper, both based their ideas on visual principles and stressed the three-dimensional architectonic character of the city plan—boundary-making, as I've called it.

---

[18] For Wagner's biography see Graf, Otto, *Otto Wagner*, Vienna: Böhlau, 1985, pp. 12–38. See also Harry Mallgrave's introduction to *Otto Wagner, Modern Architecture*, Santa Monica, CA: The Getty Center for the History of Art and the Humanities, 1988, pp. 61–73.
[19] Graf, *Otto Wagner*.
[20] See Sitte's introductory chapter of *Der Städtebau*, and Wagner, "The Development of the Great City," pp. 485–500. See also Schorske, *Fin-de-Siècle Vienna*, pp. 24–115.
[21] Wagner, "The Development of the Great City," pp. 485–500.
[22] Graf, *Otto Wagner*, pp. 101–23. See also Schorske, *Fin-de-Siècle Vienna*, pp. 24–80.

The Ringstrasse, a vast, continuous circular space, with a series of isolated buildings, posed a sharp contrast to Vienna's old medieval core. The sense of isolation and unrelatedness created by the spatial placements of the Ringstrasse buildings troubled both Sitte and Wagner. The vertical masses seemed subordinated to the flat and horizontal movement of the street. Of the new buildings and open spaces along the Ringstrasse, the Votive Church site provided Sitte with the best example of the clumsy handling of space. It occupied a prominent location within an open space facing the Ring and was the center of a public square. Seen from only one angle, it was lost in the vastness of its surroundings. A configuration achieved through the juxtaposition of buildings facades was considered to be an egregious error of the Ringstrasse planning program.

In contrast to the open expanse of the Ringstrasse, Sitte pointed to the sense of enclosed aggregation of form and space. This idea became the center of his "space-art" (*Raumkunst*) concept. In many weekly writings in newspapers after publishing *Der Städtebau*, Sitte tirelessly presented his ideas to save Vienna from becoming a monotonous town. He continually focused on the spatial configuration of the incrementally developed towns that seemed to be the product of chance rather than the product of will. Yet, to emulate the city that grew organically was also a paradox. On the one hand, Sitte adhered to the nature of the enclosed squares found in the old city and their aggregate surroundings, the "natural" outcome of incremental growth. On the other hand, he set ground rules that aimed at reconstructing such accidental spaces and forms. *Raumkunst* became a way of composing the natural—paradoxical though such a practice might seem. The city was to be the product of will, modeled after the natural product of chance.

In 1893, four years after *Der Städtebau* was published, Wagner won a competition for a new development plan for Vienna and established his place as the chief guardian of the city. Parts of Wagner's ideas were based on a very different premise than Sitte's. His program was focused on the non-aesthetic factors of the city such as traffic, land-use differentiation, and sanitary control.[23] In accordance with new concerns of the city council, Wagner submitted a design dominated by concerns for transportation. In addition to the Ringstrasse, he proposed a series of three other circumferential roads and rail belts, all of which would be intersected by radial arteries running toward the heart of the city. Wagner launched his project with the motto *"Artis sola domina necessitas"* ("Art has only one mistress... necessity"). It was necessary for Wagner to satisfy the demands of efficiency, economy, and the facilitation of business, which were manifested in a design centered on transportation. It was a tool that could be used to unite a widespread and otherwise fragmented *Großstadt* into a total unit. The city itself was to be subdivided into parts, which would be linked and united by the lines of traffic. Transportation belts and arteries were conceived as a grid, at once dividing and uniting

---

[23] The competition called for the designs for a general plan regulating the whole municipal area of Vienna. See *Die Wiener Ringstrasse, Bild Einer Epoch*, vols 1-2. See also Schorske, *Fin-de-Siècle Vienna*, p. 73.

the city's many areas. The city was also to be the product of will, but whose sense of totality was not based on the old artistic means like those Sitte advised, but a new aesthetic, representing the new economy, efficiency, utility, and technology.

The Case of Karlsplatz

In 1894, Otto Wagner was unanimously selected as an artistic advisor for the Vienna Transport Commission, responsible for the plan of Vienna Stadtbahn. This task subsequently translated into designs for stations, passageways, crosswalks, and bridges, with help from around 70 associates, among them Joseph Maria Olbrich, Josef Hoffmann, and Max Fabiani. One hundred years later, Pier Luigi Cervellati wrote:

> For the first and maybe only time in the history of architecture, one architect alone was entrusted with planning an entire urban railway, encompassing everything from landscaping to the rivets on the platform roof. The Vienna Transport Commission actually requested the Künstlerhaus, the Austrian empire's association of artists, to recommend some architects for the planning of the substructure, and they unanimously suggested Wagner.[24]

Figure 2.4 | Otto Wagner, Hietzing Station, Vienna, 1894; elevation, drawn by Joseph Maria Olbrich.

Both elegant and stylistically appropriate, Wagner's design is "light and airy" in a sense that it does not suppress already existing urban structures, but rather integrates itself into the city's development, history, and forms. Wagner proves with this work, which was built a century ago, that one does not necessarily have to be against the historical city in order to be modern.[25]
Figures 2.4, 2.5 (see p. 50), 2.6 (see p. 51), and 2.7

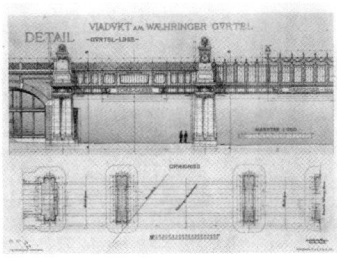

Figure 2.7 | Otto Wagner, Währinger Strasse viaduct, Vienna, 1895–6; elevation and plan.

One of the most well-known of Wagner's Stadtbahn projects was the Karlsplatz Station. Designed and built between 1898 and 1899, Karlsplatz was both representational and practical. No less important was the fact that it was spatially contained, despite the new—metropolitan—context in which it was sited. Consisting of two almost identical pavilions oriented towards an open plaza, it connected the inner city of Vienna to the iconic Karlskirche and the Technische Hochschule. The fact that the site was in front of the revered Karlskirche was already a risk. At first glance, Karlsplatz Station seemed to be alienated from its surroundings. Yet, at a closer look, the building's disposition defined and redefined its surroundings. Integrating the pavilions into the site was particularly tricky—horizontally and vertically. Wagner's disposition of the station succeeded in redefining the open plaza into a more centralized space by enclosing the platform with two pavilions and raising it above the sidewalks, making it both separated and connected to its surroundings, its orthogonals running perpendicular and parallel to the lines of the Ringstrasse. Wagner's decision to build both pavilions quite low made them much less imposing, allowing unobstructed

---

24 Zednicek, Walter, *Otto Wagner: Zeichnungen und Pläne*, Vienna: Zednicek, 2002, p. 62.
25 Zednicek, *Otto Wagner*, p. 66.

views towards the church. The space of the plaza became loosely enclosed, defined by the platform, yet open at its center. In other words, it was contained but not confined. The station could be seen both from this inner plaza and from the metro platform down below. Although the pavilions are ornate and stylized, much like Wagner's other buildings of the same period, they were designed with two contrasting fronts. From the central plaza, both pavilions appeared as beautiful objects lightly placed onto their platforms. Their heightened entrances were topped with highly ornate crowns, and oriented towards the plaza, inviting everyone to enter. Those passing through this plaza, if not going down to the metro level, usually continued toward either the Karlskirche or the Technishe Hochschule. Thus, the pavilions acted as an entry point, connecting streets and buildings from all sides. It was an entry that called for one's attention. This was the image of Karlsplatz Station that critics praised and citizens seem to have both admired and remembered.

Arriving at the station, one ceremoniously entered either of the pavilions. But one remained in the interior space very briefly, before being pushed out and downward toward the open space of the metro platform. From down below, the pavilions presented a much more austere picture, relatively simple and functional. The pavilions' outer fronts by no means demanded anyone's attention, there was nothing to notice or admire. Leaving the station was a prosaic affair. These other fronts seemed only to facilitate swift passage to other destinations. The pavilions and their platform became a threshold for different kinds of movement at different speeds. **Figures 2.8, 2.9 (see p. 52), 2.10 (see p. 52), and 2.11 (see p. 53)**

Another important project situated around Karlsplatz was the Kaiser Franz Josef-Stadtmuseum. The competition for the museum, which was to be located within the boundaries of Karlsplatz next to the Karlskirche, was held in 1901–02.[26] The competition raised the problem of redesigning the entire Karlsplatz, a project that had been envisioned by Karl Lueger, the Mayor of Vienna at the time. Karlsplatz had been known as a problematic part of Vienna, especially after the Ringstrasse development. The Karlskirche was designed by Fischer von Erlach between 1716 and 1739, in commemoration of Emperor Karl VI's patron saint, Carlo Borromeo. The site for the church was located beyond the city's old fortifications, outside town, on the opposite bank of the Wien. After completion, the facade unfolded its silhouette above the river, *glacis*, and bastion when seen from the Hofburg. But the part of the Wien that had been culverted in the 1880s, resulted in a large, shapeless area in front of the church. There was no satisfactory form of enclosure at the sides. After 1858, when the *glacis* was turned into the Ringstrasse, Karlskirche remained for many years the subject of dispute and competitions among architects. The question was simple but the task difficult: how to integrate it properly into the new ring road?[27]

With the Ringstrasse in front, and without a satisfactory form of enclosure at the sides, Karlskirche was left in the middle of a shapeless open field, disconnected from the whole of Vienna.

Figure 2.8 | Otto Wagner, Karlsplatz, Vienna, 1898–9; masterplan around the area of Karlsplatz and Naschmarkt.

26 See the discussion in Munz, Ludwig, and Gustav Kunstler, *Adolf Loos: Pioneer of Modern Architecture*, Vienna: Frederick A. Praeger, 1966, pp. 172–84.
27 See details in *Die Wiener Ringstrasse, Bild einer Epoch*, vols 1–2.

In response to the problem, Karl Lueger took an interest in the re-planning of the Karlsplatz. The Kaiser Franz Josef-Stadtmuseum played an important part in the scheme. Above all, the primary goal was to provide a definition for the Karlsplatz. As the competition specified, the museum was to visually enclose the Karlskirche, thereby forming a harmonious relationship with the church.[28] Through the competition, this prominent site acted as a catalyst for an already heated debate in Vienna between the preservers of tradition and the advocates of modernity.

In an article from 1902, Sitte critiqued various competition entries. Unexpectedly, Sitte did not mention the reorganization of the Karlsplatz area as a whole, but only focused on the design of the museum. Included among his files is a collection of nearly 30 plans compiled from the competition entries, which addressed the problem of how to enclose the square. Among the many architects who participated in the competition was Otto Wagner, who submitted several plans and a model. Most of the plans Sitte collected offered similar spatial organizations, except for a few divergent cases. They traced the perimeter of the site. Despite formally following the designated footprint of the given site, most of the proposed plans are oriented inward and turned away from the Karlsplatz, rather than providing an enclosure for it. The proposals suggested a new building that became a self-contained spatial body independent from its surroundings. **Figure 2.12 (see p. 54)**

The project that Sitte paid most attention to was designed by Max Fabiani, who offered a slight variation on the same scheme. Most competition entries proposed a scheme organized around an inner court and main stairs, with exhibition areas homogeneously distributed around them. Upon entering the building from the Karlsplatz, one would have been faced with centrally distributed space that presented little or no distinctive hierarchy between the left and the right axes, a method familiar to most museum projects including the Kunst- and Naturhistorisches Museums by Gottfried Semper and Karl von Hasenaur. Fabiani, on the other hand, presented a scheme that shifted the stairs to the left and balanced them with a large open hall connected to the exhibition space on the right. Next to the stairs is a much smaller corridor leading to what appears to be non-exhibition spaces. Considerably less celebratory than other entries, Fabiani offered a plan that seemed to be configured within an order and criteria of use rather than an order of graphic composition. Rooms are assembled with variations in size and configuration, rather than being lined up as a regulated strip of space. In Fabiani's scheme, the perimeter of the site still prevails, yet a few retractions at the building's corners show his attempt to create exterior spatial forms. The solution answered both its internal obligations and external demands. Although Sitte preferred Fabiani's scheme, the modesty of the public gesture was not completely satisfactory for him. As a response, Sitte called for the new building to pay more attention to the Karlskirche, as well as the Karlsplatz.[29] **Figure 2.13**

---

[28] Haiko, Peter, "The Franz Josef-Stadtmuseum: The Attempt to Implement a Theory of Modern Architecture," *Otto Wagner: Reflections on the Raiment of Modernity*, Harry Mallgrave ed., Santa Monica, CA: The Getty Center for the History of Art and the Humanities, 1993, pp. 53–84.

[29] Sitte, Camillo, manuscript *Am Karlsplatz: Das Kaiser Franz Joseph-Museum der Stadt Wien*, partly published in *Neuer Wiener Tagblatt*, June 12, 1902.

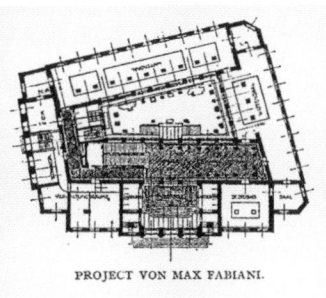

Figure 2.13 | Max Fabiani, Kaiser Franz Josef-Stadtmuseum, Vienna, 1902.

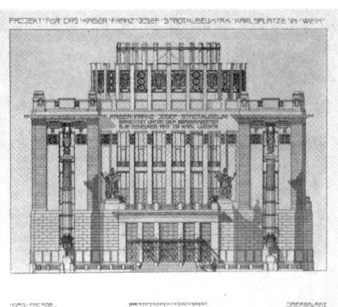

Figure 2.17 | Otto Wagner, Kaiser Franz Josef-Stadtmuseum, Vienna, 1909; front facade.

Otto Wagner's proposal for the Kaiser Franz Josef-Stadtmuseum however, demonstrated ideas that would have fulfilled Sitte's vision of providing the enclosing envelope for the Karlskirche and Karlsplatz, as well as connecting them to the fabric of the city. It clearly aimed to tackle the problem of bounded urban space. Before the actual competition, Wagner presented a museum project to the public in 1900, the year the idea of building a museum on the Karlsplatz was first suggested. He participated in the first stage of the open competition of 1901 with a preliminary project that won first prize. Later, in 1902, he submitted an essentially new scheme for the limited competition. This second stage ended bitterly for Wagner when he was not placed among the top three winners. But over the course of the next decade, through 1912, Wagner continued to refine his project, creating several variants. In 1910, despite knowing that his project was not going to be built, Wagner even successfully erected two bays of a full-scale model, so as to test the compatibility of his design with the Baroque Karlskirche. Nevertheless, all his efforts were lost, as Friedrich Schachner's design was ultimately selected.[30] **Figures 2.14 (see p. 55), 2.15 (see p. 56), 2.16 (see p. 58), 2.17, and 2.18 (see p. 32)**

The majority of Wagner's competitors, while presenting similar spatial schemes as shown in Sitte's collection, also attempted to accommodate the Karlskirche by reconstructing Baroque facades. They were committed to historicist principles. Wagner, on the other hand, specifically opposed this view.

> It is appropriate here to underscore most emphatically that erecting a museum facade in the style of the Karlskirche will necessarily lead to the most ridiculous consequences... A truly artistic conception of the problem must define the height and silhouette of the building in such a way that they become an integral part of the whole, and a solution can only be attempted on the basis of these premises.[31]

The Kaiser Franz Josef-Stadtmuseum project caused Wagner to confront and measure himself against Fischer von Erlach. Wagner's design presented a strong deviation, if not departure, from the past in terms of its facade motifs. The outcome demonstrated that he was able to work freely with "history."[32] In the various stages of his design, Wagner tried to keep a distance between his approach and Fischer's. In contrast to the historicized facades of his competitors, Wagner strove to apply his modern way of building by employing new techniques of construction. For example, masonry walls were to be sheathed with marble panels. Their thin, flat surfaces discreetly implied volume. He valued this construction method for its "easy availability, possibility of timely construction, and lowest possible price."[33] This was also an ideal way to "express the panel construction clearly in the facade."[34] Marble sheaths and their fixing bolts later appeared in the

---

[30] Haiko, "The Franz Josef-Stadtmuseum: The Attempt to Implement a Theory of Modern Architecture," p. 54.
[31] Haiko, "The Franz Josef-Stadtmuseum: The Attempt to Implement a Theory of Modern Architecture," p. 54.
[32] Haiko, "The Franz Josef-Stadtmuseum: The Attempt to Implement a Theory of Modern Architecture," p. 54.
[33] Haiko, "The Franz Josef-Stadtmuseum: The Attempt to Implement a Theory of Modern Architecture," p. 65.
[34] Haiko, "The Franz Josef-Stadtmuseum: The Attempt to Implement a Theory of Modern Architecture," p. 65.

designs of the Postsparkasse and the Church of Saint Leopold am Steinhof, becoming emblems of Wagner's dedication to functions and necessities.

Wagner's proposals, though transformed during the span of several years, all showed a uniform exterior that reflected the coherence of the interior organization. Much like the Majolikahaus and the Postsparkasse, Wagner's various proposals presented highly articulated facades. But earlier facade schemes, with their overtly embellished expression, contradict his earlier statements on how new buildings should fit in with the structure of the urban ensemble and not necessarily concern themselves primarily with localized articulation. Apart from the fact that the perimeter of the museum building fit the perimeter of the site, it is difficult to understand how Wagner's earlier scheme was determined to take part in the larger ensemble of its urban neighbors.

An attempt to compose a self-contained spatial body enveloped within its walls would certainly result in an articulated building in its own right. Such a building's facade could present its symbolic, material, and constructional value. But when the building is considered within the city, the dialogue between its well-clad body and the urban setting raised other problems—problems of spatial definition. His later schemes, however, presented a different picture. They seemed to recall an idea initiated in his earlier projects, such as the Länderbank. The plans of the Länderbank were composed to respond to both internal demands and external obligations, which represent an attempt to reconcile its inner configuration with the shifting axis of its urban setting. The building's facade reciprocated the interior pattern of inhabitation. The Länderbank was a testament to Wagner's ability to compose both interior space and exterior form. But as Wagner became highly successful in his career, the concern for architecture's double obligations seems to have become less important, only to be picked up again in his later proposals for the Kaiser Franz Josef-Stadtmuseum. **Figure 2.19**.

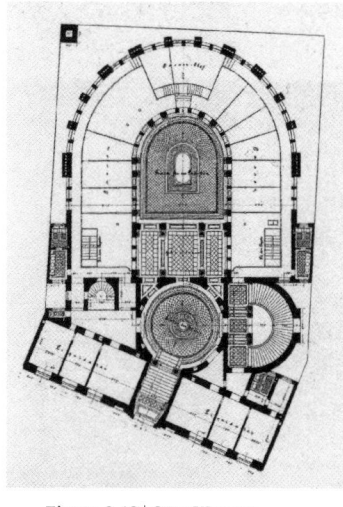

Figure 2.19 | Otto Wagner, Länderbank, Vienna, 1883–4; plan.

At first glance, Wagner's Kaiser Franz Josef-Stadtmuseum seems at once subservient to the Karlskirche and alienated from the other components of the area. Yet, the design also demonstrated scalar correspondences with the church and area, in the dimensioning and articulation of its entrances. Later designs between 1910 and 1912 clearly yielded the building to the square. It became much less ornate and self-sufficient. Wagner created a sense of non-identical resonance between his building and the church, as well as other buildings around the square, enough for his design to define itself and redefine other buildings around it. The building's facade was more planar. Both the size and the pattern of its openings clearly demonstrated his efforts to create a dialogue with surrounding buildings. Together with the backdrop of Karlskirche and the Technische Hochschule, Wagner's Stadtmuseum contributed to the creation of a continuous surface around the square, articulating it as a contained spatial entity within the city.

Wagner's full-scale facade model for the Kaiser Franz Josef-Stadtmuseum also indicates his attempt to integrate the building into its surroundings. In the end, his seemingly alienated building spoke the language of the city. Facade design was not only a matter of self-configuration, as his works often seemed, but also a question of urban order. The order and hierarchy of urban space was articulated by both the building's form and its cladding. It is a great pity that the design was never realized.

Despite their differing views, Wagner's proposal for the Kaiser Franz Josef-Stadtmuseum was a direct answer to Sitte's repeated calls for the creation of enclosed urban space that addressed both Karlskirche and Karlsplatz. But paradoxically, Sitte's own proposal for the reorganization of the Ringstrasse, while highly inspiring as a civic gesture to create habitable space, also presented a problem. Two projects to enclose the space in front of the Votive Church and the Rathaus were proposed in *Der Städtebau*. The buildings meant to enclose the Votive Church and the Rathaus are rendered as anonymous spatial constructs, inarticulate in terms of their internal organization, yet highly articulate in terms of their external disposition. The enclosing buildings appeared as enveloping walls or masses delimiting the open space. It seemed that the Votive Church as well as the Rathaus should be accompanied by other buildings so that the square would be legibly defined. Without resolving what those buildings were to be, their shapes and forms were precisely configured. This demonstrates the conflict of interest between the internal and external obligations of architecture. Sitte expressed his overriding concern toward the external configuration of architecture in relation to the spatial pattern of the city. The task of architecture is to envelope or enclose the space of the city before taking into account its own internal business. Architecture is a tool used to create hierarchy and order in public space. Thus, in Sitte's view, all buildings must participate in the art of building cities. **Figure 2.20**

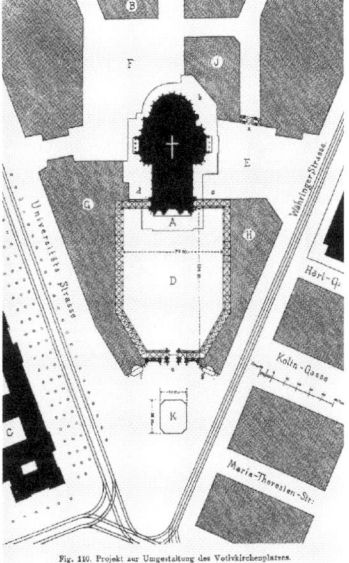

Figure 2.20 | Camillo Sitte, Votive Church area, Vienna, 1889; plan.

August Schmarsow proposed in *The Essence of Architectural Creation* that architectural space is a matter of relationships. Ensembles and their parts play decisive roles at various scales, but also boundaries.[35] The matter is not minor, for spatial creation constitutes the essence of architecture as an art. Yet, for the city the story of spatial creation can be problematic. The title of Sitte's book, *The Art of Building Cities According to Artistic Principles*, implied the problem, perhaps unknowingly. Despite the common conceit that the city is like a large house, and the house is like a small city, the works of Sitte and Wagner clearly demonstrated that the city can hardly be a unified work of art. While architecture is consciously created as a self-contained spatial body, the city cannot be similarly objectified. The space of the city is neither artistically composed, nor shaped solely by impersonal factors. Any attempt to compose the city's space will result in solutions that fail or seem profoundly reductive.

[35] For August Schmarsow and the concept of space in architecture, see Panin, Tonkao, "Space-Art, the Dialectic Between the Concepts of Raum and Bekleidung," PhD dissertation, University of Pennsylvania, 2003.

Though the city consists of aggregated bodies of architecture, it is also made up of the in-betweens. When the interior space of architecture is created, it is bounded and enclosed within its walls. The space of the city, on the other hand, is conditioned by places that are unnamed, unoccupied, and at times unwanted. The space of the city comes into being when architecture is conceived as a part of its spatial structure. Sitte and Wagner show us that in some cases the city's space can and should be structured with clear distinctions between built objects and open spaces—enclosed but unroofed and permeable. In other cases, city space is best left unclaimed and unauthored. While the space of the city is at times thought to be deliberately created, it is also a byproduct, but a byproduct that is used and occupied.

Though the creation of the space of the city is not entirely in the architect's hands, the architecture of the city carries a double obligation. The lessons of Sitte and Wagner imply that the task of architecture is to yield parts of its self-contained body to the spatial pattern of the city, structuring and being structured by its surroundings. Rather than being a void, a left-over space between carefully composed objects, a mere receptacle into which buildings are to be inserted, the space of the city may also be built-up. The space of the city, thus, lies within the relationships between the ensembles of architectural bodies that lend materiality to its boundaries.[36]

---

[36] Tonkao, "Space-Art, the Dialectic Between the Concepts of Raum and Bekleidung."

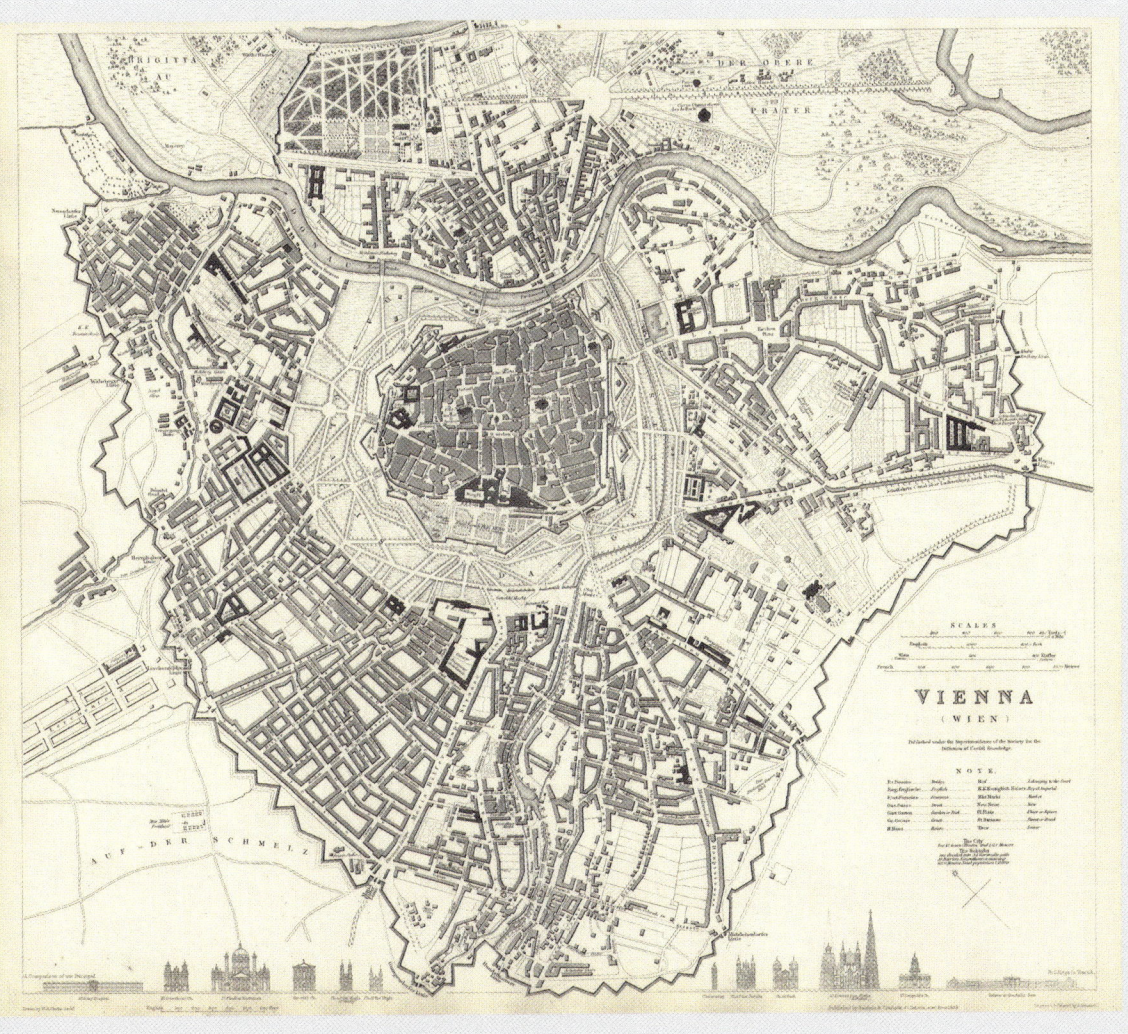

Figure 2.1 | Vienna map, 1848;
Cartographer: W.B. Clarke,
Engraver: J. Henshall.

Figure 2.2 | The Ringstrasse development, Vienna, 1860; plan.

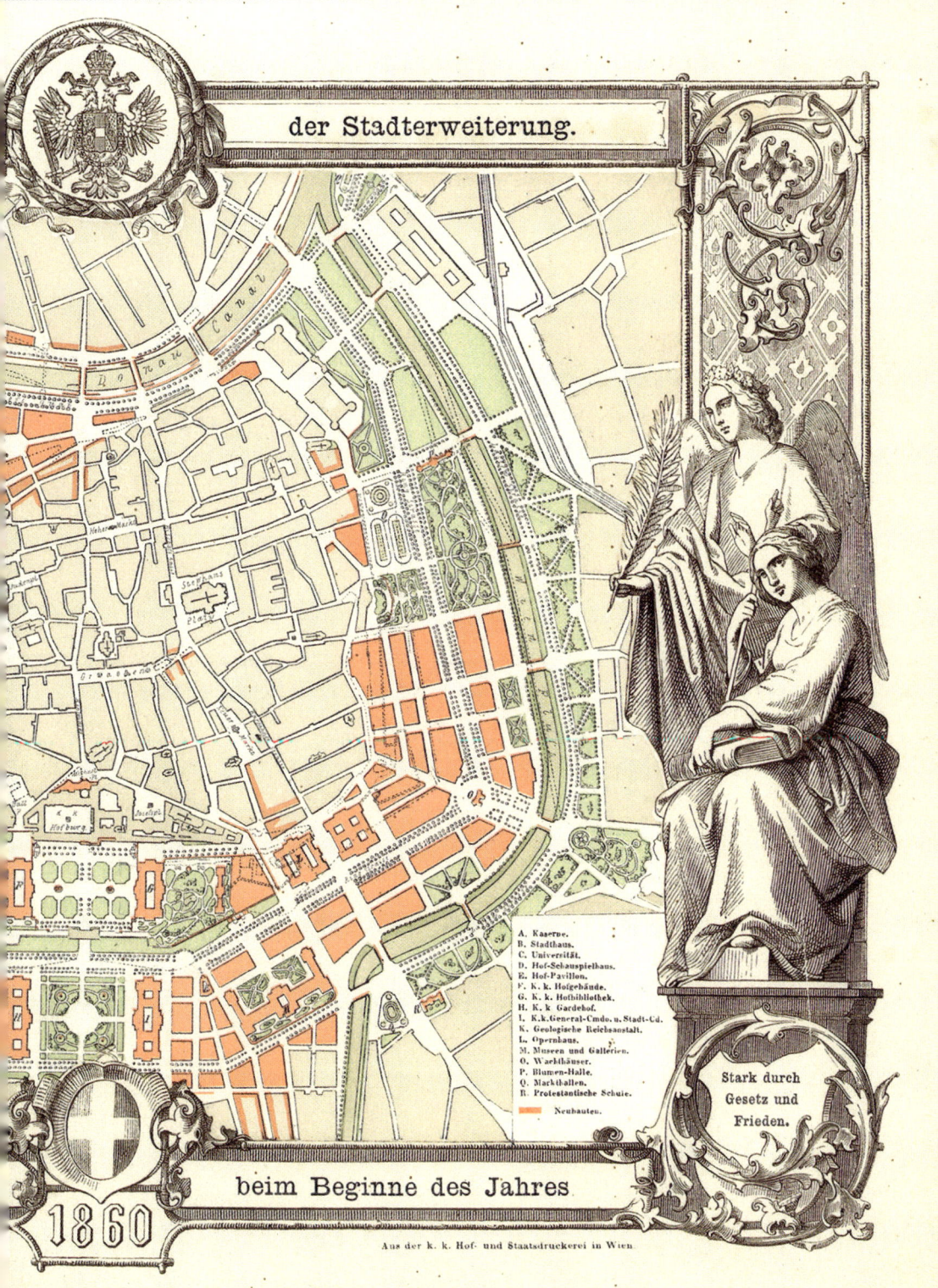

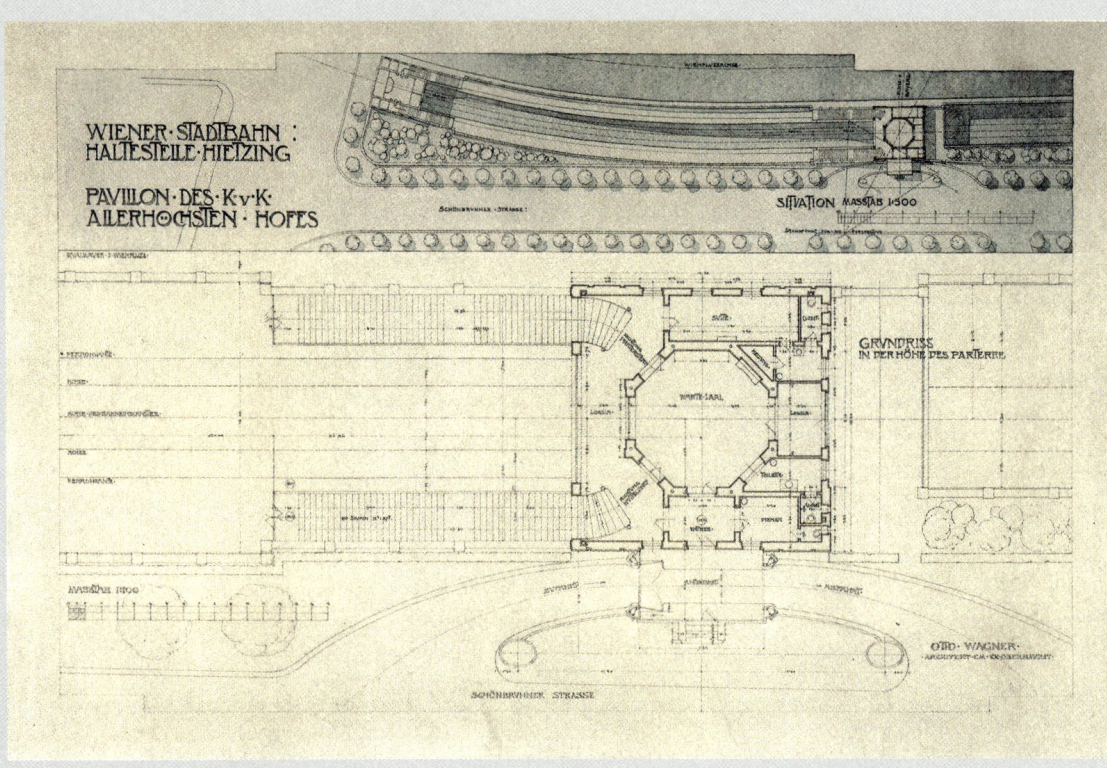

Figure 2.5 | Otto Wagner, Hietzing Station, Vienna, 1894; plan.

Figure 2.6 | Otto Wagner, Unt-Döbling Station, Vienna, 1895–6; elevation.

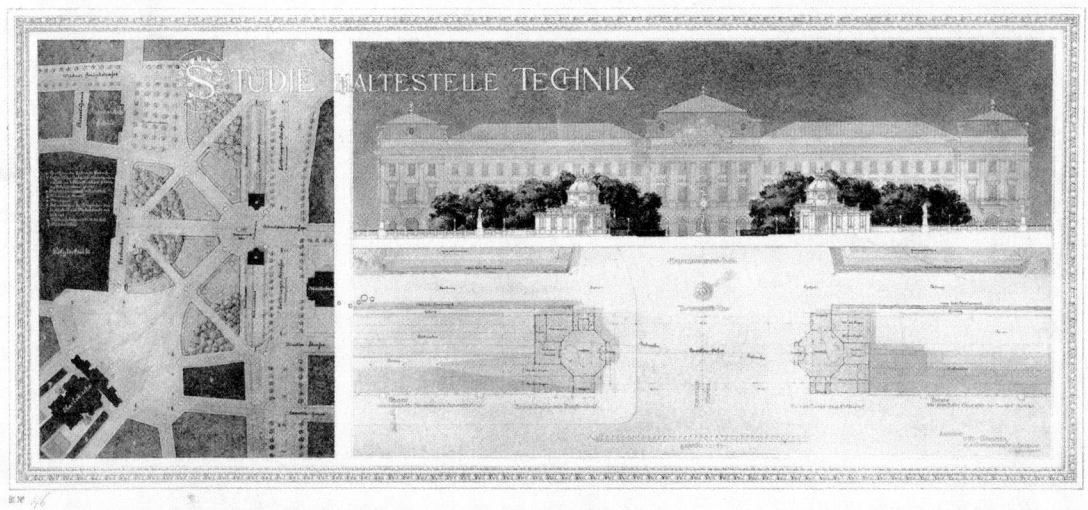

Figure 2.9 | Otto Wagner, Karlsplatz, Vienna, 1898–9, first design against the backdrop of the Technische Hochschule; plan.

Figure 2.10 | Otto Wagner, Karlsplatz, Vienna, 1898–9, final design; plan and elevation.

Figure 2.11 | Otto Wagner, Karlsplatz, Vienna, 1898–9; frontal view.

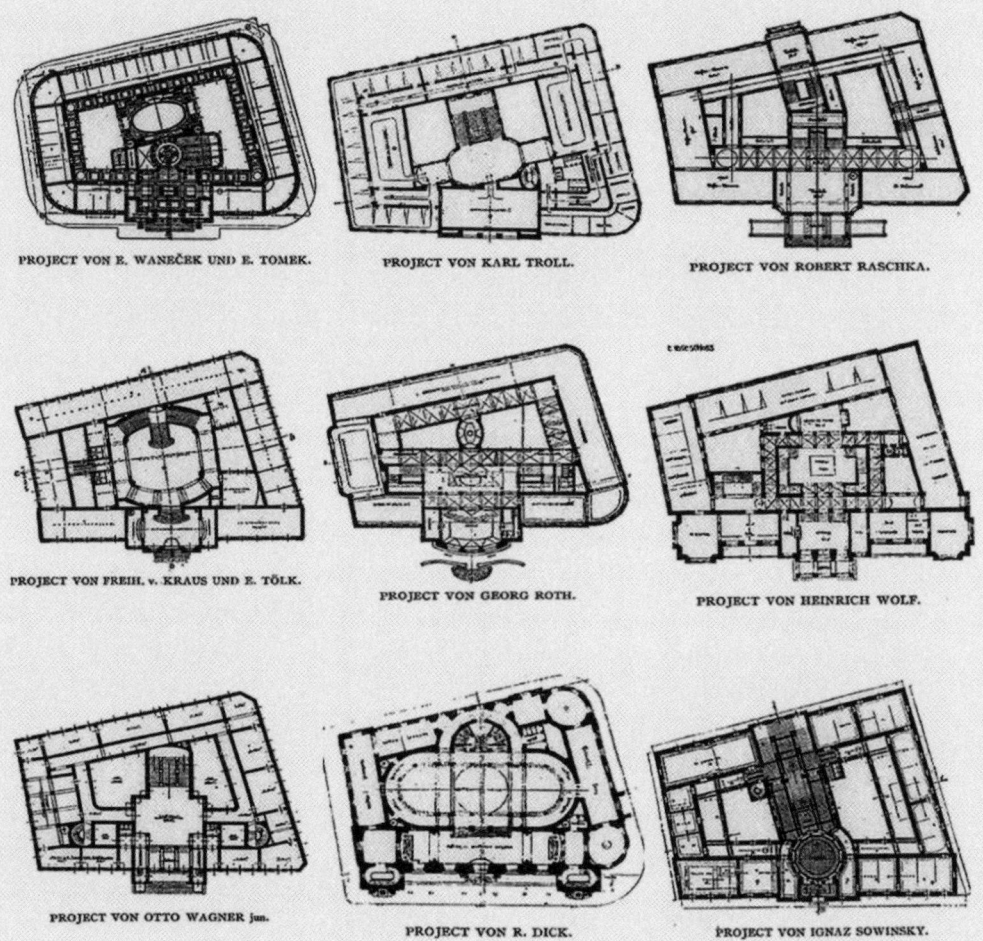

Figure 2.12 | Kaiser Franz Josef-Stadtmuseum, Vienna, 1901–2; competition entries.

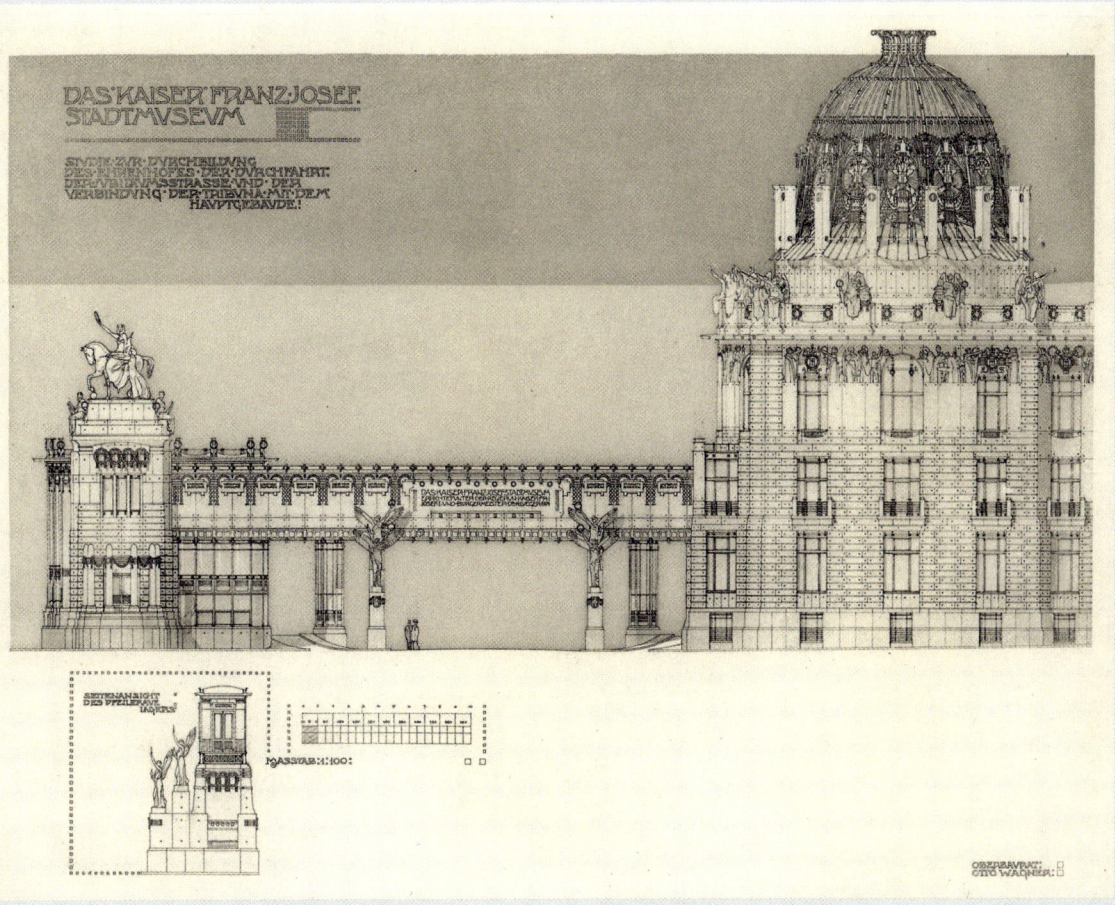

Figure 2.14 | Otto Wagner,
Kaiser Franz Josef-Stadtmuseum,
Vienna, 1903.

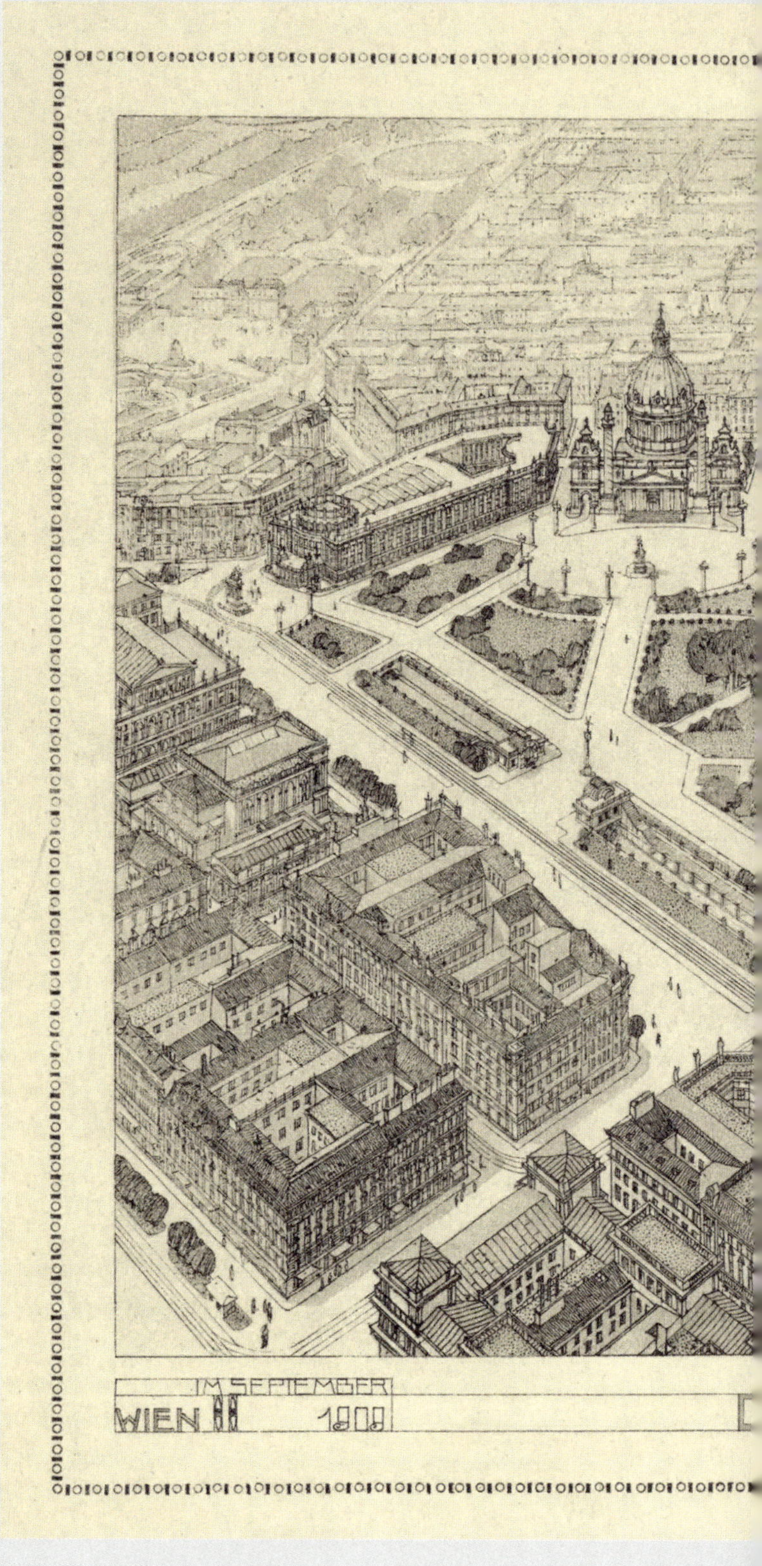

Figure 2.15 | Otto Wagner, Karlsplatz, Vienna, 1909; bird's-eye view.

Figure 2.16 | Otto Wagner, Kaiser Franz Josef-Stadtmuseum, Vienna, 1909; perspective showing enclosed Karlsplatz with the Kaiser Franz Josef-Stadtmuseum, Karlskirche and Technische Hochschule.

Esra Şahin Burat

City as Compass and Calendar

Le Corbusier's Radiant City and the Apartment Building 24NC

There is a ground upon which harmony must be based.

—Le Corbusier, *The Radiant City*.[1]

Figure 3.4 | Le Corbusier and Pierre Jeanneret, 24NC, Paris, 1931–4; east facade, as seen from rue Nungesser et Coli.

[1] Le Corbusier, *The Radiant City*, P. Knight, E. Levieux, D. Coltman trans., New York: Orion Press, 1967, p. 109. (Originally published in Boulogne as *La Ville radieuse* in 1935.)

"The sky is radiant and we have been living for two weeks in miraculous new conditions: a home that is heavenly, because everything is sky and light, space and simplicity,"[2] wrote Le Corbusier to his mother on 28 May 1934. He and his wife Yvonne had just moved to their apartment at the periphery of Paris where they would reside for the rest of their lives. The apartment building, located at 24 rue Nungesser et Coli and abbreviated by Le Corbusier as 24NC, was one he and his cousin Pierre Jeanneret had designed and constructed between 1931 and 1934.

24NC is a relatively well-known building in the history of modern architecture, examined with particular emphasis on the architect's private studio-apartment, which occupies the top two floors. The richly articulated volumes and the distinctive selection of materials, furniture, and artwork have attracted interest, too, yet they have also eclipsed the building's relationship to the architect's urban proposals, which have often been heavily criticized as strictly "Cartesian" and reductionist.[3] 24NC's personalized accents have been thought to have little in common with the standardized collective housing schemes of his visionary urban plans.[4] However, a close reading of the relationships that Le Corbusier established between 24NC's architecture and its urban context shows that the building was indeed meant to fulfill the theoretical projects of the 1920s and 1930s, which culminated in the Radiant City. The following study proposes an interpretation of 24NC not only as an exemplary manifestation of the fundamental tenets of the Radiant City project, as Le Corbusier himself described it,[5] but also as an indication of how urbanity can be projected through a single work.

Le Corbusier the Town Planner

Le Corbusier exhibited his first urban project in 1922. **Figure 3.1 (see p. 78)** Titled A Contemporary City for Three Million Inhabitants, it was a theoretical proposal without a specified site. In the foreword to the corresponding publication titled *Urbanisme*, he recounted how and why he came to be interested in town planning. During his early travels, he said, he "felt the all-powerful might of architecture," but he had "many and difficult stages" in front of him before finding "an adequate frame for it." He saw that harmony was possible only when architecture "was genuinely appropriate to its environment."[6] While Le Corbusier promoted A Contemporary City to be his "first stud[y] in town planning,"[7] he neglected to mention that his initial efforts dated back to the early 1910s, when he set out to write a book titled *La Construction des villes* (building cities), inspired by Camillo Sitte's *City Planning According to Artistic Principles*.[8] Having completed a substantial body of text, he set it aside and embarked on traveling in the spring of 1911, first in Germany and afterwards to "the Orient."

As the "official" launch of his town planning career, A Contemporary City featured differentiated zones of residential and business districts laid out in a concentric manner. At the core was the central station from which several levels of underground

---

[2] Letter in the archive of Foundation Le Corbusier, hereafter abbreviated as FLC.

[3] Expressing a common sentiment, Stanislaus Von Moos wrote, "That his curiosity for cities and for city building should have resulted in the bureaucratic abstraction of the Plan Voisin or the Ville Radiëuse was the most irritating aspect of his entire work." Von Moos, Stanislaus, *Le Corbusier: Elements of a Synthesis*, Rotterdam: 010 Publishers, 2009, p. 224.

[4] Arthur Rüegg wrote, for instance, that "although he emphasized the 'conditions de "Ville Radieuse"' in the *Œuvre complète*—thereby invoking the model-like character of the project—the design of his own residence is again far from the standardized dwelling that conformed to his visionary urban plan." Rüegg, Arthur, "Living with Objects – Learning from Objects: Le Corbusier's 'Collection Particulière'," *Le Corbusier History and Tradition*, Armando Rabaça ed., Coimbra: Coimbra University Press, 2017, p. 75.

[5] "The architects have maintained their interest in the construction of this building because the terrain fulfilled the conditions of the 'Ville Radieuse' and offered an opportunity to prove the correctness of the theses which Le Corbusier had developed in this respect." Le Corbusier and Pierre Jeanneret, *Œuvre complète volume 2 1929–34*, Basel, Boston, Berlin: Birkhäuser, 2006, p. 144; *Le Corbusier 1910–65*, W.B. Gleckman trans., Basel, Boston, Berlin: Birkhäuser, 1999, p. 64.

[6] Le Corbusier, *The City of Tomorrow*, Cambridge, MA: MIT Press, 1971, p. 4 (originally published in Paris as *Urbanisme* in 1924).

[7] Le Corbusier, *The City of Tomorrow*, p. X.

[8] Sitte's book was published in German in 1889 and in French in 1902. On Le Corbusier's *La Construction des villes*, see Brooks, H. Allen, *Le Corbusier's Formative Years*, Chicago, IL: University of Chicago Press, 1997; Schnoor, Christoph, *Le Corbusier's Practical Aesthetic of the City, The treatise 'La Construction des villes' of 1910/11*, London: Routledge, 2020.

tube networks and elevated highways radiated. The business zone of skyscrapers was surrounded by two types of collective housing: blocks with setbacks and perimeter blocks, both of which were provided with parks and sports fields. The city itself was surrounded with "protected zones of woods, fields and sports grounds," beyond which were the hills in the horizon. "Strictly speaking," wrote Le Corbusier, "the city is an immense park." The roofs of the housing blocks were also designated as "gardens and walks," and each housing unit was provided with "hanging gardens"—terraces furnished with planters. The geometric layout of these blocks permitted "broad vistas" of the urban scene, which had now become "a lively urban landscape."[9]

Le Corbusier's journey to the Orient was influential. His precedent for "covering the urban landscape with verdure" was the city of Istanbul, visited in 1911.[10] Yet he promoted the idea more as a necessity than a means of picturesque or "artistic" town planning. It was a vital remedy against "the dreadful menace of the great city which imprisons, stifles, and asphyxiates those who are cast into it."[11] The "clear and definite scheme for the provision of vegetation in the city" was one of the key tenets of A Contemporary City, one that remained unchanged and variously elaborated in the proposals of the later years. Plan Voisin of 1925 proposed replacing several historic districts of Paris with a portion of A Contemporary City. The plan consisted of "a commercial city" of skyscrapers and "a residential city" of housing blocks connected by a gridiron network of wide thoroughfares, while immense parks that filled the open spaces made the city "a vast garden."[12] Le Corbusier's further elaboration of these schemes culminated in the Radiant City, exhibited in 1930 and published as a book in 1935. In the Radiant City, the business district was pushed out of the residential zone towards the north and isolated by a green belt. The set-back blocks became the normative housing type, as they offered extended views in contrast to the closed perimeter blocks. Vehicular traffic was completely separated from pedestrian traffic, as in earlier plans, and allocated to elevated thoroughfares that would flow without interruption like great rivers.[13]

"The Contemporary Disaster"

What was it that led Le Corbusier to propose such extensive reforms in city planning, reforms that could even demand demolition of downtown Paris? Why were such drastic measures necessary? "The contemporary disaster," as he called it, consisted of two contradictory conceptions: the "urban desert" and the "garden city."[14] The former occupied the center of the city, the latter its surroundings. The "urban desert" emerged when the houses from the time of horse and cart were increased in height as the population multiplied. These tall and cramped blocks were "punched by light holes and sliced off by roads." And when the automobile arrived, cities became "deserts of stone and asphalt."[15] This kind of residential layout was unhealthy because access to sun, clean

---

9 Le Corbusier, *The City of Tomorrow*, pp. 232–6.

10 In the section where he introduced the topic of verdure in *The City of Tomorrow*, Le Corbusier quoted a Turkish proverb ("Where one builds, one plants trees") and illustrated his argument with his own sketches of Istanbul where buildings are surrounded by trees (pp. 80–1).

11 Le Corbusier, *The City of Tomorrow*, pp. 80–1.

12 Le Corbusier, *The City of Tomorrow*, pp. 275–81.

13 Le Corbusier likened the circulation of traffic to that of water and urged the city planners "to establish the correct bed for that new fluid of the modern era: the automobile." Le Corbusier, *The Radiant City*, pp. 79–80.

14 Le Corbusier and François de Pierrefeu, *Home of Man*, London: Architectural Press, 1948, p. 55. (Originally published as *La Maison des Hommes* in Paris in 1942.)

15 Le Corbusier, *Three Human Establishments*, Chandigarh: Punjab Government, Department of Town & Country Planning, 1979, p. 20. (Originally published as a volume in the ASCORAL collection with the title *Les trois établissements humains* in Paris in 1945.)

air, and greenery was very limited. "The corridor streets" created chaos and danger as the automobile and pedestrian traffic clashed, while the exhaust fumes increased the desert's sickening effects. Paris had become "tubercular." It was also wasteful and obsolete. Historic blocks that were being preserved for their "pretty iron work" lacked basic sanitation. "Mass-produced junk" overlaid with "antique" decoration[16] drained the income of the city dwellers who aspired to live in the bourgeoisie palaces they saw in movies, which in reality lacked all the basic requirements of health and wellbeing.

The other evil form of contemporary urban growth was suburbanization, exemplified by the "garden cities" of the U.S. and England, but then emerging around Paris as well. While motivated by a "dream of escape,"[17] it resulted in "exile and disillusion." Two kinds of waste resulted from dispersion: of resources, because services and infrastructure needed to be carried to each house, and of time, as commuting from center to periphery exhausted the precious hours of the solar day. Suburbanization also destroyed the collective spirit because it led to "a sterile isolation of the individual."[18] It was a waste of land, too, as the widespread pattern destroyed the natural terrain, resulting in the loss of "the object of its enterprise."[19]

Thus his fervent denunciation of "the false" alternatives. Contradictory as they were, the root cause of their troubles was the same: they both "banished nature." And "in banishing nature, the town has perished."[20]

Sun, Space, Verdure: "Happiness is a relation"
Le Corbusier's urban housing reform was based, first and foremost, on rediscovering the primordial conditions of nature and restoring the "basic pleasures" of "sun, space, verdure." They were essential and indispensable because they "penetrate into the uttermost depths of our physiological and psychological being."[21] These "ancient influences fashioned our body and our spirit,"[22] and conditioned all terrestrial life in its seasonal phases and spatial orientation. The modern city, however, neglected and abandoned them, which led to its decay and ruin. "While in nature life follows the seasons—birth, maturity, and death, spring, summer, fall and winter—and each year nature cleans up, throws out and buries, we, the intellects of the universe, are pleased to live in streets and houses that are rotting."[23] The cure required the reintroduction of the sun as a guide and the earth as a "clock," with "units" of nature as the measuring rods of all urban enterprise.[24]

Concern for the city was inseparable from involvement with nature, "in which, and upon which, we act and meditate."[25] Le Corbusier's emphasis on the dual relation of "in and upon" underlined the position of the human enterprise. "Everything in that environment passes through ... each of the individual personalities ... [a]nd whatever we are able to deduct or conclude from that environment ... is a work of art." He illustrated this idea in *The Radiant City* book with a sketch of two cones meeting at

[16] Le Corbusier's 1925 book *L'Art décoratif d'aujourd'hui*, published in Paris by G. Crès, laid out numerous examples of these.
[17] Le Corbusier, *Three Human Establishments*, p. 24.
[18] Le Corbusier, *The Radiant City*, p. 38.
[19] Le Corbusier and de Pierrefeu, *Home of Man*, p. 101.
[20] Le Corbusier and de Pierrefeu, *Home of Man*, p. 55.
[21] Le Corbusier, *The Radiant City*, p. 86.
[22] Le Corbusier and de Pierrefeu, *Home of Man*, p. 83.
[23] Le Corbusier, *The Radiant City*, p. 8.
[24] Le Corbusier, *The Radiant City*, pp. 76-7.
[25] Le Corbusier, *The Radiant City*, p. 83.

the human eye, the worlds of "universe" and "work." "Man, the medium" receives what flows in from the environment and reveals them as works of art. Each individual can "create something out of the cosmos" in his/her own way. Yet as "man is a product of nature created according to its laws," he flourishes only when his works accord with the "flux of nature." Making sense of the thesis means viewing the words nature, universe, and cosmos as synonymous. **Figure 3.2**

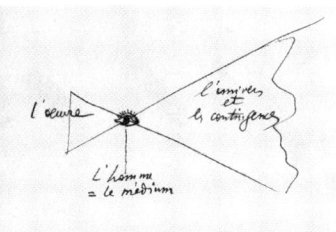

Figure 3.2 | Le Corbusier, sketch of "man, the medium."

Explaining how the favors of nature could be repaid with gifts of art was the ultimate aim of the Radiant City. Le Corbusier summed up the necessary measures in two directives: "Horizons must be reclaimed. Trees must be planted afresh."[26] The architectural and literary arguments of the urban plans elaborated these two measures, with far-reaching implications.[27] The emphasis on organic life implied embedding habitations within the workings of the natural world. The "horizon," a notion exclusive to humanity,[28] on the other hand, pertained to the perceptual and conceptualizing faculties of an observer whose vision established the prospects or cones. Together, they enrooted the meditative actions of the urban dwellers "in and upon" the contingencies of the environment, allowing their "feet [to] rest immutably upon the earth" while their gaze opened to inspirational perspectives.[29] Vegetation and horizon, therefore, encompassed the ecological and imaginative aspects of urban dwelling.

The site of 24NC fulfilled these essentials beautifully and instructively. Positioned within the loop of the Seine, edged by Bois de Boulogne (a large public park), and surrounded by gardens, sports fields, and public recreational facilities, it was a fragment of the Radiant City. Wooded hills in the west and the city of Paris in the east granted the meditational prospects for "dreaming" and "inspiration." The newly developing neighborhood had been part of Bois de Boulogne, the southern end of which was cleared and subdivided for construction in the 1920s.[30] Rue Nungesser et Coli was opened in 1929, two years before the developers purchased the plot and commissioned the architects. Following the acquisition, the developers and architects prepared an advertisement brochure to lure potential investors. Though hardly a work of art, it deserves attention because it encapsulated the essential propositions of the Radiant City and the thinking that motivated the design of 24NC.

An Advertisement that was a Thesis

The first page of the advertisement brochure featured a facade perspective as seen from the street, highlighting its all-glazed, industrial construction. Listed next to the drawing were the site's attractions: Bois de Boulogne, metro stations, and each of the several sports facilities located in the vicinity.[31] The emphasis on the surrounding stretch of parks and sports fields reflected the central tenet of the Radiant City, using the ground plane for collective recreational activities. Strolling the winding paths among trees throughout the seasons and participating in team

---

26 Le Corbusier and de Pierrefeu, *Home of Man*, p. 86 (translation altered by the author).

27 "The Five Points of a New Architecture" were put forth as the architectural "formula" of opening habitation to the effects of the horizon and live vegetation. On one important early example, the Weissenhof houses, see Şahin Burat, Esra, "Modern Rhythms: The Five Points of a New Architecture of Concordance," *Architectural Journal* 637, December 2021, pp. 20–6.

28 For an anthropological interpretation of the notion of horizon, see Van Peursen, Cornelius, "The Horizon," *Husserl: Expositions and Appraisals*, F. A. Elliston and P. McCormick eds., Notre Dame, IN: University of Notre Dame Press, 1977, pp. 182–201.

29 Le Corbusier, *The Radiant City*, p. 83.

30 Paris became a destination for artists and intellectuals from around the world when the French economy prospered after the First World War. Some newcomers entrusted the design of their houses to famous architects. Le Corbusier, a Swiss émigré, designed Villas Lipchitz-Mietschaninoff (1923-6), Villa Cook (1926), and Villa Ternisien (1923-7) not far from the site of 24 NC.

31 Archive FLC H2(2)488. The first two pages of the four-page brochure were published by Jacques Sbriglio in *Immeuble 24N.C. et Appartement Le Corbusier / Apartment Block 24 N.C. and Le Corbusier's Home*, S. Parsons trans., Basel, Boston, Berlin: Birkhäuser, 1996, pp. 25 and 87. The sports facilities listed on the first page were the Jean Bouin and the Roland Garros stadiums, the Vélodrome du Parc des Princes, a race course and a sports center with tennis courts, swimming pool, race tracks, and hockey pitches.

sports "directly outside the houses" were deemed necessary for restoring the primordial values of human nature that had been "crushed, subjugated, torn apart, [and] denatured by its subjection to the machine."[32]

The brochure also promoted the "free plan." Alongside a floor plan of two apartments with different sizes and layouts, the text advertised that "the size of the apartment and the number of rooms can be modified according to the needs of the buyer." The "liberty" of defining rooms according to changing needs and interests in the standardized blocks of the Radiant City depended on this gift of modern techniques. The next page highlighted the building's modern amenities and communal services: first-class construction materials, sound-proofing, central heating radiators, running hot water, two fitted bathrooms, elevators, laundry and drying rooms, and a garage with private parking spaces, each of which had its own raison d'être in the general scheme of the Radiant City. Provision of comfort, health, and economy was critical to the mission of the housing units serving efficiently and discreetly for the "more serious work" that would come after the work at the office or the factory: "Meditation in a new kind of dwelling, a vessel of silence and lofty solitude." This kind of disinterested, creative work could take as many forms as the individuals who lived there—a carpenter making cabinets or Le Corbusier writing a book.[33]

The brochure's site plan advertised nearby means of transport. **Figure 3.3** (see p. 80) Here the building is shown as located amid sports fields and gardens, yet still well-connected by bus, tram, metro, and train. Greenery is drawn and highlighted, but the existing blocks of Paris are eliminated. Only two structures are given a third dimension in the otherwise two-dimensional drawing: the Eiffel Tower and the facade of 24NC. The affiliation between the two structures derives from their material, situational, and functional properties: both are made of industrial materials, both rise from a bed of urban greenery,[34] and both provide viewing platforms. The full body of 24NC is abbreviated to a free facade, which works as a frame, like the tower's, through the spaces of which the gardens and parks, sports fields, landmarks, motorways, and horizons can be contemplated.[35] The disproportionately large and elaborate compass on the corner of the drawing completes the thesis: a radiant sun provides light and orientation. Le Corbusier reported that once the construction of 24NC was completed and "the building was inaugurated, the tenants spontaneously declared that a new life had started for them."[36] The ways this "new life" unfolded will be explored in the following sections.

An Elemental Ground and a Sheltered Entry

The elongated plot of 24NC has an east-west orientation, open on two shorter sides while sharing two long party walls with the neighboring buildings on the northern and southern sides. Two interior courtyards located in the center of the plan, the larger

---

[32] Le Corbusier, *The Radiant City*, p. 66.
[33] Le Corbusier, *The Radiant City*, pp. 67–8. Le Corbusier demanded the housing units be so impervious that "even a hermit in the depths of a forest could not be more cut off from other men." Monastic precedents for Le Corbusier's housing schemes have been investigated by David Leatherbarrow and Richard Wesley in *Three Cultural Ecologies*, London, New York: Routledge, 2018, chapter 5.
[34] Similar to the green plots of Parc du Champ de Mars surrounding the tower, gardens to the west of 24NC—which in reality were allotted for construction—and the sports fields to the east are highlighted in the drawing.
[35] As one climbs on the Eiffel Tower and as the visual sphere widens out, Le Corbusier claimed, "lungs expand," thoughts become "more comprehensive," "the spirit is roused," and "optimism" sets in (*The City of Tomorrow*, p. 186). The facade of 24NC sought similar effects.
[36] Le Corbusier and Jeanneret, *Œuvre complète volume 2*, p. 146. Translated in *Le Corbusier 1910–65*, p. 64.

Figure 3.5 | Le Corbusier and Pierre Jeanneret, 24NC, Paris, 1931-4; west facade, as seen from rue de la Tourelle.

Figure 3.7 | Le Corbusier and Pierre Jeanneret, 24NC, Paris, 1931-4; "a fragment of the facade and the entry porch."

"common court" to the north and the *courette* to the south, give the plan a wide "H" shape that permits six surfaces to receive light and air. The pedestrian entry on the ground floor and the vehicular access to the basement are located at the opposite sides of the plot. **Figures 3.4 (see p. 60) and 3.5** A ramp from rue de la Tourelle leads to the basement where the parking lots, common service facilities, and the rooms for domestic staff are located. The western end of the basement, reserved for the domestic staff, has a double-height English court that brings in "full western sun" and air to these rooms. The street edge of the sunken court is furnished with planters that allow verdure to flow into the basement. On the eastern end, where the parking lots are located, a recessed basement opening serves as an air vent to the garage. As a result of these openings below the street level on both edges, the primordial elements of light, air, water, and earth permeate the subterranean box of the basement. **Figure 3.6 (see p. 81)**

At ground level, the pedestrian entry is recessed from the street, resulting in a generous porch that belongs both to the street and the building. The deep and high entry space, an atypical articulation when compared to the neighboring buildings, creates "a void, allowing penetration by walkers, [ambient] light, and [direct] sunlight beneath the house".[37] **Figures 3.4 (see p. 60) and 3.7** The fluted white column situated in the center showcases the *pilotis* as the key element of the Radiant City, which allows the construction of a void space to be shared. It also provides orientation by separating the entry of the studio apartment from the main access to the building. The fact that the column was designed as a "hanging column" that rests on a transfer beam spanning between two columns in the basement (as drafted in Figure 3.6) reveals that its location owes less to statics than decorum.

Upon entry, a rising, curved path takes the visitor to the foyer. Defying the expectation of a dim space in such a location, the foyer is softly lit by translucent skylights placed under the northern interior court. While waiting for the elevator, plain surfaces that are "bathed in a tomb-like light"[38] offer a tranquil atmosphere after leaving the bustle outside.

A Standard Cell

The elevator takes the occupants to the middle floors, each of which was "constructed to suit its inhabitant, with open floor space, an open facade, and five columns running from one facade to the other."[39] Free facades admitted the vistas that the promotional brochure had promised. "In order to make best use of the exceptional location, the facades have been conceived as glass curtains placed in front of the concrete floors. Thus, each apartment possesses a wall entirely of glass, running from floor to ceiling."[40] While open to the surroundings, the housing units of the Radiant City were also envisaged to be isolated containers of creative work. Le Corbusier was aware of the conflict. "Our concern here with the inhabitants of the house is divided between contradictory

[37] Le Corbusier and de Pierrefeu, *Home of Man*, p. 116.
[38] Sbriglio, *Immeuble 24 N.C.*, pp. 22, 24.
[39] Le Corbusier and Jeanneret, *Œuvre complète volume 2*, p. 146; Sbriglio, *Immeuble 24 N.C.*, p. 88.
[40] Le Corbusier and Jeanneret, *Œuvre complète volume 2*, p. 146. Translated in *Le Corbusier 1910-65*, p. 64.

Figure 3.8 | Le Corbusier and Pierre Jeanneret, 24NC, Paris, 1931–4; living room of the first-floor apartment.

Figure 3.9 | Le Corbusier and Pierre Jeanneret, 24NC, Paris, 1931–4; dining area of the second-floor apartment.

41 Le Corbusier, P. Stirton and T. Benton, "Glass the Fundamental Material of Modern Architecture," *West 86th: A Journal of Decorative Arts, Design History, and Material Culture*, vol. 19, no. 2, fall/winter 2012, p. 298. The article originally appeared in 1935 in *Tchéco-Verre*, vol. 2, nos 1–4.
42 Le Corbusier, Stirton and Benton, "Glass the Fundamental Material of Modern Architecture," p. 297.
43 Le Corbusier and Jeanneret, *Œuvre complète volume 2*, p. 147 (top left photo), p. 153 (all four photographs).
44 Le Corbusier employed photographic tricks to reinforce the expression. The camera is positioned above the parapet level for pictures of the dining tables to include more view, while it is kept at the parapet level for the living room shots.
45 Le Corbusier, *The Radiant City*, p. 12.
46 Le Corbusier, *The Radiant City*, p. 9.

alternatives: that of the pleasure in seeing the play of the sky, trees, or general views outside, and secondly, that desire to be secluded from the outside and especially to have some privacy. It is here that combinations of translucent glass and clear glass can be involved and that the role of the creative imagination can be manifested."[41] Accordingly, the window walls of 24NC were made of "judicious combinations"[42] of Nevada glass brick, frosted glass, wired glass, clear glass, metal mesh, and textile awnings, inviting or excluding aspects of the milieu as needed. The layout of the furniture as represented in *Œuvre complète* also reflected the two "contradictory alternatives."[43] The dinner table looks out on the surrounding landscape, so that what is shared on the table is perceived to be an extension of that landscape. Yet the armchairs are oriented towards the interior. The occupants of the living room are shown, without exception, immersed in some personal, "disinterested" activity, as if isolated in their cocoons, until they gather at the table to share the meal, the view, and the stories.[44] **Figures 3.8 and 3.9**

The two prospects of the apartments at 24NC, one towards the encompassing milieu and the other towards the inner horizons of the self, reflected the two facets of "man, the medium". The two wings of Le Corbusier's own premises, which occupied the whole seventh floor, laid out the two cones of his sketch on the floor plan with specific domains for receiving (nature) and revealing (art). **Figure 3.10 (see p. 82)** The dining room, the bedroom, and their common terrace on the domestic side looked out on the Bois de Boulogne and the hills in the distance. The dining table was placed and oriented such that the wooded hills became part of the meal and the conversation. The bed was raised high on steel tubes and oriented such that every morning the sleepers would rise with the sun and face the sunlit hills over the parapet. The potted plants of the terrace extended the Bois de Boulogne to the apartment—and did so until a decade ago. In all these cases, what was distant was brought near and made part of the interiors, while the distant origins of what was nearby were made legible. The housing unit served as a receptacle that extended the gifts of the universe to its inhabitants. "Sun in the room, a window filled with blue, awakening to a wave of greenery."[45] Beneficiaries of the donations, inhabitants offered their gifts in return, in Le Corbusier's case the results of work in his "atelier of patient search," located in the opposite wing.

In the diagram of "man, the medium," the cone indicating work was closed, the one facing the world was open, implying that the patient search was an inward journey. Accordingly, the eastern front of the atelier-study was closed off. Here Le Corbusier fitted the window wall with frosted glass, glass brick, and plywood panels, and curtains, to exclude distractions of "man the revealer" while preserving the image of an all-glazed, aperture-like facade. The atelier was an exemplary cell and the "free man"[46] patiently working there was an exemplary citizen, as a panel that was exhibited at the Pavillon des Temps Nouveaux in 1937 demonstrated. **Figure 3.11 (see p. 84)** Titled *Habitation*, the panel illustrated the housing scheme of the Radiant City where the homogeneous grid of the cells was exemplified with two interiors from 24NC, the living room of the first-floor apartment, and the study of Le Corbusier's own apartment. The photograph of the neighbor's living room was enriched with figures of clouds and sun on the window wall ("the bearer of essential joys"), modern furniture ("domestic equipment"), and the freestanding column (the facilitator of free plan and free facade). The other standard cell of the Radiant City featured Le Corbusier himself, studying in front of a brightly illuminated window wall covered with a curtain.[47] Denying himself the views of the sports fields that stretch outside his window, he is immersed in his own work, perhaps the text of *The Radiant City*. The panel completes the "solitary action" in the cells with the collective recreational activities outside, illustrated with the images of happy and healthy citizens enjoying the "sandy beaches" and hilly landscapes on the roof, and "races and games" on the ground. Although not pictured on the panel, Le Corbusier is reported to have regularly joined his neighbors on the sports fields. Twice a week they played basketball "with passion and blows."[48]

A Roof for Rest and Recreation

Le Corbusier's apartment was accessed by either the staircase from the sixth floor, the last floor the main elevator served, or the smaller service elevator. The eighth floor, where the guestroom and the roof garden were located, was accessible from the apartment by a spiral staircase. Le Corbusier described the roof of 24NC as "a bed and a terrace." The "bed" of the guestroom was reserved for his mother or for friends. But the roof also featured a "bed" of greenery. Initially, the roof garden was promoted by Le Corbusier as a method of insulation and protection of concrete from cracks, and as a compensation for the earth that was disturbed by the building. "Too precious to be left to pigeons and cats," it was a vital element of the Radiant City because it reinstated the natural rhythms that the contemporary city had eclipsed. Le Corbusier liked to mention that his roof garden was mostly seeded and nurtured by birds, wind, and rain. He also liked to pose for photographs while pruning shrubs and tending his roof garden. As mundane as it looked, this was for him a cosmological act, nothing less than "the key of comprehension... of our situation in the world."[49] The scissors formed images of "a lost paradise," and pruning was "an occasion to put oneself in direct contact with nature." Cutting a branch while standing on earth under the sky and clouds, with the hills in the horizon, emblematized the situation of "man, the medium" in the universe. **Figures 3.12 (see p. 77) and 3.13 (see p. 88)**

When the other aspect of the space is emphasized, the "terrace," it seems as if it was designed like a roof café, complete with a canopy, paved floor, chairs, and a concrete bench, all surrounded by greenery and open to vistas. This arrangement fulfilled his desire to move cafés to the roofs, as recommended in *Towards a New Architecture*[50] and illustrated in *The City of Tomorrow*. **Figure 3.1 (see p. 78)**

[47] The photograph was a reprint of the top left photograph published in *Œuvre complète volume 2*, p. 149.

[48] Pierre Winter, who was Le Corbusier's doctor, colleague, and neighbor at 24NC, stated in an article published in *Œuvre complète* that they played basketball together twice every week for 16 years. Winter, Pierre, "Le Corbusier, Biologiste, Sociologue", *Œuvre complète volume 3 1934–1938*, Max Bill ed., Basel, Boston, Berlin: Birkhäuser, 2006, p. 14.

[49] Le Corbusier, *Three Human Establishments*, p. 75.

[50] "Cafés and places of recreation would no longer be that fungus which eats up the pavements of Paris: they would be transferred to the flat roofs..." Le Corbusier, *Towards a New Architecture*, New York: Dover, 1986, p. 60.

The concrete bench placed adjacent to the skylight of the living room, the chimney of the living room's fireplace, and the mechanical room of the service elevator, formed a compact assembly of objects surrounded by trees and shrubs. **Figure 3.14** (see p. 86) That the composition of this ensemble was important for Le Corbusier can be concluded from both its elaborate articulation in the drawings and frequent portrayal in his books. We find the same ensemble in *New World of Space* of 1948 where the accompanying text reveals that there is more to it than what appears at first sight.

> When the inexplicable appears in human work, that is, when our spirit is projected far from the narrow relation of cause and effect and when a lively feeling lifts us up and carries our thoughts from the base object to the cosmic phenomenon in time, in space, in the intangible, in what is visible of roots that bury themselves all around and nourish us with the essence of the world—then the inexplicable is the miracle of art. In this moment a definite object, freshly created there before our eyes, has a form which is the same for all of us. It is like a piece of radium ... a concentrated power, it is a work of art ... It is the minute of silence in our work.[51]

As a genuine "work of art" where "base objects" recalled a "cosmic phenomenon," the roof garden ensemble was the "minute of silence" in the work. Originating from the same bed and nourished by the same primordial forces, flowers, trees, the work of art similarly "made something out of the cosmos" in a new creation.[52] The roof garden was a place of rest and recreation, the words "rest" and "recreation" taken in both a literal and primordial sense. It was the epitome of the passage from a nurturing bed to a radiant object under the rule of the seasons and all the elements they organized: the sun, rain, winds, birds, and last but not least, "subsoil and fertilizer," as the first drawing of *The Radiant City* indicated on the "Contents" page. A productive garden flourished on the buried remains of the season that had passed.

The Cemetery Garden
Frequent allusions to the idea of the elevated garden as a place of life, death, and regeneration are found in Le Corbusier's accounts of his journey to the Orient. The urban cemeteries of Istanbul in particular appear to have provided a model for the roof garden as a place of rest and recreation, ruled by the rhythms of the natural world. During his seven-week Istanbul journey with August Klipstein, the cemeteries fascinated him the most, as the "disproportionate amounts of time and film," sketches, travel notes, writings, and correspondence devoted to them reveal, a fascination that has perplexed historians.[53] Already in his 1910 manuscript of *La Construction des villes*, he planned a chapter on cemeteries in which he criticized the new ones for their "commercialized taste." Instead, he proposed that "the cemetery can become a

---

51 Le Corbusier, *New World of Space*, New York: Reynal & Hitchcock, 1948, p. 117.
52 The same text appeared earlier in *L'Art décoratif d'aujourd'hui*, accompanying an image of Saturn (captioned "Saturn: a true creation").
53 Brooks, *Le Corbusier's Formative Years*, p. 273. Brooks wrote that he has "no explanation for Jeanneret's fascination for cemeteries and tombstones, or why so many of his sketches, postcards, and particularly photographs are of them. His notes and letters frequently speak of them." (Note 17 on p. 267 and p. 269.)

park … [which] would oblige one to remain *stillstehen* [standing still] amidst the hurly burly of life, and this could only have a beneficial influence."[54] The "cemeteries of Constantinople" provided an example in this respect, as his primary reference on gardens, Georges Riat's *L'Art des Jardins*, singled them out for serving as public gardens and walks.[55] His readings of the Istanbul diaries of former French travelers, such as Gérard de Nerval's *Voyage en Orient* (1851), Pierre Loti's *Aziyadé* (1879),[56] which Riat quoted at length,[57] and Claude Farrère's *L'Homme qui assassina* (1906),[58] praised the "refreshing" cemeteries that host "all the pleasure-grounds" of the city,[59] the cemetery-gardens that are squeezed in between the houses, and the streets where "the living and the dead are next to each other."[60] These provided Le Corbusier with a wealth of imagery to pursue during his "journey of reverie."[61] The old district of Eyüp, known for its historic burial grounds that merged seamlessly and endlessly into the residential and commercial quarters, fulfilled his "dream."[62] In the text of his last book, which he finalized in his apartment at 24NC shortly before his death,[63] he described how the cemeteries blended into the urban fabric.

> Stamboul is submerged in tombs. Everyone loves them. The tombs extend right into the courtyards of the houses. One Turkish Sunday, I saw a fellow … seated in his garden, his back against the white column of a tomb; he was just daydreaming… but as for me, I was struck by this … in the little courtyards of many residences in Rodosto and elsewhere I had already seen little lanterns at the very threshold of the doors keeping vigil over the household dead. Constantinople is a wilderness; people build houses, plant trees, and where there is any place left, they bury their dead.[64]

A sketch he captioned "Eyoub 1911" illustrates such a street, where courtyards serve as burial grounds of the "household dead." **Figure 3.15 (see p. 89)** Elevated above street level, the cemetery-courtyards are also thriving gardens. The volumes of the house are clearly delineated, but the use of their interiors is ambiguous: the rooms of the living, the beds of greenery, and the places of rest of the dead are similar in their architectural articulation. All are simple prisms that struggle to contain, or crack under the pressure of hidden battles within, struggles like those of plants emerging from their beds. The volumes that enclose the plots, the people, or the buried are indiscriminate, except for the corner volume with windows. All that comprises the courtyard-cemetery-roof-garden in Eyüp anticipates the roof of 24NC.

Another image from the cemeteries in Eyüp, this time a photograph taken by Le Corbusier in 1911, likewise included the characters of 24NC's roof garden ensemble: stacks attached to white boxes that lie in the midst of verdure under the shade of a canopy; except in the Eyüp version, the shining boxes are tombs,

---

[54] Schnoor, *Le Corbusier's Practical Aesthetic*, p. 384.

[55] Riat, Georges, *L'Art des Jardins*, Paris: LH May, 1900, p. 362.

[56] Pierre Loti (1850-1923) was a French naval officer who rose to fame with his first novel *Aziyadé* and became a prominent novelist. William Ritter, Le Corbusier's mentor, corresponded and collaborated with Loti. Donzé, Fernand et al., "Loti, Pierre, 1850-1923," *William Ritter, au temps d'une autre Europe*, Nouvelle revue neuchâteloise 61, spring 1999, pp. 45-6.

[57] Riat quoted selections from *Aziyadé* and published an illustration that anticipated the cemetery photographs Le Corbusier took during his journey (Riat, *L'Art des Jardins*, pp. 362-8).

[58] Claude Farrère (1876-1957) was a French naval officer who became a prominent novelist following the footsteps of Loti, whom he regarded as his mentor. Le Corbusier referred to Farrère's novel as the book that made him "adore, in advance, the dead city" (letter to W. Ritter, March 1, 1911, FLC Archive). His own account of Istanbul was greatly influenced by the novel.

[59] De Nerval, Gérard, *Voyage en orient*, Paris: Charpentier, 1851, p. 165. Nerval described the festive family picnics that took place by the tombs of the loved ones. Nerval's title was borrowed by Le Corbusier with a slight alteration.

[60] "Les morts et les vivants voisinent." Farrère, Claude, *L'Homme qui assassina*, Paris: Paul Ollendorf, Société d'éditions littéraires et artistiques, 1908, p. 133.

[61] Letter to W. Ritter, March 1, 1911. On the other narratives of the Orient that influenced Le Corbusier, see Zaknic, Ivan, *Klip and Corb on the Road*, Zurich: Scheidegger & Spiess, 2019, pp. 226-39.

[62] Letter to L'Éplattenier, July 18, 1911, FLC Archive.

[63] *Le Voyage d'Orient* was published posthumously (in Paris by Éditions Forces Vives) in 1966. Le Corbusier reread the text and submitted it for publication shortly before his death. His final note to the manuscript reads: "Completed at Naples on October 10, 1911, by Charles-Édouard Jeanneret. Reread on July 17, 1965, 24 rue Nungesser et Coli, by Le Corbusier." Le Corbusier, *Journey to the East*, I. Zaknic ed. and trans., Cambridge, MA: MIT Press, 2007, p. 240.

[64] Le Corbusier, *Journey to the East*, p. 123.

the chimney stacks are tombstones, and the canopy is a tree. **Figure 3.16 (see p. 86)** Like the roof garden, however, the cemetery-garden is situated on high ground, at the level of surrounding rooftops. The clay chimneypot of Le Corbusier's chimney evokes the carved stone caps of the tombstones, a creative interpretation of the ubiquitous element of the Parisian roofscape. In the photograph, a man is standing among the dead, leaning on a tombstone without a carved cap, probably of a nameless grave. His body completes the unfinished tombstone with his own torso and hat, as if his body is his own tombstone. His restful posture re-enacts the story in the *Journey to the Orient* of the man daydreaming, with his back against the tombstone in his garden, and Le Corbusier's own description of Eyüp as a "dream." The scene was an on-site portrayal of these allusions which, in fact, had their origins in the Istanbul diaries.[65] The powerful image remained with Le Corbusier. He re-enacted it in various sites[66] and interpreted it not only on the roof of his own apartment, but also on the roofs and terraces of many of his projects from the 1920s onwards.[67] The elevated cemetery-garden encapsulated the two essential measures of the Radiant City: verdure and horizons. It coupled organic life—resting in earth and flowering according to season—with human imagination, which is "seated" in the same nurturing bed, yet capable of journeying through the seasons in a daydream.

On the roof of 24NC, the overturned flowerpot recalled the man with the hat[68] daydreaming on a bench. The skylight behind the bench, on the other hand, evoked the "lanterns[69] that kept vigil over the household dead" resting below.

The Living Room of the Dead

In *Œuvre complète*, Le Corbusier stated that his roof garden was "in communication with the seventh floor."[70] The section drawing of his apartment and an earlier section of the living room show the precision with which this "communication" was established. **Figure 3.17 (see p. 87)** The elevator box-tomb descends into the living room, the chimney-tombstone is connected to the fireplace, and the lantern-skylight allows light to penetrate the confined room below. The living room is crammed into the space between the shaft of the service elevator and the mechanical room of the main elevator. "What you so ostentatiously call my living room measures only 2.2 meters," Le Corbusier remarked.[71] A carefully composed photograph shows him reclining on a chair under the skylight and next to the elevator shaft and the fireplace, while holding a book and looking outward. **Figure 3.18 (see p. 86)** Another scene accentuates the nocturnal character of the location and the illumination from the "lantern" above, this time from a wall lamp. **Figure 3.19 (see p. 90)** The other corner of the living room forms another setting of "reverie" by the tomb, one that opens towards distant horizons. Here the sofa is placed adjacent to the mechanical room of the elevator, which forms a large, tomb-like cube in the room that recalls the white cube of his "first painting,"

---

65 Gérard de Nerval wrote in *Voyage en orient* that the tombstones in the cemeteries of Istanbul, "the height of a man, having a ball for a head surmounted by a turban," as seen through the trees under the play of the sunlight, gave the illusion of living men (p. 166). The contemplative posture of the man, on the other hand, recalled Pierre Loti's emotional experience at the cemetery where his life appeared as a dream as he was holding the marble stele of his lover's tomb. Loti, P., *Aziyadé*, Paris: Calmann Lévy, 1879, chapter 4. Loti adopted the brimless, felt hat (*fes*) during his stays in Istanbul. The stele in the foreground of the photograph resembles that of Aziyadé's tomb which Loti reconstructed at his house in France.

66 In comparable examples, Le Corbusier photographed Klipstein at a cemetery in Scutari (Üsküdar) sitting cross-legged in front of a large tree, with an analogous ensemble in the background, where a tombstone topped with a hat stands on a marble slab in front of a tree. At the Acropolis, each of them posed with a hat while leaning on the fallen columns and gazing at the horizon. These photographs were published by I. Zaknic in *Klip and Corb* on pages 142 and 194.

67 Various combinations of lantern, bench, chimney with chimneypots, and tomb-like planters can be found on the roofs or terraces of La Roche House (1923), Houses in Pessac (1925), Esprit Nouveau Pavilion (1925), Villa Ternisien (1926), the "Minimum" House project (1926), Cook House (1926), Guiette House (1926), Villa at Garches (1927), Weissenhof Stuttgart (1927), the Wanner apartment blocks project (1928-9), Villa Savoye (1929-31), Beistegui Apartment (1930-1), Clarté apartments (1930-2), Rentenanstalt Zurich (1933), and Une maison de weekend (1935).

68 Le Corbusier borrowed the analogy from Gérard de Nerval, who likened the hats of the dervishes in Istanbul to upside-down flower pots. De Nerval, *Voyage en orient*, p. 228.

69 Le Corbusier's image of the lanterns lighting up the family tombs can also be traced to Nerval, who reported that the family picnics at the cemeteries continued into the night and the fluttering lights of their lanterns fleetingly animated the tombstones of the loved ones. De Nerval, *Voyage en orient*, p. 173.

70 Le Corbusier and Jeanneret, *Œuvre complète volume 2*, p. 148.

71 Sbriglio, *Immeuble 24 N.C.*, p. 34.

La Cheminée.[72] Le Corbusier staged himself on the sofa "his back against the white column of a tomb" and reading a newspaper—stories of the ups and downs of modern life—under the light from the high window of the northern wall or from the "lantern" fixed to the white cube (drafted in Figure 3.10), with a prospect towards the dining room and its all-glazed facade.[73] The casket-wide living room was thus designed and portrayed as a subterranean chamber "in communication" with the cemetery-roof garden in the vertical and the "cone" of reception in the horizontal. Serving as a family graveyard that prompted recollection and reflection in the center of the house,[74] it closely resembled the courtyard of the house in Eyüp. **Figure 3.15 (see p. 89)**

A comparison of Le Corbusier's sketch of the Eyüp house and the section of his apartment reveals startling similarities: a central courtyard-roof garden-cemetery flanked by two higher volumes. In the sketch, one of these volumes has windows,[75] similar to the western wing of 24NC which was open to the views of the neighborhood, the park, and the hills in the distance. The other high volume of the house in Eyüp has no windows, resembling the eastern wing of 24NC, the secluded domain of "man the revealer." The closed volume of the sketch has traces of red paint—the color of creativity in the Corbusian palette—in contrast to the green traces of the volume of reception at the other end. Plants are growing above the cracks of the roof of the red volume, which are recalled by the plant emerging from the roof of Le Corbusier's atelier, promoted as a measure "to protect concrete from cracks." **Figure 3.13 (see p. 88)** The cracks give a glimpse of the battles that take place inside, the fruits of which emerge as "works of art." In Eyüp, the closed box is supplied with a fountain beneath, repeated in Le Corbusier's atelier as a spout with a basin to the right of the entrance, drawn in the plan.

In both houses, the cemetery-gardens in the center accommodate various agents of vertical movement, such as stems, steles, ducts, wells, shafts, and vents. Rises and falls through them are occasioned by the engagements with the milieu. At 24NC, the gifts of the universe received on one side and the offerings given in return on the other are weighed in the center, the locus of reverie of "man, the medium." In the existing state of "mechanized and triumphant times," this "weighing [of] the values of conscience" and "the instinctive sense of justice" that triggered it had been sent "down the drain" for "a rush of riches."[76] The graveyard-garden located in the center was an attempt to awaken that instinct, as if in a "chariot of death," which advertised in *The Radiant City* that justice prevailed "in life after death."[77] The visionary states of life, death, and afterlife were serviced by the conduits that ascended and descended between the floors of 24NC. On the days that one gave more than he received, the spirit rose up through the chimney flue and the body sprouted as a tree, yet if a debt incurred, the service elevator gave access to the basement. Here a garbage room was located next to the elevator and a boiler room down the hall, the "communal services" of 24NC.

---

[72] Le Corbusier erroneously yet purposefully called *La Cheminée* of 1918 his "first painting." I propose that the painting encapsulates the cemetery theme in the context of his living room at 20 rue Jacob, outlining what is left behind after death: a tomb-house-temple (the white cube) and books (stories, "nothing is transmissible but thought") above the horizon, and fragments (details of the mantelpiece) below. An affiliation between *La Cheminée* and 24NC has been proposed previously. See Carl, Peter, "Le Corbusier's Penthouse in Paris, 24 Rue Nungesser-et-Coli," *Daidalos* 28, June 1988, pp. 65–75.

[73] Le Corbusier appears in several photographs that show him in this posture in the living room. Those taken by Willy Rizzo in 1953 can be cited as exemplary. One of them was published in a richly illustrated article (Maurice Diricq, "Génial et amer, admiré et injurié, architecte du bonheur, visionnaire de la cité future: Le Corbusier," pp. 26–7) in *Paris Match*, January 30, 1954.

[74] Pierre Loti too built "tombs" in his house in Rochefort, next to which he would rest on a divan and read in isolation. He decorated a skylit room like a *türbe* (family mausoleum), with tiled walls and coffins draped with textiles and furnished with caps. Next to the coffins stood Aziyadé's tomb brought (or copied) from a cemetery in Istanbul. On Loti's house, see Liot, Thierry, *La maison de Pierre Loti à Rochefort: 1850–1923*, Chauray: Editions Patrimoines médias, 1999.

[75] A crude sketch of the same house as viewed from the opposite side shows a third window on the facade looking onto the greenery and the tombstones that populate the foreground (FLC 1792 verso).

[76] Le Corbusier, *The Radiant City*, p. 15. "It is better to give than to receive. There is pleasure in giving. Put out one hand to receive a little, put out the other to give away more: then the circuit of life moves in a positive direction and leaves each conscience with its piece of contentment."

[77] Le Corbusier, *The Radiant City*, p. 14. The painting that Le Corbusier reproduced in *The Radiant City* and captioned "Chariot of Death" was the panel of "Triumph of Death" (1460s) which he had seen at the Pinacoteca Nazionale in Siena.

It is highly probable that Le Corbusier's sketch of the house in Eyüp does not correspond to any real location.[78] Instead, the sketch puts forth a mythical precedent, a dreamed-of prototype of the conceptual, functional, and volumetric scheme of his apartment at 24NC. The notion of the cemetery-garden, however, was not an idiosyncratic element of his apartment; larger themes of urbanity were at play. Helpful here is his story of a café in Istanbul, narrated in *Journey to the East*.

Allegory of the Café

Titled "A Café," the story described a coffeehouse in Istanbul located in front of an old mosque close to the Grand Bazaar. **Figure 3.20 (see p. 91)** Le Corbusier wrote that he found it by chance, as he was "fleeing anywhere to escape the Bazaar." A place where "everything is cool and quiet," the café was in stark contrast to the feverish bazaar. The most "touching" parts of the café were the mounds that lay among the tables and the benches. These mounds were tombs of saints, each "bordered by a stone wall with a fine iron railing; a lantern hung to some tree which had sprouted there burns every night to illuminate the tombstones whose worn inscriptions no doubt recall the virtues of brave men now resting between the roots of the great sycamore which rises like their soul to heaven. They must rest here among the living, so as to familiarize them with Sweet Death."[79] His story and the sketch reassemble the key elements of his apartment, but in the setting of an urban café: a bench for dreaming next to a tomb (enclosed within a wall of stone and iron), a canopy, trees that sprout there, a lantern that illuminates the tomb of the "brave man" resting below, and "inscriptions" that recall past stories.[80] The drawing's circular frame, together with the "great sycamore's" profile, enclose the ensemble within a spherical horizon of accents and descents.

The allegorical character of the story becomes evident when we discover that the particulars were adjusted to fit into the narrative.[81] Regardless, the story transposes the cemetery-garden to a bustling urban context as a place of burial and regeneration "to remain *stillstehen* amidst the hurly burly of life." Le Corbusier's urban plans proposed similar places of rest and recreation, pause and recalibration amid the incessant flow of the modern city. In defense of Plan Voisin's erasure of the old districts of Paris, he argued that certain landmarks would be preserved as relics amidst a "framework of trees and woods." These "green parks with their relics are in some sort cemeteries, carefully tended, in which people may breathe, dream, and learn."[82] Not only the roof gardens, therefore, but the whole urban ground was envisaged as a recreational and communicative cemetery-garden. He was more explicit in *The Radiant City*. "Death is the Sacrament of life. Without death, life has no meaning. Death implies a limit, a stage, a cycle, the whole, the achievement. Suddenly all is gone. Why don't we want to lead human achievements to the cemetery?—tools,

---

[78] The house in the sketch appears to be a creative combination of his impressions of the houses he studied in the Balkans and those of the cemeteries of Eyüp. His photographs and sketches of the Balkan houses show architectural elements that strongly resemble the house in the sketch. See, for instance, the images published by Giuliano Gresleri in *Le Corbusier Viaggio in Oriente*, Venice: Marsilio Editori, 1984, on pages 146–8, 153–4, 166–7.

[79] Le Corbusier, *Journey to the East*, pp. 135–6.

[80] The theme of news and stories that prompt reflection has precedents in Le Corbusier's early readings. Gérard de Nerval likened the legends told by professional storytellers in the cafés of Istanbul to serials in French newspapers, and narrated at length the dramatic story of an architect hero as told in a café. In *Aziyadé*, the section that follows Loti's dream by the tomb is a newspaper article that reports the naval officer's (Loti's own) heroic death in a battle. In realization of Le Corbusier's allegorical re-enactments of the theme in his apartment, *LIFE* magazine reported the news of the "Death of a Great Architect – 'Le Corbu'" with the photograph in Figure 3.18 on page 86 (September 10, 1965, p. 40).

[81] While Le Corbusier wrote that he found it "by chance," the café of Mahmud Pasha was mentioned by Claude Farrère as "the most adorable of the little Turkish cafés." It was where Farrère and Loti spent many evenings when they both served in the French cruiser that was stationed in Istanbul in 1903–4 (Farrère, C., "Message de M Claude Farrère, de l'Académie Française, à l'Assosiation Culturelle Franco-Turque d'Istanbul à l'occasion du 100ème anniversaire de la naissance de Pierre Loti," *Bulletin Officiel du Touring et Automobile Club de Turquie*, January 1950, pp. 23–4). The café was a meeting point for local poets, writers, and intellectuals. Le Corbusier and Klipstein seem to have wanted to join the club of learned men meeting there, following the footsteps of the French sailor-novelists. Mahmud Pasha Mosque (1463) had two identical domes covering the main rectangular space, not "a single large dome that rested on four bare walls." Le Corbusier seems to have preferred the building to have a simpler volume and a pure geometric shape.

[82] Le Corbusier, *The City of Tomorrow*, pp. 287–8.

houses, cities."[83] With "uninterrupted stretches of vegetation from which would rise only the pure prisms of the houses,"[84]—of the dead and the living alike—the Radiant City was the allegory of a creative burial ground fertilized by the remains and the parables of the late season.

Urbanity as Ecological Imagination

The Radiant City was Le Corbusier's "sacred book," the writing of which was a battle. "I'm still there, every morning, I worry to die skinning myself, rereading myself a hundred and once! What patience is needed to bring a work into the world,"[85] he wrote to his mother in November 1934. While being drafted in the tranquil atmosphere of his new, "heavenly" home, he professed in the opening essay that the book was "not a literary work written ... in the serene study of things." On the contrary, the book was about "the battering of life today; the rapid and violent growth of the modern phenomenon of urbanism; the explosion of accumulated anxieties and the outbreak of hysteria; dilemmas; a healthy, courageous and optimistic viewpoint; a belief in the future of a new civilization."[86] The chapters that followed were an exposition, with vivid examples and dramatic literary style, of the perils of the age. Machine civilization had advanced and become a menace. In the face of the "contemporary disaster," the Radiant City offered "minutes of silence" and "a breadth of vision" to situate the battles of urban life in a cosmological framework, so that one did not lose his way and his time in the violent flow of the modern city. Envisaged for productive and contemplative mortals, the Radiant City was meant to be a calendar and a compass for its citizens, as the promotional brochure for 24NC illustrated. The sun-compass and the calendar-gardens provide orientation and temporality to the urban surge signified by the bus and the metro lines, while 24NC and the Eiffel Tower present framed views of the spectacle to the reflective city-dweller, offering prospects of both ascent and descent.

In *Journey to the East*, the chapter that followed "A Café" was "Sesame,"[87] where Le Corbusier told the story of the bazaar, the place of "worst horrors:" It is a labyrinth, a dark maze "without a glimpse of sky," where one gets lost without a compass. Yet it is full of "disconcerting ingeniousness." One does not enter the shops, but is sucked in. And "once inside the great machine, the hustle begins." "Vampire" merchants shout endlessly, "babbling like a machine-gun," stuffing their merchandise in one's hands one after the other. Tempting with so many words, making promises, swearing oaths, they stupefy. "You cannot be cold-blooded any longer... too many delightful evocations... You are intoxicated... This torrent, this flood ... brutalizes and annihilates you." At the end one is lost, walking out with a bundle of merchandise under the arm, "filled with remorse." It is frenzied during the day, but "at sunset, the heavy doors are drawn... the great clamor subsides," and crushed souls escape to the cemetery-garden-café to recover themselves.

---

83 Le Corbusier, *The Radiant City*, p. 203.
84 Le Corbusier, *Precisions on the State of Architecture and City Planning*, E. S. Aujame trans., Cambridge, MA: MIT Press, 1991, p. 50. (Originally published in French in Paris, 1930.)
85 "Mon sacré livre 'Ville Radieuse'..." Letter dated November 4, 1934, FLC Archive.
86 Le Corbusier, *The Radiant City*, p. 7.
87 The title "Sesame" referred to the phrase "Open, O sesame" in the story of *Ali Baba and the Forty Thieves*. Le Corbusier, *Journey to the East*, pp. 137-42.

The bazaar was an allegory, like that of the café, one that complemented and justified it. Together they illustrated the contrast between the machine-bazaar and the cemetery-café; the brutal, intoxicating dominion of uncontrolled fight for gain and the necessity for the tranquil garden to cope with its effects.[88] Incessant assaults of the industrialized free-market economy, allegorized by Le Corbusier as the machine-bazaar, were hardly stoppable. While recognizing its pervasiveness,[89] Le Corbusier hoped that this unproductive fight could be restrained within spatial and temporal boundaries, oriented towards higher motives, and replaced by the enthusiasm of team sports and creativity of disinterested work. He pushed the domains of industry and business away from habitation by means of strict zoning and isolated them with green bands. He proposed unlimited gardens above and below for rest and recreation in a cosmological framework. He let the unstoppable machines run their course at full speed, but only in their allocated beds. He made the housing units places of refuge and recuperation from the torrents. The housing blocks were "arks" modeled after ocean liners.[90] Considering all things, he aimed at a "theoretically water-tight formula."[91] In the end, he was not the prophet of a new age, the age had advanced and strayed far, but of the looming disaster, in the face of which he tried to instill hope. Nevertheless, the modern man whom he passionately tried to awaken and empower failed to control the gushing rivers that flooded the world's cities. Perhaps the most illustrative realization of Le Corbusier's allegory, the global environmental catastrophe that ensued from the unrestrained machine-bazaar, would have been no surprise to him; rather, the inescapable and the just return to the cemetery-garden for a fresh beginning.

---

[88] Tim Benton likened the serenity of the café of Mahmud Pasha as depicted by Le Corbusier to his experience at the Monastery of Ema, the former being "the oriental variant of ... a settled and peaceful existence" (Benton, T., "Voyage d'Orient," *Le Corbusier: Architect of the Century*, London: Arts Council of Great Britain, 1987, p. 57). I would suggest calling it an urban variant, for it transposed the monk and his contemplative garden to a busy commercial center the experiences of which provided him ample opportunity for reflection.

[89] He wrote that based on the laws of supply rather than demand, modern industry's endless production of waste and the market's relentless efforts to sell that waste made "free competition" a frightful fight. Le Corbusier, *The Radiant City*, pp. 68-9.

[90] Le Corbusier, *The Radiant City*, pp. 115-8.

[91] Le Corbusier, *The City of Tomorrow*, p. 160.

Figure 3.12 | Le Corbusier and Pierre Jeanneret, 24NC, Paris, 1931-4; Le Corbusier in the roof garden, 1952.

City as Compass and Calendar

Figure 3.1 | Le Corbusier, A Contemporary City for Three Million Inhabitants, 1922; "The center of the city seen from one of the terraced cafés surrounding the Grand Central Station square."

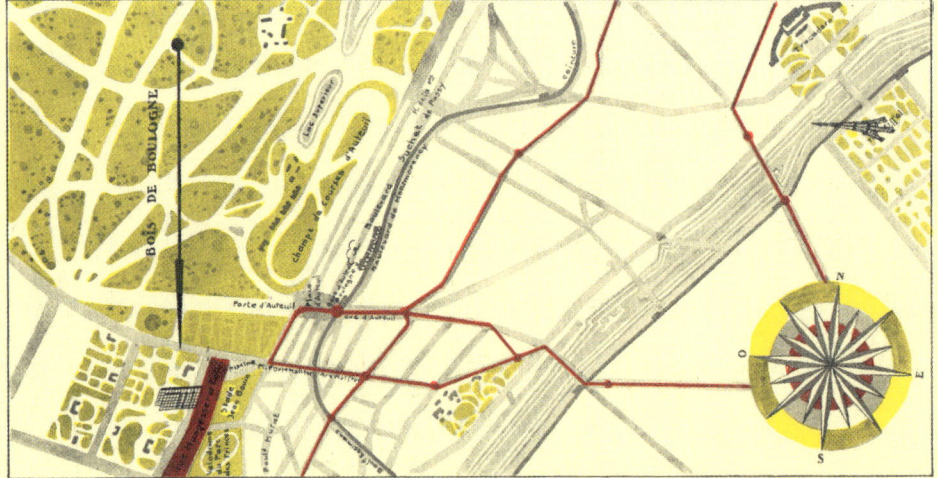

Figure 3.3 | Promotional brochure of the Société Immobilière de Paris-Parc des Princes, early 1930s; site plan showing the means of transportation to the city center.

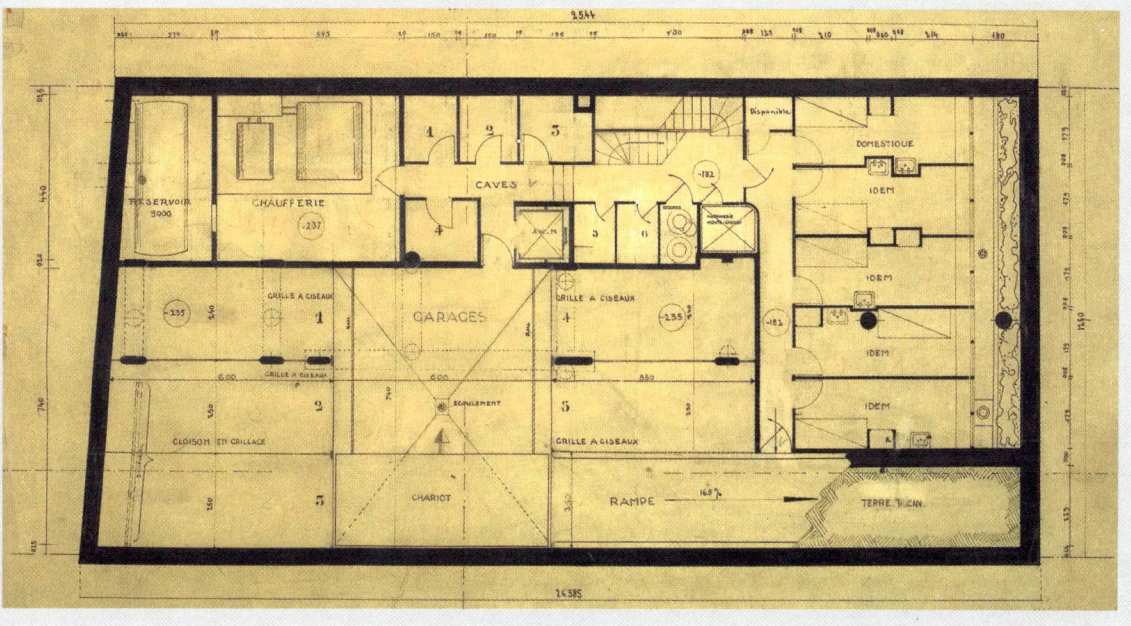

Figure 3.6 | Le Corbusier and Pierre Jeanneret, 24NC, Paris, 1931–4; plan drawing of the basement, dated October 12, 1931 (corrected February 26, 1932).

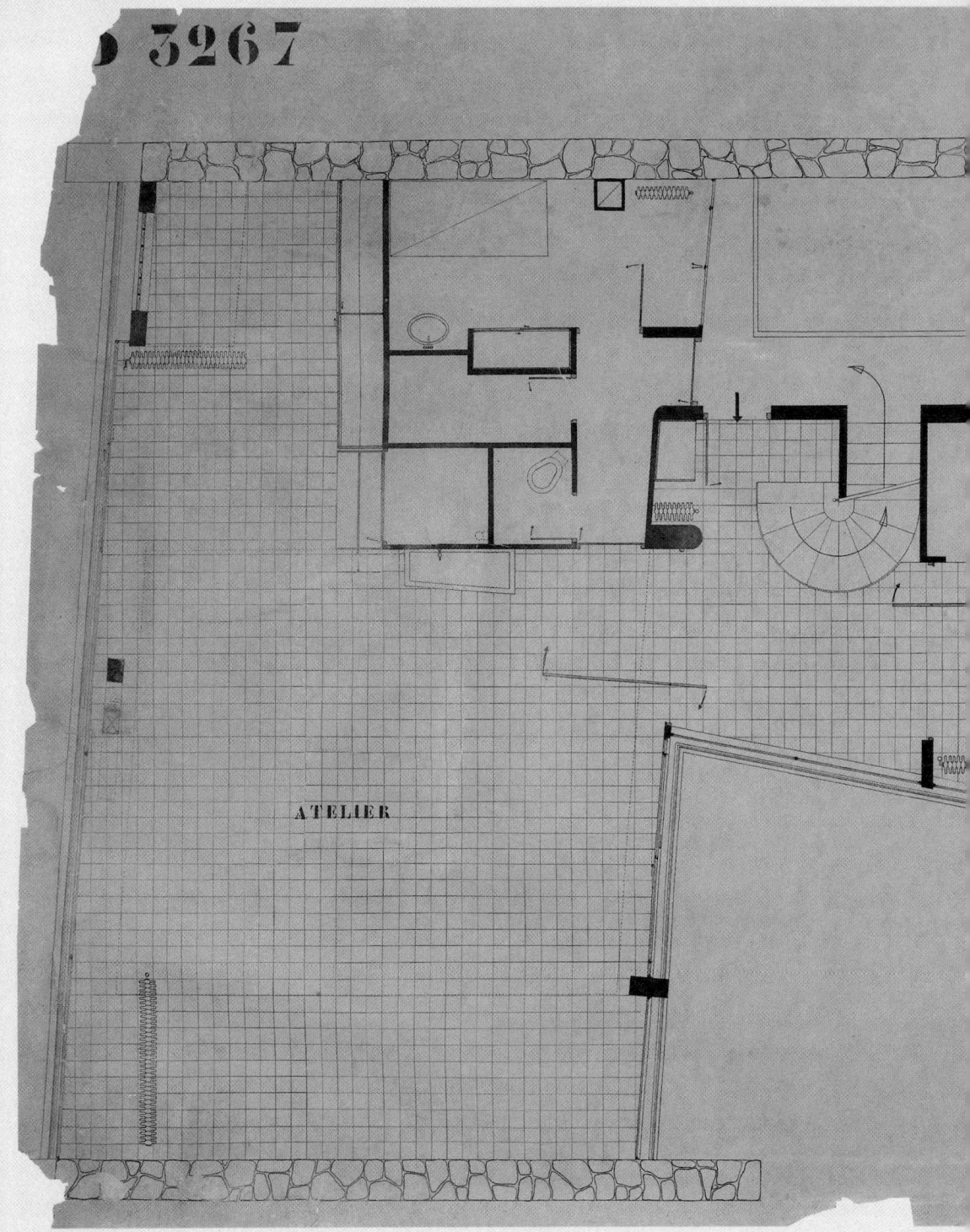

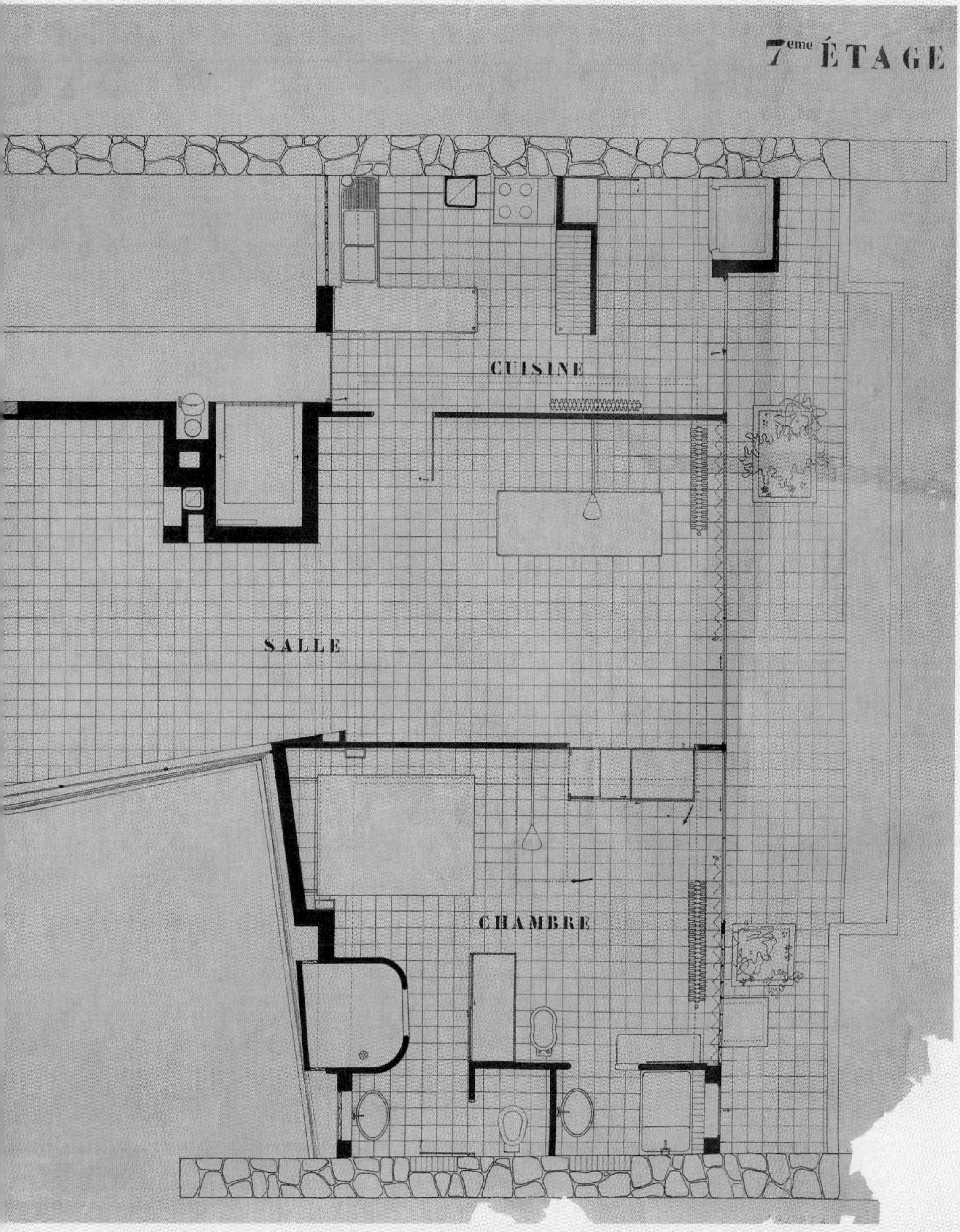

Figure 3.10 | Le Corbusier and Pierre Jeanneret, 24NC, Paris, 1931–4; plan of the seventh floor.

City as Compass and Calendar

Figure 3.11 | Le Corbusier, reconstruction of the photo collage panel titled *Habitation*, exhibited at the Pavillon des Temps Nouveaux, Paris International Exposition, 1937.

Figure 3.14 | Le Corbusier and Pierre Jeanneret, 24NC, Paris, 1931–4; view of the roof terrace.

Figure 3.16 | A cemetery, Istanbul, 1911; photograph by Le Corbusier, inscribed "Constantinopel, Cemetery Eyüp."

Figure 3.18 | Le Corbusier and Pierre Jeanneret, 24NC, Paris, 1931–4; Le Corbusier in his living room, 1946.

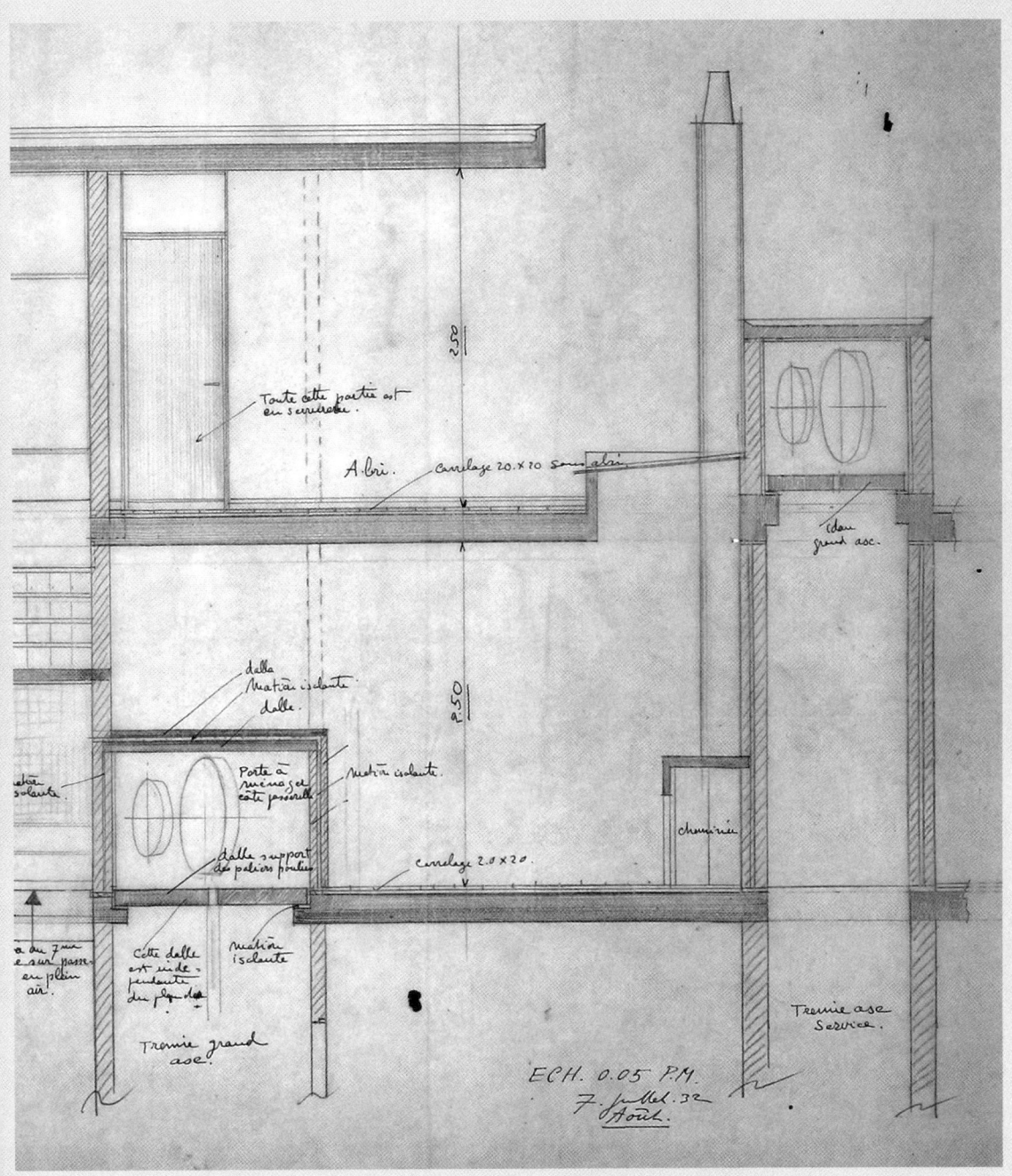

Figure 3.17 | Le Corbusier and Pierre Jeanneret, 24NC, Paris, 1931–4; detail from an early section drawing of the living room and the roof garden, dated July 7, 1932.

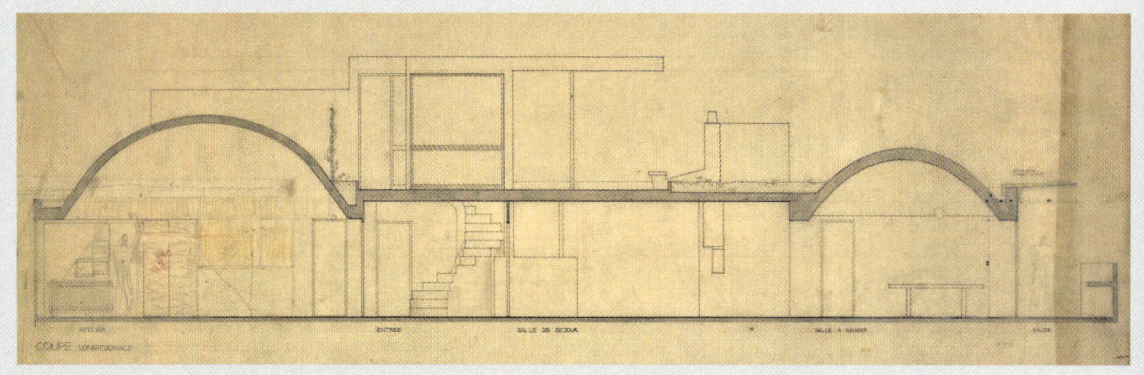

Figure 3.13 | Le Corbusier and Pierre Jeanneret, 24NC, Paris, 1931–4; longitudinal section drawing of the seventh and the eighth floors.

Figure 3.15 | A house with a courtyard; sketch by Le Corbusier, captioned "Eyoub 1911."

Figure 3.19 | Le Corbusier and Pierre Jeanneret, 24NC, Paris, 1931-4; Le Corbusier in his living room, 1954.

Figure 3.20 | A café, Istanbul, 1911; sketch by Le Corbusier, captioned "Le café de Mahmoud Pasha."

Juan Manuel Heredia

Urban Topography and the Workers' City

Juan O'Gorman's Labor-Union Architecture for Mexico

If, as Joseph Rykwert states, "our experience of buildings is always political, every building adds or diminishes the common good," the experience of the Mexican Cinema Workers Union building in Mexico City was political in a double sense.[1] Designed in 1936 by Juan O'Gorman in the aftermath of the Mexican Revolution, it both addressed the physical needs of a nascent political organization and represented them to the passerby and the city beyond. Although nowadays transformed beyond recognition, the building stood relatively undisturbed for three decades, adding to the common good of the city and inspiring others along the way. Through the careful examination of a series of photographs, drawings, and texts that reveal its urban and cultural significance, this chapter reconsiders and revaluates this forgotten building by O'Gorman.

Figure 4.1 | Juan O'Gorman, Mexican Cinema Workers Union building, Mexico City, 1936–7; exterior.

[1] With those words Rykwert concluded his lecture, "The Profession and the Art," when receiving the RIBA Gold Medal in 2014.

Two Photographs

The first photograph I'd like to consider, taken on Wednesday December 12, 1939 (the feast day of the Virgin of Guadalupe) shows Calle Orozco y Berra in Colonia Guerrero, a neighborhood to the north west of the city's historical center. **Figure 4.2 (see p. 108)** Recently opened to alleviate the congestion of vehicular traffic caused by the nearby railway station, the street was never completed as planned. It was stopped before it could connect with Avenida Buenavista, where the station was located. Partly because it terminated in a dead-end alley it had a rather tranquil character. The photograph, admittedly unspectacular, was taken from Avenida Guerrero (where Orozco y Berra began) next to the Church of San Fernando, part of a Franciscan establishment built in the mid-18th century. During the following century, this establishment was expropriated by the liberal government of Benito Juárez, and its gardens transformed into a civil cemetery.[2] This was not any cemetery though, but the resting place of Vicente Guerrero, the Afro-Mestizo leader of the War of Independence against Spain, and of Juárez himself, the first and still only indigenous Mexican president, famed for, among other things, defeating the last attempt at imposing a foreign ruler in the country.[3]

Inspecting the image more closely one can see on the left a 19th-century house that was, presumably, once inhabited by a family but was at the time of the photo used as a clinic to treat venereal diseases. No doubt it was the opening of the street that led to the destruction of the neighboring building, but traces are still visible on the party wall, now serving as a billboard. To the right, across the street, one can see a newly constructed apartment building with shops on the ground floor. Farther away, similar structures are also visible. These buildings easily fit José Luis Benlliure's derogatory definition of much speculative "modern" architecture of the time: "boxes with holes" ("*cajones con agujeros*").[4] Crossing the street in the direction of the building appears a young man sporting a jacket and beret, walking with the ease that only a certain familiarity with the *barrio* can give. Founded in 1874, Colonia Guerrero was one of the first subdivisions outside the city limits and for more than a century it has retained the character of a working-class neighborhood.[5] Its identity comes largely from the national heroes buried in the cemetery, one of whom gives the neighborhood and its principal artery their names.[6] Although originally planned for an incipient middle-class, the *colonia* soon changed its destiny, as it was filled with lower- and lower-middle-class tenements and *vecindades* (low-income housing developments usually organized around a courtyard). It is therefore often referred to as a *barrio bravo* (rough/ courageous neighborhood) and it is somehow fitting that the word "Guerrero" literally means warrior.

Near the corner, in the foreground of the image, two teenagers finish crossing Guerrero Avenue. One of them stops briefly before reaching the sidewalk to reposition the cardboard box that he carries on his head. An adult with an open coat, disheveled appearance, and no apparent business awaits them, cigarette in hand, as he leans on

---

2 In 1859 President Juárez promulgated the Law for the Secularization of Cemeteries.

3 Juárez ordered the execution in 1867 of Maximilian I of Hapsburg, the short-lived "emperor" sent by Napoleon III three years prior at the request of Mexican conservative enemies of his government.

4 Benlliure, José Luis, "Sobre la arquitectura y su enseñanza en México en la década de los cuarentas," *La práctica de la arquitectura y su enseñanza en México*, Alexandrina Escudero ed., Mexico City: INBA, 1983, p. 11.

5 On the origins and development of the colonia see Reese, Carol McMichael, "The Urban Development of Mexico City: 1850-1930," *Planning Latin American Capital Cities, 1859-1950*, Arturo Almandoz ed., London: Routledge, 2002, pp. 139–69.

6 The western side of Colonia Guerrero is officially named Colonia Buenavista. Yet both were originally conceived as one, and the latter is normally considered part of the former.

a telephone post. Behind this group, in the middle distance, one can distinguish a policeman looking fixedly on the opposite sidewalk, where a well-dressed group composed of three adults and one girl walk, accompanied by an older girl (probably a servant) carrying a box and a bag with some difficulty. Surely, they are headed to the Church of San Fernando to listen to a mass in honor of the Virgin of Guadalupe, who 408 years prior appeared to Saint Juan Diego on a hill four miles to the north of this spot. Further back in the image one can notice some older, some newer, buildings, a few vacant lots, a couple of cars, more people, and the street itself, as it terminates in the dead-end alley.

Looking more closely, one can get a glimpse, a few meters behind the policeman, of a small crowd gathering at the entrance of a building. Due to the angle of the view, the building cannot be fully discerned, but given the number of people out front it must be public in purpose and use. Any doubt soon dissipates as one looks skyward: a convex volume painted in a dark color indicates that it is O'Gorman's building for the Mexican Cinema Workers Union (Sindicato Mexicano de Cinematografistas or SMC).

A second photograph taken two years earlier, on Monday, November 1, 1937, shows Calle Orozco y Berra from a similar vantage point. **Figure 4.3 (see p. 109)** The building in the foreground of the previous image has not been erected, its site is still empty. Boarded-up, it provides support for another billboard. The photograph depicts a more quotidian scene of people going about their daily business. To the left, an old man reclines against the wall of the old house that became a clinic, with a poster behind him reading *Llamamiento* (Call) and signed by the "Committee for the Provision of Ambulances to Spain" (Comité pro-ambulancias para España), one of the many international organizations giving aid to the Spanish Republic in those years. The proximity of the poster to the union building may not be accidental, for in those years the Mexican labor movement, and the SMC in particular, demonstrated great solidarity with the Republic then imperiled. In fact, after its defeat and the beginning of the Second World War, the building became a center of reunion for the communist and antifascist Spanish and German communities in exile in Mexico.[7] So it is likely that the poster was put there by someone going to or coming from the building. To the right, an old, well-dressed couple make their way between the gravel and dirt of a sidewalk in the process of construction. Partially hidden is a construction worker laboring in a ditch. Next to this group are two child laborers helping the worker's excavations, measurements, and assemblies. One of them, wearing denim overalls, gets briefly distracted as he looks frontally into the camera. The worker seems to be communicating with another, likewise half-hidden, at the opposite end of the block. A bit farther away two more workers labor at the corner of Salgado alleyway, and behind them another crowd, a larger group gathering at the entrance to O'Gorman's building. Equally difficult to discern, the building is blocked by yet another "box with holes," finished

---

[7] See Reimann, Aribert, *Transnational District: European Political Exile in Mexico City, 1939–1959*, Cologne: KUPS, 2020, p. 36.

just a few weeks before the photograph was taken. Despite the similarity between the images, this one offers a better view of the building, for it shows it at a slightly wider angle and with a little more detail.

Both photographs were commissioned by the city's Department of Urban and Sanitary Works to record the improvements made by the city government to the streets. For this reason, the foci in the images are the streets, not the buildings. The marginality thus granted to architecture is, therefore, revealing, for not just the street but the activities it accommodates get highlighted. In turn, these activities occur in correlation with the buildings, thus bringing the latter back into prominence. In the case of the SMC building, the number of people around it indicates its centrality within the vicinity. Located along the northern sidewalk of Orozco y Berra, the building was—as both images show—one of the first to be erected along the new street. And if not the first to be erected, O'Gorman's building was at least the first that endowed the street with a definitive scale and character, as can be deduced from the second-rate structures that soon followed. The difference between these and the SMC building lay in its decidedly public and political program, and the way that program was interpreted.

The Union and its Building

Completed the same year that he decided to prematurely retire from architecture and dedicate his life to painting, the SMC building did not deserve much commentary from its author, perhaps because in those years architecture for him began to transform into "a Frankenstein."[8] Indeed, O'Gorman famously retired from architecture as a profession after realizing that the functionalist doctrine he had so fiercely espoused and promoted since the late 1920s had been co-opted by forces that transformed his search for economy for the sake of social betterment into a search for economy for the sake of profit and capital accumulation. A transformation exemplified by the "boxes with holes" that eventually came to surround the SMC.[9]

Regrettably, there is little available documentation of both the project and the building. The only known original drawing is a perspective now kept in one of the few archives of the architect's drawings. **Figure 4.4 (see p. 110)** Labeled number 8, the drawing was certainly one in the set that O'Gorman drew and presented to his clients for approval. Sadly, no other drawings in that set are known or have been made public, the worst-case scenario being that they were destroyed by O'Gorman along with most of his professional archive.[10]

But luckily there is another set in an article about the building published the year of its completion that includes all the plans, one facade, and a variation of that perspective.[11] **Figure 4.5 (see p. 111)** The article also includes one of the few photographs of the building as newly completed. **Figure 4.1 (see p. 92)** Besides the mostly technical information included in it (probably supplied

8 "'Abandoné la arquitectura porque se me convirtió en un Frankenstein': O'Gorman, Juan," *La palabra de Juan O'Gorman: selección de textos*, Ida Rodríguez Prampolini, Olga Saenz and Elizabeth Fuentes eds., Mexico City: UNAM, 1983, pp. 212–6.

9 O'Gorman's 1949 canvas *Mexico City Landscape* (*Paisaje de la Ciudad de México*) offers an alternative pictorial insight into this transformation. See Zavala, Adriana, "Mexico City in Juan O'Gorman's Imagination," *Hispanic Research Journal*, vol. 8, no. 5, 2007, pp. 491–506.

10 There is no comprehensive archive of Juan O'Gorman's architectural works. It is believed that he destroyed it, the surviving drawings being dispersed and kept by the government, universities, family, clients, and friends.

11 "Juan O'Gorman: dos de sus obras," *Arquitectura y Decoración* 3, October 1937, pp. 57–64.

by O'Gorman himself), the only known commentary made by the architect was written more than 30 years later and concerned the origins of the commission and the quality of the construction.

> In 1934 I designed and built the premises of the Cinema Workers Union, commissioned to me by the Mexican Workers' Confederation (Confederación de Trabajadores de México, CTM) whose Secretary-General was then Vicente Lombardo Toledano ... An extremely intelligent man [he] realized the value and meaning of functional architecture for Mexico and asked me to do the project ... on a piece of land he had purchased in Calle Orozco y Berra in Mexico City. I did the project, which was approved by the Secretary-General [of the CTM] and by the Secretary of the Cinema Workers Union. The construction of the building took approximately six months and the contractor was my dear friend, the engineer Luis Gutiérrez Cañedo, who did a work of very good quality.[12]

Although O'Gorman stated that the building was built in 1934, it was in fact constructed later, between 1936 and 1937. But his remarks regarding the instrumental value that functional architecture held for Mexican political leaders are true and relevant. They belong to a passage in his autobiography where he discussed his early work, and came after similar remarks narrating how, in 1932, Mexico's minister of education found his functionalist doctrine (until then only tested in a handful of domestic commissions) suitable for the construction of public schools.[13] In a similar fashion, in the cited passage O'Gorman claimed that the leader of the CTM, the principal confederation of Mexican labor unions, found his functionalist architecture suitable for the design of labor-union buildings. Although O'Gorman did not make any major value-judgment on his building, it is significant that he thought of it positively, if only in terms of its construction. Other than that, there is no other public commentary about it made by him.

The historiography that discusses the SMC building is insufficient. In the most positive assessments, historians see it as an example of Mexico's "radical functionalism," but mention it only in passing as one of the key union buildings promoted by the vigorous Mexican labor movement that gained ascendancy under the presidency of Lázaro Cárdenas (1934–40).[14] The lengthiest, but at the same time most negative commentary, came from historian Rafael López Rangel, who lambasted its pragmatism and "architectural poverty" ["*pobrismo arquitectónico*"] that in his view was the main cause of its alteration given that it "did not meet with shared approval among its users ... much less among the popular masses and the general public."[15]

Indeed, O'Gorman's building was a representative of Mexico's "radical functionalism," a movement that he founded and led,

---

12 *Juan O'Gorman, autobiografía, antología, juicios críticos y documentación exhaustiva sobre su obra*, Antonio Luna Arroyo ed., Mexico City: Cuadernos populares de pintura mexicana moderna, 1973, pp. 123–4 (translation by author).
13 *Juan O'Gorman*, pp. 116–9.
14 See González Lobo, Carlos, "Arquitectura en México durante la cuarta década: el maximato, el cardenismo," *Apuntes para la historia y crítica de la arquitectura mexicana del siglo XX: 1900–1980*, vol 2, Víctor Jiménez ed., Mexico City: INBA, 1982, pp. 95–7; López Rangel, Rafael, *La modernidad arquitectónica mexicana, antecedentes y vanguardias, 1900–1940*, Mexico City: UAM, 1989, pp. 155–9; De Anda Alanís, Enrique X, *Historia de la arquitectura Mexicana*, Barcelona: Gustavo Gili, 1995, pp. 188–9; Olsen, Patrice Elizabeth, *Artifacts of Revolution: Architecture, Society, and Politics in Mexico City, 1920–1940*, Lanham, MD: Rowman and Littlefield, 2008, pp. 150–1.
15 López Rangel, Rafael, *La modernidad arquitectónica Mexicana*, pp. 155–9 (translation by author).

and that shocked not just "the masses and the general public," but also the country's architectural establishment because of its concentration on technical and practical matters and its disavowal of anything deemed "artistic."[16] The radicality of this attitude is perhaps best exemplified by O'Gorman's school buildings, works reduced to their structural and formal minimums, devoid of any superfluity, and described by U.S. critic Esther Born as "stripped for action."[17] When looking at them, it is actually difficult to recall a more austere, stark, even crude architecture produced anywhere else in the world at this time. Although for López Rangel, the transformation of the building was related to the "changes in the union's organization and the services it provided," as well as to Mexico's proverbial *charrismo sindical* (union corruption through state co-optation),[18] the historian put the greater part of the blame on O'Gorman's attitude of intentionally seeking "poverty." That the building felt increasingly inadequate to its users was true, insofar as it suffered several modifications throughout its life, especially since the mid-1940s, when the two internal courtyards that gave natural light to the corridors, stair, and service spaces were closed off. During the early 1970s, moreover, the building went through an extensive makeover and expansion that completely transformed its external appearance and internal arrangement.[19]

Without differentiating the previous changes from the final and definitive one, López Rangel categorically stated that the building's transformation meant that its members "erased its discourse" (*borraron su discurso*). This observation is significant, for it endowed the building with speech or written abilities, and that, as such, this discourse was purposefully silenced or "erased". The word "erased" is in fact apt, as the building's elaborate facade (presumably the mouthpiece of its discourse) was not simply replaced by another—more appropriate one—but simply eradicated, then substituted by a conventionally glazed and "mute" surface, clear evidence of its suppression. As already mentioned, however, this transformation dated to the 1970s. During the previous three decades the building functioned more-or-less as originally conceived, even if it went through significant changes. Throughout this time, the facade remained one of its most resilient features, as the one that gave it identifiable form. Its "discourse," furthermore, was highly articulate: it told an edifying story that was understood, if only tacitly, by those who commissioned it and those who passed by. More importantly, it provided the union with a physical setting for its activities, activities that the union requested the architect consider seriously, but that were, nevertheless, creatively reimagined by O'Gorman in his design. Although for López Rangel the building's radical transformation stemmed less from the union's operative and ideological changes than from a fundamental schism between architecture and the public, the evidence suggests a different, more complex, and interesting story.

Founded in 1923, the Mexican Union of Cinema Workers was not, as its name might suggest, a national union of workers

[16] On Mexico's radical functionalism see Carranza, Luis E., *Radical Functionalism: A Social Architecture for Mexico*, London: Routledge, 2021.

[17] Born, Esther, *The New Architecture of Mexico*, New York: William Morrow—The Architectural Record, 1937, pp. 23-4.

[18] On *charrismo sindical* see Trejo Delarbe, Raúl and Anibal Yanez, "The Mexican Labor Movement: 1917-1975," *Latin American Perspectives*, winter 1976, pp. 145-6.

[19] These included turning the assembly hall into a commercial movie theater, plus adding another movie theater in the expansion.

involved in the production of movies, but a more modest local union of workers involved in the operation of movie theaters.[20] **Figure 4.6 (see p. 112)** Upon its founding, the union grew rapidly in tandem with the building boom of movie theaters in the expanding city and as movies became the preferred, affordable, form of entertainment for Mexico's urban populations. Emerging during a period of reconstruction and in an atmosphere pervaded by claims of social justice, the union soon became part of the CTM. Founded just a few months before the project was given to O'Gorman, the CTM quickly became Mexico's largest confederation of workers, replacing and absorbing previous umbrella organizations. Its main task (beyond the protection of its affiliates) was guaranteeing an electoral base for the ruling party and the Mexican state. As Jaime García Mendoza and Omar Alí Salazar Blas have explained, the union's adherence to the CTM "provoked changes in its political organization [and] in return for this integration the Mexican state gave [its leaders] governmental posts and gratifications of all kinds."[21] This adherence gradually challenged the union's independence so by the late 1950s it had become a prototypical *sindicato charro*. The benefits and privileges that its members enjoyed, many of them hard-fought and well-earned, were able to endure and expand at the cost of collaborating with the state in the policing of dissidents and a diminishing solidarity with other unions seeking independence from the CTM. This tension came to a head in 1968 when, together with the CTM, the union took sides with President Gustavo Díaz Ordaz, whose government ordered the massacre of protesting students in the Plaza de Tlatelolco on the northern edge of Colonia Guerrero, a mile away from the building. It would seem, therefore, that by the 1970s the building's original "discourse" had become irrelevant to the union, as it effectively transformed from a beacon of working-class and international solidarity into a state-legitimizing apparatus. The new facade, an extensive, homogeneous, and repetitive curtain wall, delivered in this sense a more appropriate message of political alienation.

A Vertical Promenade

Given the union's modest origins, the site chosen for the construction of its building was not as prominent as it would have been in the case of a more powerful union, and it is somewhat fitting that it was located amid the working-class dwellings of Colonia Guerrero. Occupying a 240-square-meter lot, the building was a compact volume connected through a stair and service tower to an auditorium at the back. The principal volume had five levels, each with its own facade treatment, but all sharing the same heights and general proportions. **Figure 4.7** The construction system consisted of a concrete frame with concrete slabs, and both infill and load-bearing cement-block walls. The exterior walls were plastered in cement and painted an intense vermilion color. The interior and courtyard walls were similarly plastered and painted, the first in clear green, the second ultramarine blue.

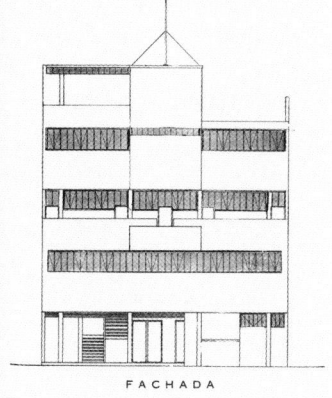

Figure 4.7 | Juan O'Gorman, Mexican Cinema Workers Union building, Mexico City, 1936-7; facade.

[20] On the union see García Mendoza, Jaime and Omar Alí Salazar Blas, *Inventario del archivo del Sindicato de trabajadores de la industria cinematográfica, sección 1*, Cuernavaca, Mexico: Facultad de humanidades Universidad Autónoma del Estado de Morelos, 2010, pp. 11-20; and Sierra Orozco, Eduardo, "El Sindicato de Cinematografistas del Distrito Federal. Desarrollo y Perspectiva," graduate thesis, Universidad Nacional Autónoma de México, 1985.

[21] García Mendoza and Salazar Blas, *Inventario del archivo del Sindicato*, pp. 12-13.

Although the ground floor was almost completely open, it did not include (as is typical in multi-story urban buildings) any commercial premises, instead rather communal ones. This level consisted of an open vestibule with free-standing columns. Towards the back, an open stair served as a focus and gave orientation to those entering the building, whether they were continuing into the assembly hall (*salón de actos*) or ascending to the main offices. The ground floor also contained the union's medical services, which were aligned to the street and expressed outwardly, via a semi-cylindrical volume reminiscent of Le Corbusier's Maison Cook. This borrowing was not gratuitous, for it served as a marker of entry, as it did in Le Corbusier's Cook residence. At a deeper level the semi-cylinder reciprocated the spaces that it enclosed, again like its precedent. Indeed, in a seminal essay Kurt Forster argued that the curvilinear elements in Le Corbusier's buildings of the 1920s often enclosed rooms where the human body was more intimately exposed or engaged (bathrooms, bidets, stairs, ramps, etc), thus indirectly rehearsing the classical analogy between human body and building.[22] In the case of the SMC building, the human body was even physically acted on, for the medical services included both a consultation room and an operation table.

Unlike other institutional buildings, this one could not afford the luxury of having a front esplanade. The ground floor, however, acted as if it were one, but turned inwards and shaded. Its openness gave the building a strong connection to the sidewalk, their separation consisting of merely three steps leading to the vestibule. Thanks also to the slow vehicular traffic, during special celebrations the union closed-off and appropriated the street in a practice that replicated the parties of nearby *vecindades*. The project could in fact be seen as an elaboration of that housing typology.

Typical *vecindades* consisted of two rows of dwellings of one to two levels, each flanking an elongated courtyard, with an open stair usually placed in a symmetrical axis to the entry. Originating during the 18th century but consolidated during the late 19th (during the first wave of the country's industrialization), *vecindades* became the standard form of housing in many Mexican cities. Despite the problems normally associated with them (overcrowdedness, precarious construction, unhygienic conditions, etc.), due to their simple arrangement and shared amenities and services, these buildings tended to promote a strong sense of community and solidarity among their inhabitants. *Vecindad* parties were normally set up in the courtyards but often overflowed into the street. Although usually thrown by individual families (occasions ranging from birthdays, to *quinceaños*, to weddings), these parties were in fact collective celebrations where the courtyard and street became one, colorfully decorated with paper adornments, garlands, and artificial lights.

Extant photographs of the union's anniversary parties attest to their similarity to those festivities. **Figure 4.8** In some, members appear dancing in the middle of the street to the rhythm of the

Figure 4.8 | The union's band and dancers occupying the street and seen from the balcony, 1954.

22 Forster, Kurt W., "Antiquity and Modernity in the La Roche-Jeanneret Houses of 1923," *Oppositions* 15-16, 1979, pp. 142-3.

Figure 4.9 | The union building artificially lit and decorated for the Union's 21st anniversary celebrations, 1954.

union's marching band, throwing streamers and confetti at each other; in others they are eating typical Mexican dishes prepared and distributed on the sidewalk and against the background of the building. In still other images the facade of the building is seen decorated and artificially lit. **Figure 4.9**

O'Gorman was very aware of the history and tradition of *vecindades*, not only because they were prevalent in the neighborhood but also because, as a student, he drew them as case studies. One such drawing set survives from his student years.[23] Moreover, while working with Carlos Obregón Santacilia, O'Gorman was probably involved in the design of a housing complex modeled precisely on the *vecindad* typology.[24]

The first floor of the SMC building was reserved for its four logistical departments: archive and statistics, organization and propaganda, treasury and administration, and treasury for emergencies and deaths. Each of these was given an individual office, all adjoining a corridor and a waiting area. Two of the offices had doors opening into the corridor, while the other two opened only through cashier windows, yet all were connected internally. Towards the street, this floor showed a Corbusian ribbon window across the entire width of the building. The ribbon window, however, did not have the standard horizontally sliding panes but traditional awnings, surely due to limitations of technique and availability. Their up-and-down movement demanded greater involvement on the part of the user and endowed the facade with an added sense of verticality.

The second floor contained the delegates' offices, which corresponded to the five branches of the union: janitors and nightguards, ticket-clerks, employees, reel inspectors, and operators. Their offices, set back from the street, formed a continuous terrace or "balcony" to which each of the delegates had independent access. That shared, open, and elevated space allowed discrete conversations, while looking at the street and at their comrades gathered below. In the center of the balcony a convex protrusion created a podium or "tribune" for proselytizing speeches. The surviving perspective shows a leader commanding that podium, wearing a cap and denim overalls, his left hand raised, pointing east and up, haranguing his comrades (absent in the drawing) recalling El Lissitzky's famous collage of Lenin at his tribune.

Not appearing in any of the drawings, but included in the union as built, was a more radical symbol of insurgency: a series of vertical embrasures rhythmically cut into the balcony's parapet. Not just symbolic but practical too, these elements were added by O'Gorman at some point during the design or construction process so that workers could defend themselves in the event of an assault by the state or reactionary groups.[25] Although common in the early colonial period (where they served to protect colonizers from indigenous rebellions), embrasures were, by the late 18th century, rare in Mexico's civil architecture. O'Gorman, however, recovered their use for union buildings, perceptibly sensing that Mexico was

[23] These drawings are discussed and reproduced in O'Rourke, Kathryn, *Modern Architecture in Mexico City*, Pittsburgh: Pittsburgh University Press, 2016, pp. 8–11, 171–8.

[24] On the building see Rivera, Diego, "The New Mexican Architecture: A House of Carlos Obregón," *Mexican Folkways*, vol. 2, no. 6, 1926, pp. 19–20. See also O'Rourke, *Modern Architecture*, pp. 171–8.

[25] This was first highlighted by Carlos González Lobo in "Arquitectura en México durante la cuarta década."

Figure 4.10 | Casa de los Mascarones, Mexico City, late 18th century.

Figure 4.11 | Juan O'Gorman, Frances Toor House, Mexico City, 1935.

26 Burian, Edward R., "The Architecture of Juan O'Gorman: Dichotomy and Drift," *Modernity and the Architecture of Mexico*, Austin, TX: University of Texas Press, 1997, pp. 127–49.
27 Rowe, Colin, "The Provocative Façade: Frontality and Contrapposto," *Le Corbusier, Architect of the Century*, London: Arts Council of Great Britain, 1987, pp. 24–8.
28 Cetto, Max, "Juan O Gorman," *Contemporary Architects*, Emanuel Muriel ed., New York: St Martin's Press, 1980, p. 594.

passing through a period of social upheaval similar to the conquest, yet inverting their meaning from colonizing to liberating. One of his possible references while adding these elements was a famous country house located just a few blocks to the west of the building. Built in the 18th century in what was then the western edge of the city, and colloquially known as Casa de los Mascarones or simply Mascarones (in view of the *mascarones* ornamenting its exterior), this house also showed narrow vertical slits, in this case cut along the base of its elaborate Baroque facade. **Figure 4.10**

Admittedly not embrasures but openings providing light and ventilation to a semi-basement, these elements gave added character to an already peculiar building. Both Mascarones and the SMC building shared a southern orientation that was positively acknowledged by their architects who gave their facades an emphatic profile and figure. It would seem that O'Gorman's abstract volumetry was the opposite of Mascarones' figurative facade, but as Edward Burian has convincingly argued, a strong bio-morphism and anthropomorphism runs throughout his career, and not only, as its usually thought, in his later "organic" work.[26] **Figure 4.11**

Viewed in this way, the Corbusian references of his architecture acquire even greater significance. O'Gorman's borrowings from Maison Cook were not limited to some isolated features, but the whole building could be considered an elaboration of Le Corbusier's canonical project. Both exemplify what Colin Rowe termed the "provocative facade," a type of elevation that exploited the tension between "frontality and *contrapposto:*" between regularity, symmetry, and formality on the one hand, and irregularity, asymmetry, and informality on the other.[27] The SMC building rehearsed this mode of articulation, but given its institutional character it tipped the scale towards "frontality" rather than "*contrapposto*." O'Gorman, moreover, playfully resituated and reconfigured its Corbusian elements, as we saw already with the semi-cylinder. Similarly, the facade's urban alignment differed from Maison Cook's suburban setback, favoring a more direct connection to and recognition of its urban setting; specifically, the sidewalk and dead-end street. Inspecting the project from bottom to top, one witnesses several other creative transpositions, all of which were legible in the facade. Further, these were not limited to a Corbusian vocabulary, but were indicative of other architectures, both proximate and distant, as we already saw in the cases of *vecindades* and Mascarones. As Max Cetto once noted in reference to O'Gorman's Corbusianism, but applicable to these other instances as well: "if he copied he made the right choice."[28]

Significantly enough, the facade of the SMC building was exactly aligned to that of the Church of San Fernando. **Figure 4.12 (see p. 114)** Begun in 1736 to the design of Jerónimo de Balbás, this church was a typical example of Mexico City's Baroque architecture. Like many structures of its kind, San Fernando's facade featured a high and centered stone relief honoring its patron, Saint Ferdinand, the 13th-century Spanish king who was

Figure 4.13 | Jerónimo de Balbás, Church of San Fernando, Mexico City, 1736–55.

Figure 4.14 | Juan O'Gorman, *Retable of Independence*, Museo Nacional de Historia, Mexico City, 1960–1; detail.

29 See McAndrew, John, *The Open-Air Churches of Sixteenth-Century Mexico, Atrios, Posas, Open Chapels, and other Studies*, Cambridge, MA: Harvard University Press, 1965.
30 The tercet reads "*Da la materia a tanta arquitectura; una piedra que en sangre está bañada; que para Cruz es la mejor tintura*" ("Matter gives to so much architecture; a stone that is bathed in blood; that for the cross is the best tincture"). Translation by the author. See *Poetas novohispanos (segundo siglo 1621–1721) parte primera*, Alfonso Méndez Plancarte ed., Mexico City: UNAM, 1995, p. 120.

canonized in the 17th century for enforcing the conversion and/or expulsion of the Muslim "infidel" population from the Iberian peninsula. **Figure 4.13**

The adjoining Colegio de San Fernando was in fact the Mexican seat of the Collegio de Propaganda Fide, the papal institution in charge of the education of missionaries for the tasks of conversion and evangelization around the globe. The first major episode in this worldwide effort of conversion took place in Mexico in the 16th century. In this case, "open chapels" occupied similarly elevated places in church complexes. Not exactly adorning their facades but adjoining them, these chapels were basically elevated podiums with altars from which priests could address the converted (or soon to-be-converted) as they gathered in multitudes in the large atria they faced.[29]

Differences in ideologies and configurations apart, the union-building's proselytizing podium acted similarly, establishing a subtle correlation between the emancipatory messages of revolutionary and religious leaders. Catholic priests had always been important in Mexico's political history. Both the secular, but mostly the regular, clergy were at the forefront in the defense of the indigenous population against the abuses of the colonial government and the *conquistadores*. The War of Independence fought against Spain in fact started when the Jesuit-educated priest Miguel Hidalgo y Costilla, waving the standard of the Virgin of Guadalupe, called the people to arms in front of the church of the town of Dolores in 1810. It is perhaps a coincidence that the most famous representation of this historical event is the large mural painted by O'Gorman himself in the Museo Nacional de Historia in Mexico City. **Figure 4.14**

The church and the union building could be connected in another meaningful way. San Fernando was built using the local red *tezontle* stone and the light-brown *recinto* stone that are typical of Mexico City's Baroque architecture. Normally left exposed, these materials gave the city a distinctive physiognomy very early on. In 1655, just as the country had overcome the most violent period of conquest and colonization, the poet Ambrosio de Solís Aguirre wrote a tercet allegedly describing *tezontle* as a "stone that is bathed in blood."[30] Painted the color of the communist flag, O'Gorman's building was also "bathed in blood," no longer that of the native population but of its descendants as they joined the ranks of the international proletariat. The facades of church and union building were even articulated similarly, for in the same way that *tezontle* dominated the surface of the church and *recinto* used for its framing and figurative elements, O'Gorman's building was mostly painted red, while the podium and a few other areas received a lighter tonality. **Figure 4.15 (see p. 113)**

The third floor contained the spaces for the highest ranks in the union's organization: the committee of justice, office of labor affairs, and office of the secretary-general. All these had a common waiting area that, although quite compact, was cleverly arranged and furnished with built-in seats providing a minimal area for rest.[31] This floor was realigned towards the street while repeating the curving protrusion below in the form of a convex volume that served as backdrop for the union's signage. Displaying its name, year of founding, and year of erection, this sign consisted of metal letters attached to the wall but slightly separated from it, thus casting a moving (cinematic) shadow during the day. At night, the letters were also visible thanks to artificial lights that accentuated their profile, evoking the marquee of a movie theater. Placed symmetrically within the facade, and vaguely reminiscent of a human forehead, this convex volume reasserted the central and lofty hierarchy of the union's principal leaders. In Maison Cook, the *promenade architecturale* featured, as one of its culminating moments, a curving volume that appeared convex toward the living room and concave towards the cantilevered balcony of the last floor. O'Gorman, as it were, turned this volume inside-out, re-centering it while simultaneously bringing the balcony one floor down in the form of the leader's tribune. The idyllic view to the landscape as a reward for completing the promenade was replaced by a more realistic view of the city, but holding a similar promise of liberation.

Just behind the convex volume was the reception office of the secretary-general, an ample space with only a thin, horizontal window that allowed natural light to penetrate deep into the interior. Although the perspective prefigured some spatial release for this room in the form of lateral windows, the final design suppressed them, giving greater focus to the moment of reception. Turning left, one entered the secretary-general's private office. Further ahead lay the office of the secretary of labor affairs. To the right of the reception office was the larger room for the committee of justice. In plan, this room featured a rectangular area abutting the western wall. Most probably equipped with a wooden platform, this area was framed by a pair of columns. Given the use of the space, this framing device, encountered as soon one entered and turned toward the platform, offered a tacit image of balance for those deferring to the authority of the committee for the airing of their grievances.

The fourth and last floor contained the library, a reading area, and a sundeck. In the project it consisted of four spaces arranged sequentially and having increasing degrees of openness. Whereas the library was almost entirely enclosed, the reading area (to which it opened by means of full swinging doors) consisted of an outdoor room only protected from sun and rain by a flat roof. Next to it, an open area with a pergola and a planter anticipated the full openness of the sundeck that had a view to the city. In the structure as built, this sequence was slightly abbreviated, yet increased the porosity still further. In the project, O'Gorman also proposed to screen the sundeck with one of his famous cactus fences (as he had done in his houses), but here a conventional planter was used instead. Overall, the architectural program at this level symbolized the combination of spiritual and physical wellbeing to which every worker in the union was thought to ideally aspire.

31 Similar built-in benches also appear on the second floor.

Figure 4.16 | Raising the strike flag, early 1970s.

At the top of the building O'Gorman placed a constructivist-inspired flagpole (another of his favorite motifs) that in the perspective rendering was represented with a communist flag waving high above. This was not simply a crowning adornment, but an inherent and active element of the program of uses, some of which were ritualized. Every time the union went on strike, a formal ceremony was held on the roof, during which the red-and-black anarcho-syndicalist flag (the one used for strikes in most parts of the world) was proudly raised, announcing a definitive end to the time of collective bargaining. It was also a request for solidarity with the city and its citizens. **Figure 4.16**

Curiously, the perspective exaggerated the proportions of the building by almost doubling its width. While it would seem that this was due to O'Gorman's desire to represent the building as larger than life, it was probably also a result of the fact that the property initially included an adjacent lot to the west. If so, O'Gorman simply adjusted the initial design by compressing it to fit into the available land. Be that as it may, an unfortunate fact is that the perspective also omitted the main stair on the ground floor, which as the facade drawing and plans show, was one of the most prominent aspects of the design. Moreover, the only known photographs of the exterior of the finished building were either taken at an angle that made it impossible to see the stair, or showed the entrance closed-off by a metallic rolling curtain (yet another crude industrial motif), probably added for security reasons, yet also quite appropriate given its recurrent use in neighboring buildings. What is clear from the facade, the plans, and the published description of the building, however, is that the stair received a good amount of natural light coming from the small courtyard to the west. In this way, an intense overhead luminosity would have descended through the patio and the staircase, bathed their surfaces, and promised a vivid experience of ascent for those entering the building. One final aspect gave the project added internal coherence and urban expression, an interphone and loudspeaker system that O'Gorman installed throughout the building, so that the deliberations taking place in the assembly hall could be heard in the office spaces, the internal corridors, and on the street. Thanks to this technology, the institution, like the facade, had a voice on the street.

Despite the lack of much original documentation, the available sources demonstrate that with this building—the last of his professional career as an architect—O'Gorman created a thoughtful arrangement of spaces for a set of corresponding human situations that were typical of labor unions, but not entirely expected by their members in their final form.[32] The facade, moreover, registered and represented the hierarchy of these situations through the differentiated treatment of levels, forming a crescendo of architectural choreography: from full openness towards the city on the ground floor, to the intricacies of bureaucracy on the first floor, and the realm of political

[32] On the notion of human situations in architecture see Vesely, Dalibor, "Between Architecture and the City," *Phenomenologies of the City: Studies in the History and Philosophy of Architecture*, Henriette Steiner and Maximilian Sternberg eds., London: Routledge, 2015, pp. 151–65.

Figure 4.17 | Detail of Figures 4.2 and 4.4.

representation on the second, then, the delegation of political power on the third, culminating on the top floor where a sense of community, solidarity, and liberation was restored, in an elevated position. In this sense, it is nothing short of amazing that the photograph with which I began this chapter shows—when enlarged—at least three of those situations at the time of their occurrence, a happy coincidence between the reality imagined or represented by the architect, and the reality lived, reimagined, and re-presented by the workers: the union members crowding the entry, a union leader looming over them from the podium, and a group of workers raising a flag: perhaps the communist, maybe the anarcho-syndicalist, probably the union's own, possibly the Mexican, or (who knows?) even the Virgin of Guadalupe's. **Figure 4.17**

Imagining the Workers' City

Despite its relatively short lifespan, O'Gorman's building had an important progeny. As already mentioned, his was the first in a series of labor-union buildings promoted by the Mexican labor organizations that found favor and impulse under Cárdenas's presidency. **Figure 4.18 (see p. 116)** Upon completing this project in 1937, O'Gorman immediately set about designing the headquarters of the National Union of Telephone Workers (Sindicato Nacional de Telefonistas), as well as the larger and more ambitious central headquarters of the CTM. Although unexecuted and eventually built to other architects' designs, these projects further elaborated the themes he explored in the SMC building: the open ground-floor, the vertical sequence of similar but differentiated floors, the proselytizing podium, the liberating roof-deck, the prominent signage, the defensive embrasures, the crowning flagpole, etc. Moreover, they were also unapologetic variations of Le Corbusier's architecture, the project for the CTM even being a compact version of the Tsentrosoyuz building, again appropriately, a union of unions. Planned to be constructed in front of the Monument to the Revolution and proportioned to its scale and massing, this project achieved the highest degree of civic and institutional character of any of O'Gorman's early projects and anticipated much of his later work.[33] **Figure 4.19 (see p. 117)**

This character notwithstanding, it is significant that without any established typology from which to derive his SMC building design, O'Gorman largely relied on a domestic precedent, Maison Cook, downplaying or suppressing some of its features, while transforming and highlighting others that offered better prospects of an urban architecture. And once built and published, this building set the standard in Mexico for this type of commission. The reach of O'Gorman's project can be appreciated in the many labor-union buildings constructed in the following years and decades, not only in Mexico City but also in other parts of the country. When looking at them together one can begin to understand that the reinterpretation of exemplary models can become a creative and projective strategy

[33] The CTM was his first project that envisioned modulated masonry cladding for a facade. In this sense it prefigured his university library building of 1952.

for architects who play a role in the formation of cities. Perhaps the earliest and most famous of these buildings following O'Gorman's footsteps is Enrique Yáñez's 1939 headquarters for the Mexican Union of Electrical Workers (Sindicato Mexicano de Electricistas), one of the most powerful labor organizations in the country. A disciple and follower of O'Gorman, Yáñez redeployed many of the elements present in the SMC building but reconfigured them in his own way.

Significantly enough, most of these buildings were located in or near Colonia Guerrero, in close proximity to the Monument to the Revolution. Begun in 1933 and completed in 1938, this monument was an adaptation of the steel-structure of Mexico's Federal Legislative Palace, an impressively large edifice initiated in 1910 during Porfirio Diaz's dictatorship but definitively halted by the Revolution. Once converted into the monument honoring the historical event that caused its demise, it became the focus of a new civic square that mirrored the city's old and traditional civic square, *el Zócalo*, located on axis to the east. Around this square and monument the vigorous Mexican labor movement of the 1930s imagined buildings that would represent it to the nation. O'Gorman's Mexican Cinema Workers Union building was the first to give visible form to this imagined and to some extent realized workers' city. **Figure 4.12 (see p. 114)**

Figure 4.2 | Calla Orozco y Berra, Colonia Guerrero, Mexico City, December 12, 1939.

Figure 4.3 | Calla Orozco y Berra, Colonia Guerrero, Mexico City, November 1, 1937.

Figure 4.4 | Juan O'Gorman, Mexican Cinema Workers Union building, 1936–7; perspective.

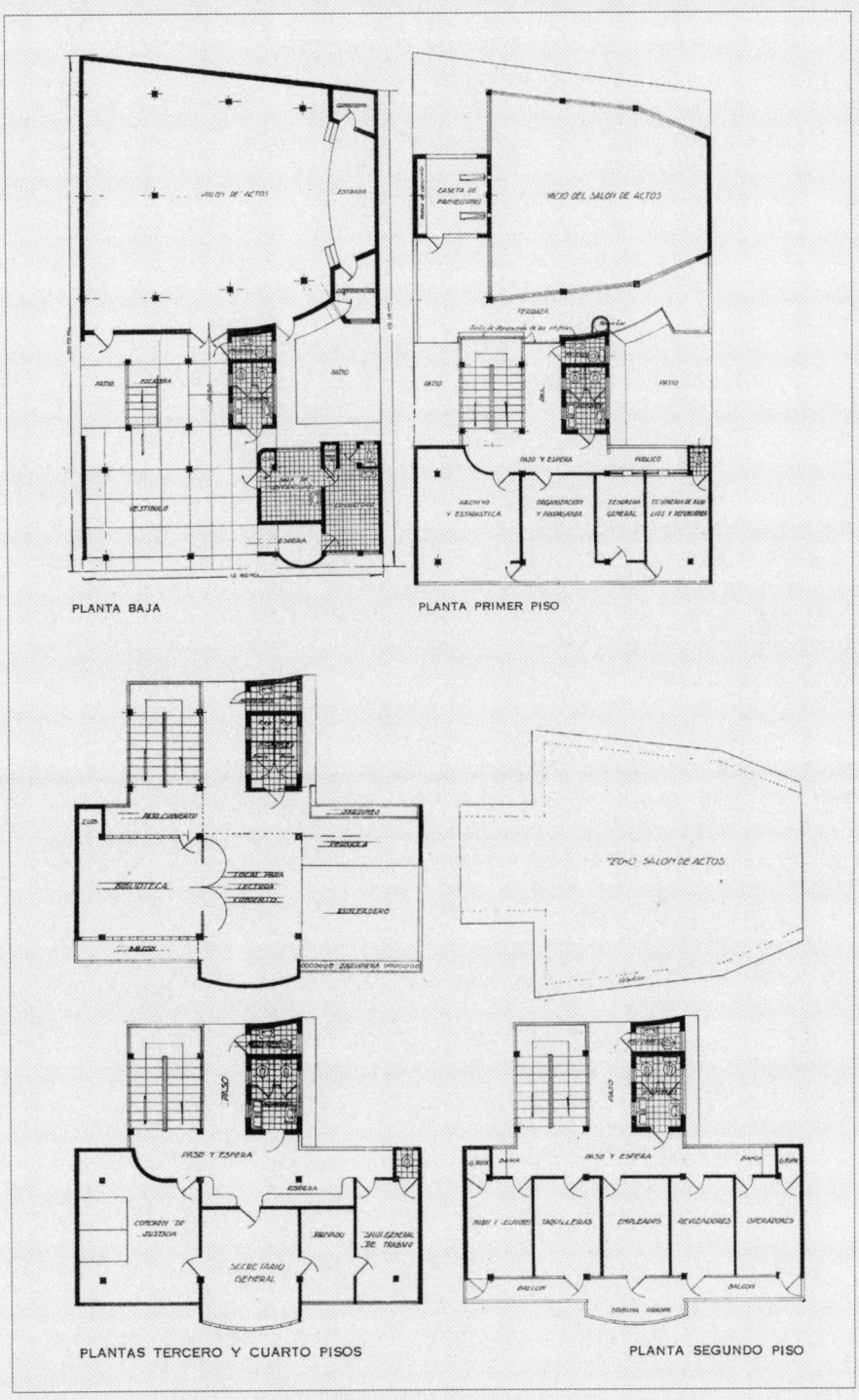

Figure 4.5 | Juan O'Gorman, Mexican Cinema Workers Union building, 1936; floor plans.

Figure 4.6 | Members of the union, c. 1923.

Figure 4.15 | Juan O'Gorman, Mexican Cinema Workers Union building, Mexico City, 1936–7.

Figure 4.12 | Aerial view of Colonia Guerrero, Church of San Fernando (bottom center), SMC building (bottom right), and Monument to the Revolution (center right), c. 1945.

Figure 4.18 | Juan O'Gorman, Project for the National Union of Telephone Workers building, Mexico City, c. 1937; perspective.

Figure 4.19 | Juan O'Gorman, Project for the CTM headquarters, Mexico City, c. 1937.

Daphna Half

Assembling Differences

Tel Aviv Culture Complex by D. Karmi, Z. Rechter, Y. Rechter, and A. Karavan

In 1953, the cornerstone was laid in Tel Aviv for Heichal HaTarbut, concert hall and home to the Israel Philharmonic Orchestra. **Figure 5.1 (see p. 131)** It was born out of the initiative of the Tel Aviv Municipality, the orchestra, and its co-partners: the national government, the Jewish Agency for Israel, the General Organization of Workers in Israel, the America-Israel Culture Foundation, and Frederick R. Mann, a music patron from Philadelphia. The project, co-designed by the practices of Dov Karmi and Zeev Rechter, was ultimately inaugurated in 1957. Among those attending the inauguration ceremony were Prime Minister David Ben-Gurion, President Yitzhak Ben-Zvi, former Prime Minister and Foreign Affairs Minister Moshe Sharett, and many foreign diplomats. Leonard Bernstein conducted the opening concert, which included the pianist Arthur Rubinstein, the violinist Isaac Stern, and the cellist Paul Tortelier.

Figure 5.10 | Rechter-Zarhi-Peri Architects in collaboration with Avraham Karavan, Yaakov Garden, Tel Aviv, 1965; garden's second-story view toward concert hall.

As an institution of cultural and national import, adjacent to the existing Habima National Theatre, the building was conceived as part of a new Culture Complex which was planned in the decades that followed national independence, the 1950s and 1960s. The buildings in the complex were both independent entities and part of the wider urban territory, to which they responded and with which they negotiated: the physical urban landscape, of course, but equally the social, cultural, and political conditions that brought that landscape to life.

Such an approach to architecture generally, and Tel Aviv specifically, was recommended by a planner who had an important role in the city's development, Sir Patrick Geddes. In *Cities in Evolution: An Introduction to the Town Planning Movement and to the Study of Civics,* Geddes discussed the planner's response to the circumstances that preceded his work, as opposed to "top-down" planning. Although he referred to planning the entire town, the practice was scalable, which is to say relevant to the making of buildings in towns. "Town planning is not something which can be done from above, on general principles easily laid down, which can be learned in one place and imitated in another... It is the development of a local life, a regional character, a civic spirit, a unique individuality, capable of course of growth and expansion yet always in its own way and upon its own foundations."[1]

Geddes established the foundations for Tel Aviv's masterplan in the mid-1920s, during the period of the British Mandate for Palestine. He first came to Palestine upon the invitation of the International Zionist Organization in 1919 in order to develop plans for Jerusalem's future development and the Hebrew University.[2] In 1925, Meir Dizengoff, Tel Aviv's Mayor, commissioned him to draw a masterplan for the rapidly growing coastal city. The plan delineated north-south "main ways" and east-west ancillary "home ways" and defined lot sizes interspersed with open spaces and gardens. It also included a centralized campus for future cultural institutions, assembled into a 40-dunam site (a dunam is 1,000 square meters) symbolically termed "Cultural Acropolis."[3]

Geddes's Acropolis was never realized. The Local Town Planning Commission replaced the centralized scheme with one affording a multiplicity of dispersed centers, which was an urban principle advanced by Municipal Head Engineer Yaakov (Ben Sira) Shifman. Ben Sira's approach specifically acknowledged the question of scale in architecture, which became pivotal in the Karmi-Rechter design of the complex, which in its 70-year history has become a seminal cultural and civic node in the city.[4]

The Idea of a Civic Center

The concept of a civic center occupied many architects after the Second World War, not only those in Israel. It became specifically relevant in the context of reconstruction after the destruction of many European cities in the war. While many reconstruction projects subscribed to the prevailing paradigm of the Functional City,[5] social critics and progressive planners, such as the American cultural critic

---

[1] Geddes, Patrick, *Cities in Evolution: An Introduction to the Town Planning Movement and to the Study of Civics*, London: Williams and Norgate, 1915, p. 205.

[2] Hyman, Benjamin, "British Planners in Palestine 1918-1936," dissertation submitted to London School of Economics and Political Sciences, January 1994, p. 106.

[3] Geddes, Patrick, *Town Planning Report—Jaffa and Tel Aviv*, Tel Aviv Municipality Archive, 1925. On page 51 of the report, Geddes addresses the issue of the centralized cultural campus under the title: Cultural Institutes for Tel Aviv. See also: Hysler-Rubin, Noah, *Patrick Geddes and Town Planning, A Critical View*, New York: Routledge, 2011; Marom, Nathan, *City of Concept: Planning Tel Aviv*, Tel Aviv: Babel, 2009, pp. 153-4 [Hebrew].

[4] In the Town Planning Scheme the public square had already been outlined. The scheme shows the square as the convergence of Rothschild Boulevard and Chen Boulevard. Rothschild Boulevard was one of the first boulevards in Tel Aviv. It already existed when Geddes outlined the city's masterplan.

[5] Although the Athens Charter was only published in 1943, Le Corbusier's book *La Ville Radieuse*, which was published in 1933, already presented the ideals of the Functional City. The tenets of the Athens Charter were also published in various architectural journals: in the Paris *Gazette des Beaux-Arts* in 1933, and in the *Technika chronika—Les Annales Techniques* in Greece, which was then published in Spain, Italy, Switzerland, Holland, and Belgium. In the 1930s, CIAM (Congrès Internationaux d'Architecture Moderne) groups throughout Europe published the ideas of the Functional City in their affiliated journals (*Opbouw* and *L'Équerre*, for example).

Lewis Mumford, insisted on addressing the previously neglected socio-cultural aspects of urban life.[6] Joined by other voices from within CIAM (Congrès Internationaux d'Architecture Moderne), architectural historians and practitioners began questioning the adequacy of Functional City principles according to which a city had to accommodate four main functions: dwelling, work, recreation, and circulation. They thought that in addition to accommodating these functions, a civic and cultural core should be created, wherein a "sense of community" could be expressed. This became a fundamental theme in Post-War architectural debates. It informed CIAM's eighth congress in Hoddesdon, England, in 1951, where the civic center—the "city's nucleolus"—was symbolically termed the main theme of the congress: "The Heart of the City."[7]

In 1946, the Tel Aviv Municipality initiated a public competition for planning a civic culture center adjacent to the Habima National Theatre (1934–45).[8] This was part of municipal planning policy that sought to establish multiple, decentralized civic centers throughout the city that would impart a sense of community to each neighborhood. The model for this policy, as advanced by Ben Sira, was London. Ben Sira pointed to London's advantage over other metropolises, and contended that "it was essentially a consolidation of several towns and villages, in which central spaces for public practices and a public spirit still existed, compared with cities that grew around one central urban core."[9] He appreciated London's multiplicity of public centers, each contributing to the expression and consolidation of civic identity, and would consequently adopt this structural principle in urban development policies for Tel Aviv in the following decades.[10]

The site for what was to become the Culture Complex measured 20 dunams and included a mound with old sycamore trees. It was situated in a condensed residential neighborhood at the convergence of three prominent arteries, Rothschild, Chen, and Ben-Zion Boulevards, and negotiated the different ground levels along its borders, which were incorporated in the architectural plans. **Figure 5.2 (see p. 132)**

It eventually accommodated three seminal cultural institutions: the existing National Theatre, Heichal HaTarbut (literally, "The Culture Palace," also named after its benefactor the Mann Auditorium[11]), and the Helena Rubinstein Art Pavilion (an extension of the Tel Aviv Museum of Art, commissioned to Zeev Rechter and his son Yaakov, completed in 1959). **Figures 5.3 (see p. 133) and 5.4 (see p. 133)** The program of the Culture Complex underwent development through different stages, and included a number of commercial uses in small spaces leased by the Tel Aviv Municipality to accommodate local residents.[12] These included a bookstore, a flower shop, a greenhouse, a coffee shop, and a taxi station.[13] Two open public spaces were also integrated in the complex: a public square (forecourt to the auditorium) and a partially enclosed public garden, planned in 1964 by Yaakov Rechter and his firm Rechter-Zarhi-Peri Architects in collaboration with the head municipal landscape architect Avraham Karavan. **Figure 5.5 (see p. 134)**

---

6 Mumford, Lewis, *The Culture of Cities*, London: Secker & Warburg, 1938.

7 This was the title of the co-edited publication *CIAM 8: The Heart of the City*, Ernesto N. Rogers, Josep Lluís Sert and Jaqueline Tyrwhitt eds., New York: Lund Humphries, 1952. The question of the city "Core" as a significant component for establishing and practicing community life was also expressed earlier in an essay Sert wrote in 1944, where he argued that scaled-down pedestrian civic centers ought to be incorporated in city planning in order to establish a "sense of differentiation" in cities that had been subjected to unplanned expansion. His argument is closely linked to the question of scale that occupied Yaakov Ben Sira. See Sert, "Human Scale in City Planning," *New Architecture and City Planning*, Paul Zucker ed., New York: Philosophical Library, 1944, pp. 392–412; Sert, "CIAM 8: Core of the City," *Transformation 2*, 1951, pp. 114–6; Mumford, Eric, *The CIAM Discourse on Urbanism, 1928–1960*, Cambridge, MA: MIT Press, 2002, pp. 201–14.

8 The Habima National Theatre was planned by Hungarian émigré Oskar Kaufmann.

9 Ben Sira, Yaakov, "Master Plan for Tel Aviv-Jaffa," *Handasa We'Adrikhalut*, 1954, p. 13. [Hebrew]. This point was also made by Steen Eiler Rasmussen in *London the Unique City* published in Danish in 1934. The first English edition was published in 1937.

10 At the end of the 1930s Tel Aviv's population approached 150,000. In the early 1950s it grew to 241,000. The Culture Complex and the debates over its planning, materialization, and reception in public opinion were, therefore, tied to the county's and the city's growth and its symbolic weight in constructing new civic and national identities.

11 In 2013, the building was renamed the Charles Bronfman Auditorium.

12 In 1964, the America-Israel Cultural Foundation sought to establish its headquarters in the complex, in place of the allotment for commercial uses (see letter from the foundation to Mayer Mordechai Namir. Tel Aviv Municipality Archive, section 4, מ/10/1.)

13 Tel Aviv Municipality Archive, section 4, מ/10/1.

Figure 5.6 | Dov Karmi and Zeev Rechter, Heichal HaTarbut concert hall, Tel Aviv, 1957; bird's-eye view of concert hall and Yaakov Garden.

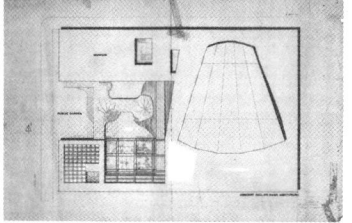

Figure 5.7 | Dov Karmi and Zeev Rechter, Heichal HaTarbut concert hall, Tel Aviv, 1957; site plan.

14 Interview with Ada Karmi Melamede, Dov Karmi's daughter, in July 2014.

15 For years the square was a parking lot. It was converted into its original intended purpose in 2013. Tel Aviv Mayor Mordechai Namir guaranteed the lot's designation as an open public space, reassuring Tel Aviv residents that it would become a public garden "organically extending Yaacov Garden." "A Two-Storey Garden Will be Inaugurated in Tel Aviv Today," *Herut*, May 1964.

16 Different degrees of social interaction have informed theories on public space. Ben Sira expressed this idea when considering the values of urban life: "...Allowing for the individual's seclusion, when he so desires, and enabling his association with a greater community, when he feels the need... a need for privacy—on the one hand, and social activity—on the other..."(Ben Sira, Yaakov, "The Urban Development: The Size of a City," *Symposium on the Problems of Planning and Development, Handasa We'Adrikhalut* 5, 1943, p. 10. [Hebrew].

The site was surrounded by a dense pattern of dwelling units, typically three to four stories high, and was framed by Karmi's earlier plans for the concatenated four-story residential buildings along the east side of Huberman Street. Karmi rejected Tel Aviv's parcellation policies, in which the divisibility of the block into smaller lots generated "disassociated buildings" on a set-back building-line. Instead, he sought to establish a contiguous border that would help define the public square.[14] The limits of the public square were meant to define an open-air enclosure that would accommodate and represent public life. This was no simple undertaking, for the entrance to the Habima National Theatre never faced the square, and the building's opaque mass remained a hindrance to the overall balancing of the elements surrounding the square. The concert hall remained the only building whose entry required passing through the square, which was critical for the building's architecture and its social and cultural standing.[15]

The project's surrounding residential fabric was both a physical backdrop and an indication of the habitual social practices that had an impact on the architects' overall shaping of the complex. The synthesis of national institutions that draw visitors from beyond the neighborhood and city, with services and spaces that accommodate the residents in the local neighborhood, point to the planner's working premise that acknowledged the complex's different users. The design demonstrated a stratified concept of the public domain in which a range of "publics" was accommodated, and a variety of uses addressed. As a result, the architects reconciled different architectural scales that corresponded to the activities that took place on site: from collective and festive gatherings related to the cultural institutions, to local mundane practices associated with the small shops and enclosed garden.[16] The architectural ensemble was moderated to accommodate large group associations as well as an intimate rendezvous or a secluded repose from the busy urban surrounds. It was predicated on the idea of a simultaneous presence of a multitude of objectives and perspectives, catering to innumerable purposes. It underscored *praxis* and was to be experienced *in* everyday life. **Figures 5.6, 5.7 and 5.8**

The collaborative work between Karmi and Rechter (who, together with Arieh Sharon, are considered the founding fathers of Israeli Modernism) generated distinct buildings and open spaces all of which simultaneously shared formal commonalities. To an observer unfamiliar with their uses, the projects might be interpreted as distinct parts of a single whole, for while the institutions maintained their individuality, their mutuality was reinforced by obvious intercommunication. The buildings and garden were assembled and contained within an extended field of columns and beams that shared a common circumferential cornice and roof. When this structural system soared over Yaakov Garden it became a horizontal *brise-soleil* that enabled the old sycamore trees to extend through and beyond it. **Figures 5.9 and 5.10 (see p. 118)**

Figure 5.8 | Rechter-Zarhi-Peri Architects in collaboration with Avraham Karavan, Yaakov Garden, Tel Aviv, 1965; model.

Figure 5.9 | Rechter-Zarhi-Peri Architects in collaboration with Avraham Karavan, Yaakov Garden, Tel Aviv, 1965; garden's second story.

Figure 5.13 | Dov Karmi and Zeev Rechter, Heichal HaTarbut concert hall, Tel Aviv, 1957; interior views of foyer and concert hall.

Figure 5.15 | Dov Karmi and Zeev Rechter, Heichal HaTarbut concert hall, Tel Aviv, 1957; south and east elevations.

17 Karmi, Ram, "Don't touch Heichal HaTarbut", *Haaretz*, June 27, 2005.

This grid of columns and its frame were a rational, pre-defined, regulating structural system that was imposed on the site. It exemplified the completeness of the ensemble but also allowed adaptations to the conditions that preceded the project. The architects moderated this readily identifiable type-form to acknowledge a given situation (the existing trees for example) and enhance awareness of it. The pliability of the formal architectural type also enabled the accommodation of a variety of functions for the range of users described above. This principle of pliability did not compromise the type's clarity, organizational principle, or the intended functions of the spaces. Nor did it subject the type to a formless ambiguity. It pointed, rather, to a hybrid or combinatorial idea of abstraction and engagement, sufficient to make the spaces in the complex legible, but also susceptible to specific and changing contexts that are not necessarily foreseen from the onset.

The Concert Hall

The flagship building in the complex was Heichal HaTarbut (Culture Palace). Its porous and airy columnar structure contrasted with the massive volume of its concert hall. While the regularity of the first alluded to atypical and extended space, the concert hall grounded one in the experience of a concentrated perception of a musical performance. Accordingly, the two systems employed different materials. Various finishes of exposed concrete, bush hammered concrete stucco, stone, and glass were used in the spaces that flow through the columnar structure, while "warmer" materials (also acoustically sounder) such as wood and upholstery refined the interiors of the concert hall, which some have compared with a musical instrument.[17] The building sustained a tension between these two schemes; the first "belonged" to the city, the second "belonged" to the separated and protected atmosphere of the concert hall. **Figures 5.11 (see p. 136), 5.12 (see p. 137), 5.13 and 5.14 (see p. 138)**

The concert hall's protruding roof was noticeable, but hardly prominent or immediately obvious. Although it contained more than 2,700 seats, its vastness was barely apparent from the building's exterior. The structure did not exceed the height of its neighboring buildings and receded inward from the building's boundary. The formal independence of the concert hall body was mediated by contextual adaptations through the building's trabeated structural system and its foyer, which was contained within a horizontal, prismatic volume enclosed by plate glass. **Figure 5.15**

Karmi and Rechter planned second-story balconies on the north east and south east frontages by recessing the glazed foyer. A third west-facing balcony negotiated between the foyer and Yaakov Garden. In these instances, open space is realized by subtracting volume from the mass of the building, reshaping the figure/ground relationship, and serving to integrate the building with its context. In the balcony that adjoined the garden, this manner of integration is manifest in the use of the space by non-concert goers. By providing the balconies, which were contained within the building's trabeated system, the architects maintained the building's skeletal appearance and reduced its presence on the street. The rhythmic and regulating columnar system, the moderation of the auditorium's mass-form by encompassing it within the horizontal glass enclosure, and the articulation of the building's interface with its attendant urban space by mediating, in-between spaces, which also afforded direct and peripheral views to the surrounding neighborhood, eschewed any trace of Beaux-Arts monumentality. It was essentially a project that defied monumentality, or one that sought to redefine the idea of monumentality. **Figure 5.16 (see p. 140)**

Modest Monumentality

Ideas on the appropriate kind of monumentality informed the debates concerning the building. But, while Sigfried Giedion's sense of a "new monumentality," for example, involved a celebratory demonstration of new materials and structures, employing architectural "effects" for theatrical display in the spirit of urban festivals and world fairs,[18] the civic center in Israel conveyed a profoundly different message. Discernible in Heichal HaTarbut and its reception in public opinion, was a new civic monumentality that was intrinsically bound to the question of propriety and modesty in collective representation.

Referring to the building as a Culture *Palace* may seem odd given this accent on architectural simplicity and restraint. At the very least, that type of building—a ruler's residence—misrepresents the idea of a public institution reflecting a co-operative ethos or value system, through which the public identifies itself. In the case of Israel in the 1950s, this value system was predicated on Social Zionism. Because the first years of independence were marked by material scarcity, the welfare state and austerity regime implemented a strict rationing policy that affected the building industry as well. The call to "reduce the standard of living" and the appeal to make do with materials at-hand were considered a "political necessity."[19] Under this value system, a rejection of the historic monument's subject of representation was accompanied by a dismissal of its formal methods. Not only were monuments no longer signifiers of ruling regimes, their means of representation had to reflect the new socialist modern state and its cultural values of frugality and austerity. Thus, an earlier symmetrical scheme that included a more rigid use of forms and an arrangement less pliable to extraneous factors was abandoned. This kind of rigid, ostentatious monumentality was a sign of impropriety, and several local architects deemed it incongruous with the ethos of the new socialist and modernist Israeli nation.[20] **Figure 5.17 (see p. 141)**

Tel Aviv head engineer, Ben Sira, identified this new intention in public institutions as a "reduced tendency to astonish and belittle the individual compared with the awe-inspiring structures of a ruling society."[21] Aba Elhanani, an architect and prolific architectural critic and historian, expressed this cultural atmosphere in his

---

[18] Sigfried Giedion, Josep Lluís Sert, Fernand Léger, "Nine Points on Monumentality," (1943) was intended to be published in a volume for the American Abstract Artists. It never appeared in this form. Similar content appeared in Giedion, Sigfried, "The Need for a New Monumentality," *New Architecture and City Planning*, Paul Zucker ed., New York: Philosophical Library, 1944, pp. 549–68. The original co-authored text would appear in Giedion, *Architektur und Gemeinschaft*, Hamburg: Rowohlt, 1965, pp. 40–2. Followed by the English edition: *Architecture, You and Me*, Cambridge, MA: Harvard University Press, 1958, pp. 48–52.

[19] Ben Sira, Yaakov, "On The Planning of Housing," *Handasa We'Adrikhalut*, 1953, pp. 17–20. [Hebrew].

[20] The debate regarding the Israeli House of Parliament also concerned the question of what style of architecture was appropriate to represent the newly founded state. Dov Karmi was active in the debate and was finally chosen with his son, Ram, to "modernize" Yosef Klarwein's initial monumental and symmetrical proposal. See the editorial column in *Handasa We'Adrikhalut*, 1953, p. 1. [Hebrew]. See also Hetis-Rolf, Shila, "The House of Parliament in Givat Ram: Planning and Construction," *Katedra* 96, July 2000; Efrat, Zvi, author and editor, Elhyani, Zvi, co-editor, *The Israeli Project: Building and Architecture, 1948–1973*, Tel Aviv Museum of Art, 2004, pp. 741–8.

[21] Ben Sira, Yaakov, "On the Architecture of Our Time," *Tel Aviv Municipality Newsletter*, 1947–8, p. 27.

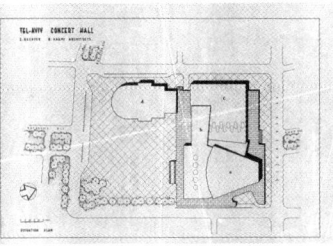

Figure 5.18 | Dov Karmi and Zeev Rechter, Heichal HaTarbut concert hall, Tel Aviv, 1957; site plan.

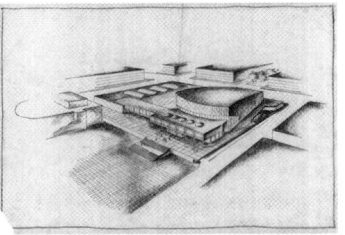

Figure 5.19 | Dov Karmi and Zeev Rechter, Heichal HaTarbut concert hall, Tel Aviv, 1957; perspective.

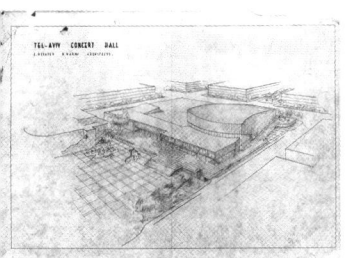

Figure 5.20 | Dov Karmi and Zeev Rechter, Heichal HaTarbut concert hall, Tel Aviv, 1957; perspective.

22 Elhanani, Aba, "The Culture Palace and its Adjacent Public Square," newspaper clipping recorded in the Ram Karmi Archive, folder titled "Dov Karmi 1962-1968."
23 Elhanani, Aba, "The Culture Palace and its Adjacent Public Square."
24 "Monumental Building," *Tvai* 3, 1967, pp. 17-22.
25 "Yaacov Gardens will be Inaugurated Today in Tel Aviv," *Davar*, May 1964.
26 Azaria, R., "The Culture Palace— a Public Domain Intended for the Public's Enjoyment," *Maariv*, October 1957.

critique of the newly completed concert hall. He maintained that the building's "splendor" was achieved by its "restrained use of simple and easily recognizable materials, and the abstention from any superfluous effects..."[22] Elhanani thought the building was "a reflection of one of architecture's principles of economy of means and the honest expression of the building 'as is' with no camouflage or embellishment."[23] His praise of the building underlined the value system he thought the building reflected, by exhibiting a new reserved or modest monumentality that required suppression of its architects' individual expressive gestures. This conception also entailed the idea of engagement and acceptance of contingencies of place: the physical backdrop of the location (buildings and topography) as well as the historical moment's economic constraints and particular social fabric. These questions would appear in the third issue of the architectural periodical *Tvai*, in which Elhanani and fellow architects S. Gilad and A. Erlich discussed the question of monumentality.[24]

Interdependency of Distinct Urban Spaces

Unlike the National Theatre, which stood autonomously and defined the western border of the public square, the concert hall, the Helena Rubinstein Pavilion for Contemporary Art, a number of commercial uses, and Yaakov Garden were assembled and contained within a single substructure, one that allowed the architects to refer to the complex as "one architectural unit."[25] The composition underscored a sense of association and awareness among its parts, articulated through mediating spaces that provided opportunities for functional interface. Urbanity and the civic public realm thus corresponded to plurality, mutual awareness, and inter-relatedness. It enabled overlapping experiences, formal and functional juxtapositions, and offered public space to a variety of potential users. **Figures 5.18, 5.19, and 5.20**

The idea of appealing to a "public of all sorts" was key to Heichal HaTarbut, which was perceived as a catalyst through which music would reach wide audiences, including all ages and socio-economic levels.[26] Although early design schemes included an elevated platform that distinguished between the building and the adjoining square, the executed plans omitted it, and established a common ground between them. This gave the building a quotidian nature, not elevated from but engaged with the ordinary city life that took shape in the boulevards and forecourt it bordered. Its entrance and main orientation were anchored to the square, likewise facing (though not symmetrically) Rothschild Boulevard. Proponents of a "classical arrangement" in which the auditorium would be axially positioned in relation to Rothschild Boulevard questioned Karmi and Rechter's off axis parti. In a statement complemented by an analysis of the site presented to the municipality in March 1953, Yohanan Ratner, Dean of the Technion's School of Architecture, addressed the formal arrangement of the masses and supported the architects' scheme, which he described as "classical not classicist" since the building "will be seen not frontally and directly but angularly and indirectly, like the Parthenon."[27]

The building's recessed glass in the longitudinal south facade, where the entrance was situated, offered an elongated shaded space that stretched along the open square and drew it into the boundaries of the interior foyer. The building's foyer became an extension of the public square and vice versa. Interior and exterior public gatherings were spectacles for mutual display, and crowds assembling in the ground foyer, before and after performances or during intermission, trickled out onto the public square, thus enacting the contiguity between ordinary city life and the festivity of attending a musical performance. The square mediated between the paces of movement in the streets and boulevards, and the building. Presently, it is visited daily by local families and serves as a venue for different cultural attractions throughout the year, many of which extend from the lively atmosphere that has come to characterize Rothschild Boulevard. It is also a platform for political demonstrations, and accommodates the philharmonic orchestra's complimentary musical performances, which are open to the public. In the multiplicity and overlapping of its uses, some of which could not have been anticipated by the planners, the square (or auditorium forecourt) was another recognizable architectural type-form that, like the grid of columns, was sufficiently abstract to allow for some variation of, even disruption to its initially intended function. The square's abstract type-form lent itself to unforeseen uses, and allowed them to take place in it, and reshape it, as they indeed still do today. This is what affords the project its afterlife, and what makes it contextually embedded.

Heichal HaTarbut's connection with Yaakov Garden was another opportunity for spatial and functional crossings. Here, too, the public attending a concert could convene on the upper foyer and drift onto the west-facing balcony and into the garden's upper level. The boundaries between one space and another were impossible to delineate. Since the garden also accommodated local residents and pedestrians passing by and offered its visitors a space to convene or play in—a *locus amoenus* affording a temporary respite from urban rhythms—its users mingled and a variety of movement patterns overlapped.

Yaakov Garden

The public garden was not included in the municipality's initial brief. The original program designated this space for the Tel Aviv Museum. Local resistance to the intention to level the uneven terrain and uproot the 200-year-old sycamore trees precipitated the movement of the museum to another location. In its place, the city issued plans for a public garden.[28] The garden's area covered less than an acre and was designed on two levels, each of which linked it to a different element in its vicinity; the ground level was coplanar with the public square in front of the Mann Auditorium, and was

---

27 Yohanan (Eugen) Ratner in a letter submitted to the Tel Aviv Mayor's office on March 13, 1953. Tel Aviv Municipality archive, section 4, Heichal HaTarbut, ד/5/14. [Hebrew].

28 Pines, Shimon, "A Unique Garden is being Planted Near the Culture Palace," *Davar*, June 25, 1963.

connected to the square diagonally. The garden's second level was linked by a ramp to Chen Boulevard and Dizengoff Street and connected Heichal HaTarbut's second-story foyer to a greenhouse through a suspended bridge also branched off to connect to the mounds on which the old trees were located. **Figure 5.21 (see p. 142)**

In 1965, the Rechter-Zarhi-Peri partnership was awarded the prestigious municipal Rokach Prize for Architecture for planning the garden.[29] The judging committee maintained that "the garden's main goal was to integrate public institutions—among the more significant urban architecture of the new Tel Aviv—with old natural assets (sycamore trees), among the few remaining vestiges of young and romantic Tel Aviv." Though the multi-leveled garden was located between existing buildings and was situated on a small lot, the committee believed it conveyed "a feeling of relief for those strolling in it." The committee complimented the architectural solution that "beautifully coincided with the trees' levels, the adjacent buildings and streets, and completed the space between them with a successful combination of plant, water, and construction." It proclaimed that the garden "completed the most significant culture center in Tel Aviv, while successfully utilizing the different conditions present on site."[30] The judges praised the architects for integrating pre-existing conditions into their design process, thereby heightening awareness of them, even as this awareness was peripheral.

Though not completely walled in by its neighboring institutions, the garden bore resemblance to the enclosed garden type, which existed before its inclusion in an urban fabric. Only in the early Renaissance did the type acquire its standing as a spatial unit defined by the buildings surrounding it within the overall system of the town.[31] Before that, it typically appeared in isolated configurations such as monasteries and villas, where it was still a spatial unit within a larger spatial ensemble, but not yet one associated with the practices performed at the scale of a town. The idea of the enclosed garden's inter-relatedness with versus its absolute seclusion from its surrounding settings was also subject to changes. In the Middle Ages, as *Hortus Conclusus,* it was strictly separated from its surrounding landscape, and afforded only an *axis mundi*, or vertical link to the heavens through which it represented connection to the divine order. But because its principal role as a reference to an ideal place, a Garden of Eden, relied on the employment of concrete materials from its own physical surroundings, this strict separation was ultimately modified. The metaphysical was bound to become concrete.[32]

In the Renaissance, the type would eventually augment its strictly vertical alignment with the sky with horizontal connections to the surrounding world, drawing the once excluded horizon into the garden, exemplifying a part-whole relationship that also pertains to the issue of scaling. This transformation was, no doubt, also affected by the concrete changes of political stability, the rediscovery of pictorial space, and the development of the graphic technique of perspective.[33] Perspectival depictions of

---

[29] Beginning in 1954, the prize named after Tel Aviv's Mayor Israel Rokach was awarded for "excellent contributions in the field of architecture, and landscape and urban planning."

[30] Tel Aviv Municipality Archive, division 4, 4473, 10.02.1963 - 20.09.1965, 10/1/ב

[31] The early Renaissance was marked by a shift in the conception of a town, from a haphazard collection of built masses to a rational geometric system that could be expressed formally. Planning and shaping the overall configuration of the town became analogous to the planning of the individual architectural object. Hence the different elements of the town corresponded to the different spatial components of the villa.

[32] Aben, Rob and Saskia De Wit, *The Enclosed Garden, History and Development of the Hortus Conclusus and its Reintroduction into the Present-day Urban Landscape*, Rotterdam: 010 Publishers, 1999.

[33] For the development of perspective see Frommel, Christoph Luitpold, "Reflections on the Early Architectural Drawings," first published 1994, *The Renaissance, from Brunelleschi to Michelangelo, the Representation of Architecture*, Henry A., Millen ed., New York: Rizzoli, 1997, pp. 101–21.

space integrated distance and the organization of geometrical objects on the ground surface onto the picture plane, structuring the ensemble in correspondence to a fixed viewing point. This process rendered architecture increasingly pictorial, and space conquerable and controllable. Architecture became a subject for viewing and a setting from which viewing was encouraged. The landscape and orientation toward the horizon became the subject for exploration and aesthetic reflection, subsequently adjusting the structural rationale of the enclosed garden. This reflected a principal change in the medieval conception of space. From identifying space with a single object, a definitive and stabilized closed form, the concept of space became receptive to distance and to what lay beyond the object's defined borders. Space ceased to be predicated on the object and became constituted on the relationship between objects placed upon an extensive ground, a continuum visibly reaching the horizon.

The type's key structural constituents were ultimately called into question in the late 19th and early 20th centuries. The immured space of the garden, intermittently opened to negotiate its enclosure with specific views, now forfeited its enclosure and correspondingly its status as an autonomous space. Modernism's fascination with distance and the horizon was affected by developments in the field of architecture, with improved techniques in the production and construction of plate glass and reinforced and pre-stressed concrete.[34] It was also influenced by conceptual and cultural fascinations with the expansive, accessible and, presumably, controllable landscape. This rid the type of its essential significance and purpose. Relinquishing its principal programmatic and symbolic meaning, the enclosed garden dissolved into the landscape with which it became synonymous, and its clearly defined borders, like those of its urban counterparts—the piazza or square—succumbed to a border-less environment in which the entire landscape became a boundless garden/park. Le Corbusier's Ville Contemporaine (1922) and Ville Radieuse (1924) are cases in point. The dissolution of the relationship between built mass and constructed void in which the two performed jointly to comprise the matrix of the town rendered the extendable void—the landscape—an undifferentiated field.[35] Though Yaakov Garden is entirely modern, it is neither unbounded nor homogeneous. **Figures 5.22 (see p. 143) and 5.23 (see p. 144)**

Because Yaakov Garden accommodated local residents and visitors to the institutions on site, it was fully engaged in the practices taking place around it.[36] Its various entrances and exits also corresponded to the street network along its borders. The architects established views to the public square that were mediated by the structural colonnade. From various locations within the garden, one could even see beyond the public square to the boulevards on both ends. The garden, therefore, presented an intrinsic antinomy. On the one hand, it offered inclusion, drawing the disparate subjects of the community together, integrating them into a space defined by its adjacent buildings for which it was

---

[34] Giedion, Sigfried, *Space, Time and Architecture: The Growth of a New Tradition*, first written 1941, Cambridge, MA: Harvard University Press, 2009.

[35] For an account on the modernist landscape see Treib, Marc, "Nature Recalled," *Recovering Landscape, Essays in Contemporary Landscape Architecture*, James Corner ed., New York: Princeton Architectural Press, 1999, pp. 29-41.

[36] Tel Aviv Municipality Archive, division 4, 10.02.1963-20.09.1965, 10/1/ב, letter dated September 11, 1964, sheet no. 28.

both the actual and symbolic unifying element. Also, the carefully constructed visual links to the garden's surrounding urban setting, point to the architects' intention to associate the space with others in its vicinity—an intention reminiscent of spatial structures like the Cortile del Belvedere from the 16th century. But on the other hand, the garden also served the purpose of exclusion, suspending one's absorption in the routines of city life and counterweighing the vigor of the city by enclosing a territory within the city's fabric. Yaakov Garden was a synthesis of the enclosed garden as fully unhitched from its surroundings, and the transformation of the type into a system partially compromising its complete introversion for the sake of engaging with the outside world.[37] **Figure 5.24 (see p. 145)**

Conclusion

Analyzing the configuration of the Tel Aviv Culture Complex identified key architectural types: the grid of columns and its frame, the public square, and the enclosed garden. Two issues emerged in consideration of these types. The first concerns the architectural principles or rules that govern their formation. The second asks what adjustments to these principles allow for their co-existence and mutual involvement (when they seem so profoundly opposed to one another), as well as their association with more basic understandings of the urban milieu.

My emphasis on architectural types was intended to stress formal issues as a preliminary to the other (social, historical, political, and cultural) issues discussed. The principle of scale or proportionality, for example, was considered vis-à-vis the idea of parts participating in wholes. This principle has both physical and ethical dimensions; proportionality in terms of measurement and relationship between part and whole and among the different parts, as well as proportionality among the living components of a community and their mutual participation in the formation of that community, without one part overpowering another (measure as manner) and together comprising a whole that sustains a certain balance among the community's parts. Scale or proportionality, then, become an architectural expression of political participation.

It was these architectural types and their abstract formal articulation, which allowed the multiplicity of publics that gauged the project's urbanity and granted the flexibility that made it sit within its vicinity so gracefully. This abstraction was also manifest in the care for functions and programs. Rather than becoming over-particularized and, therefore, over-determining and restrictive, the design afforded a flexibility and, therefore, freedom precisely because it retained a certain purity of conception that allowed unanticipated forms of occupation to be no less at home than those that were initially envisaged.

This kind of formal analysis entails thinking about how the urban articulation of an architectural type has to consider what is permanent together with what this permanence sometimes overlooks or has not foreseen: situations that arise out of urban life.

[37] The garden's 2013 restoration further compromised the sense of enclosure for the sake of a direct, co-planar and widened passageway between the main entrance at Dizengoff Street and the public square. The omission of the ramp and the ideal of facilitating connection overshadowed the idea of the garden as a space for seclusion.

The type's urbanity means that things that are implicit in, even key to its conceptualization, sometimes require alteration, adaptation, and even resignation. This is how an imposed, rationalized grid, for example, yields to certain preconditions and "loosens" its rigidity. The grid-form does not, thereby, lose its typological identity, or its association to a family of related objects. On the contrary, the analogical association becomes enriched by a certain flexibility to things that are perforce impermanent.

The Tel Aviv Culture Complex was conceived as a place of formal, functional, and symbolic syntheses. It integrated diverse "publics" by accommodating a range of public institutions and re-empowering everyday life in the local neighborhood, while reinforcing the identification of public space with the social space of chance encounters, unpredictable experiences, a multitude of perspectives, and the recognition of difference.

The idea of urban space as a totality capable of assembling differences was manifest in the architecture of the complex. The trabeated substructure that assembled the different buildings as well as the garden into a legible ensemble maintained the distinctness of the spaces, but also communicated their mutual association. In this case, buildings were not conceived in isolation. Urbanity and citizenship meant participation in and awareness of a wider (shared) territory. By allowing the natural level of the ground to undulate freely, by refusing to level the mound with the old sycamore trees, and by responding to the surrounding boulevards' natural topography, the architects emphasized the idea of accepting existing settings and bringing the buildings into conversation with them. But, at the same time, by introducing the substructure's horizontal circumferential frame (a unifying element that brings the disparate elements into some sense of agreement), the architects *constructed* a steady common ground—a shared landscape—amid the irregular and fluctuating preconditions and surroundings. While the complex revealed an unmistakable attunement to conditions that preceded it, it did not fully acquiesce to them. It condensed conditions within a wider territory, but also established a platform that stabilized them, thus creating a stage for public life. **Figure 5.25 (see p. 146)**

Figure 5.1 | Dov Karmi and Zeev Rechter, Heichal HaTarbut concert hall, Tel Aviv, 1957; view from Yaakov Garden.

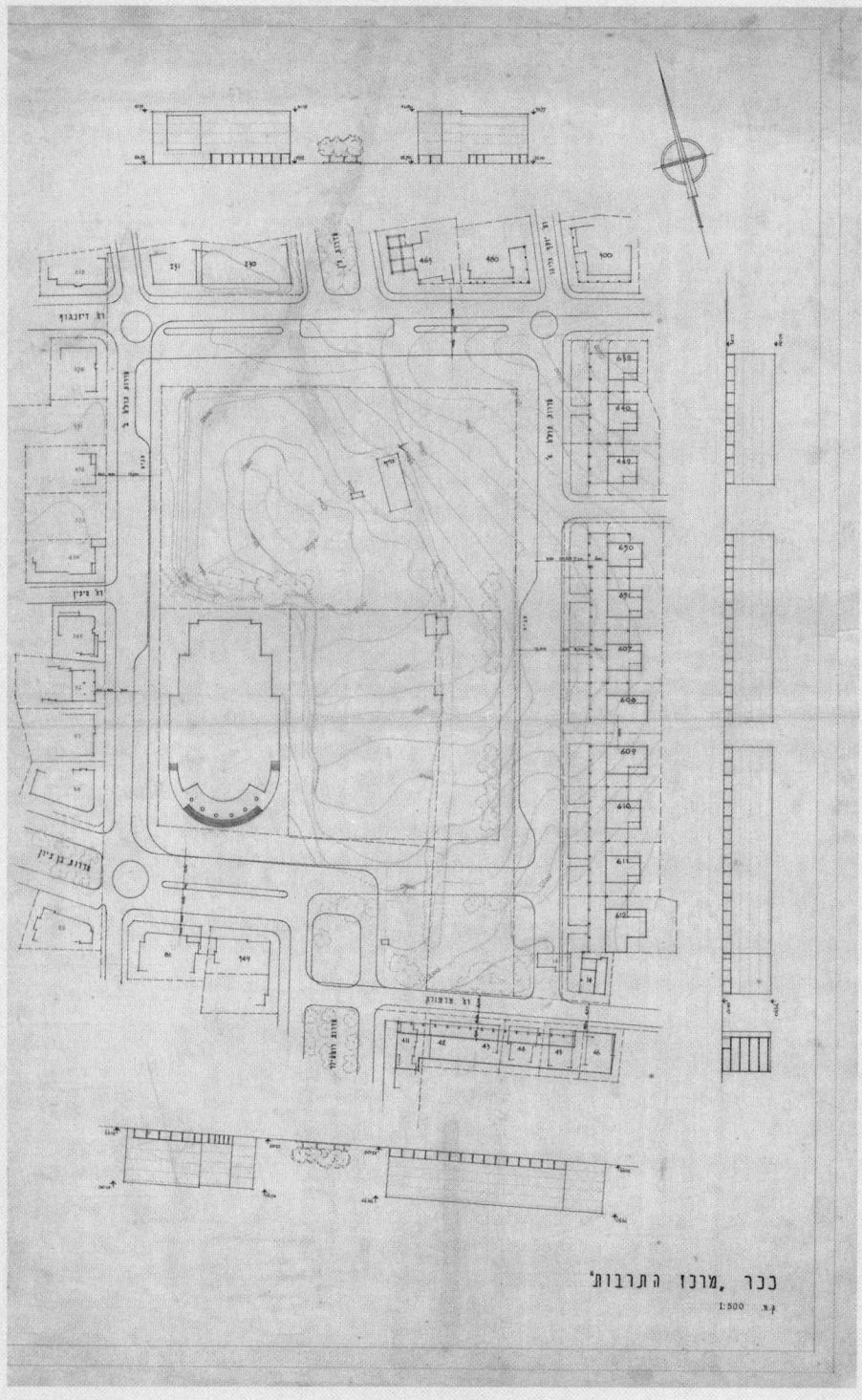

Figure 5.2 | Dov Karmi and Zeev Rechter, Heichal HaTarbut concert hall, Tel Aviv, 1957; survey plan.

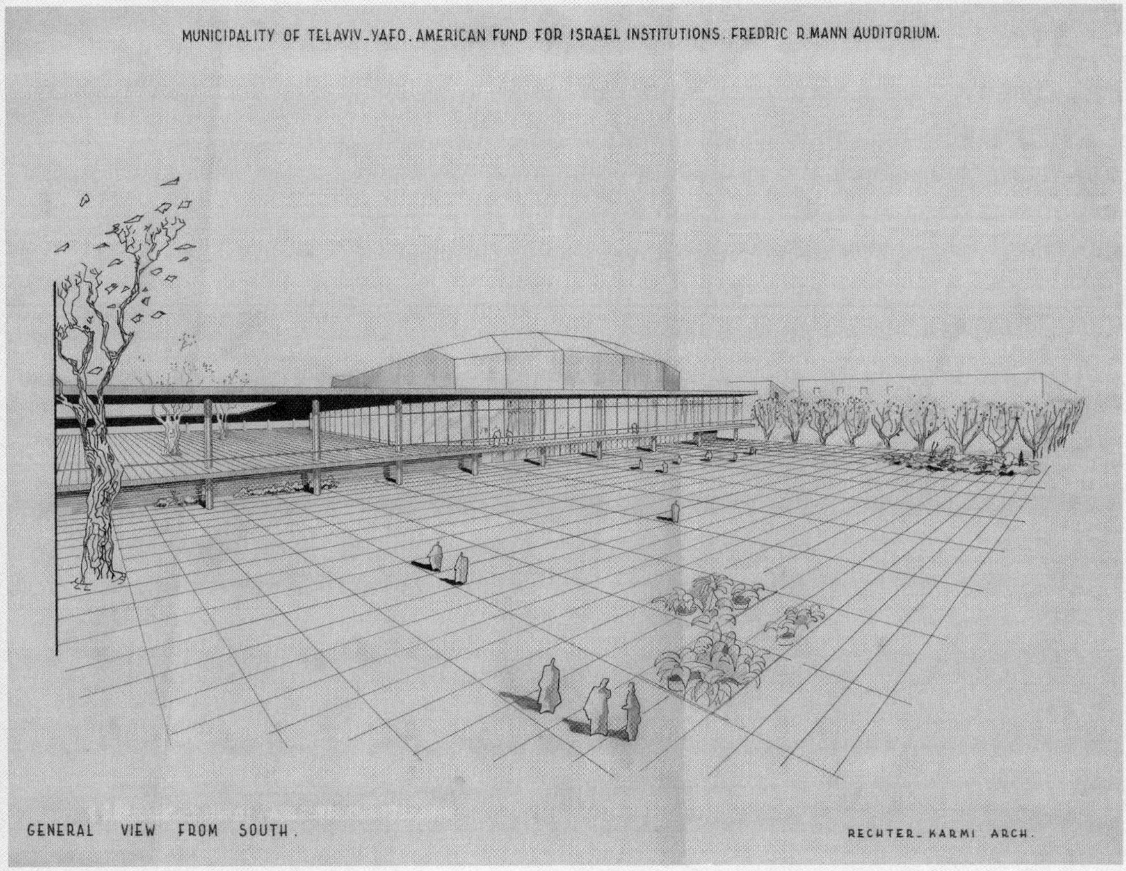

Figure 5.3 | Dov Karmi and Zeev Rechter, Heichal HaTarbut concert hall, Tel Aviv, 1957; perspective.

Figure 5.4 | Zeev Rechter and Yaakov Rechter, the Helena Rubinstein Art Pavilion, Tel Aviv, 1959; north elevation.

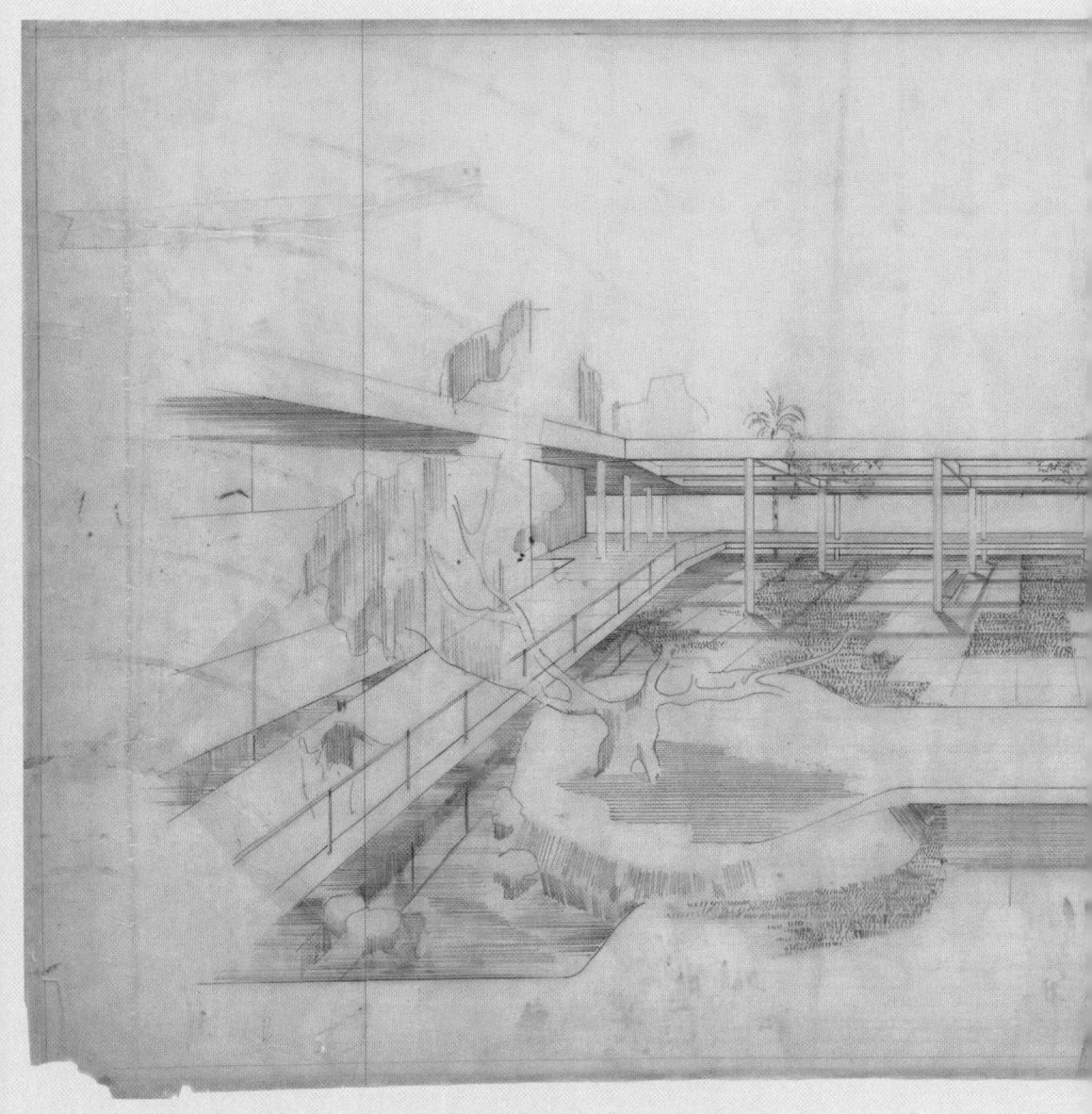

Figure 5.5 | Rechter-Zarhi-Peri Architects in collaboration with Avraham Karavan, Yaakov Garden, Tel Aviv, 1965; perspective looking south.

Figure 5.11 | Dov Karmi and Zeev Rechter, Heichal HaTarbut concert hall, Tel Aviv, 1957; interior view of concert hall.

Figure 5.12 | Dov Karmi and Zeev Rechter, Heichal HaTarbut concert hall, Tel Aviv, 1957; interior view of foyer.

Assembling Differences

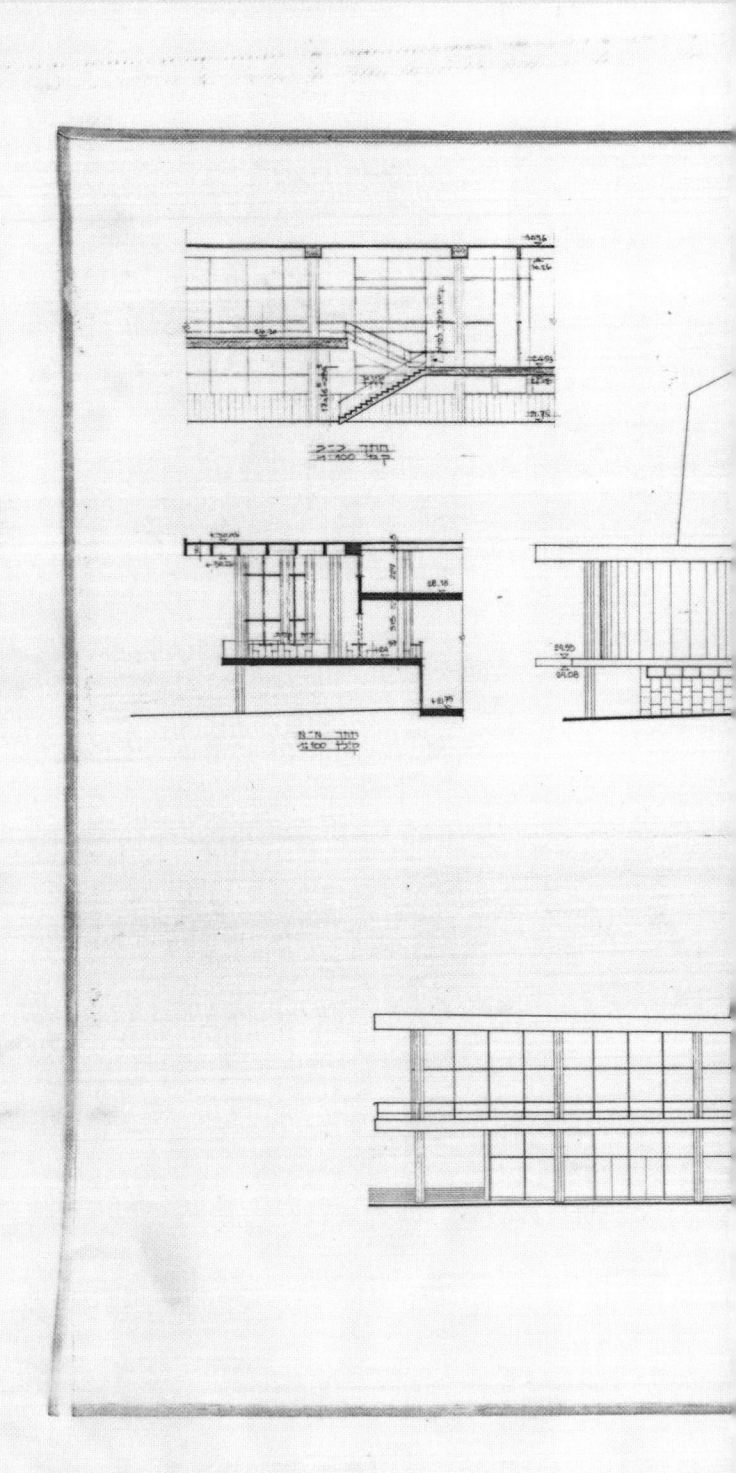

Figure 5.14 | Dov Karmi and Zeev Rechter, Heichal HaTarbut concert hall, Tel Aviv, 1957; elevations.

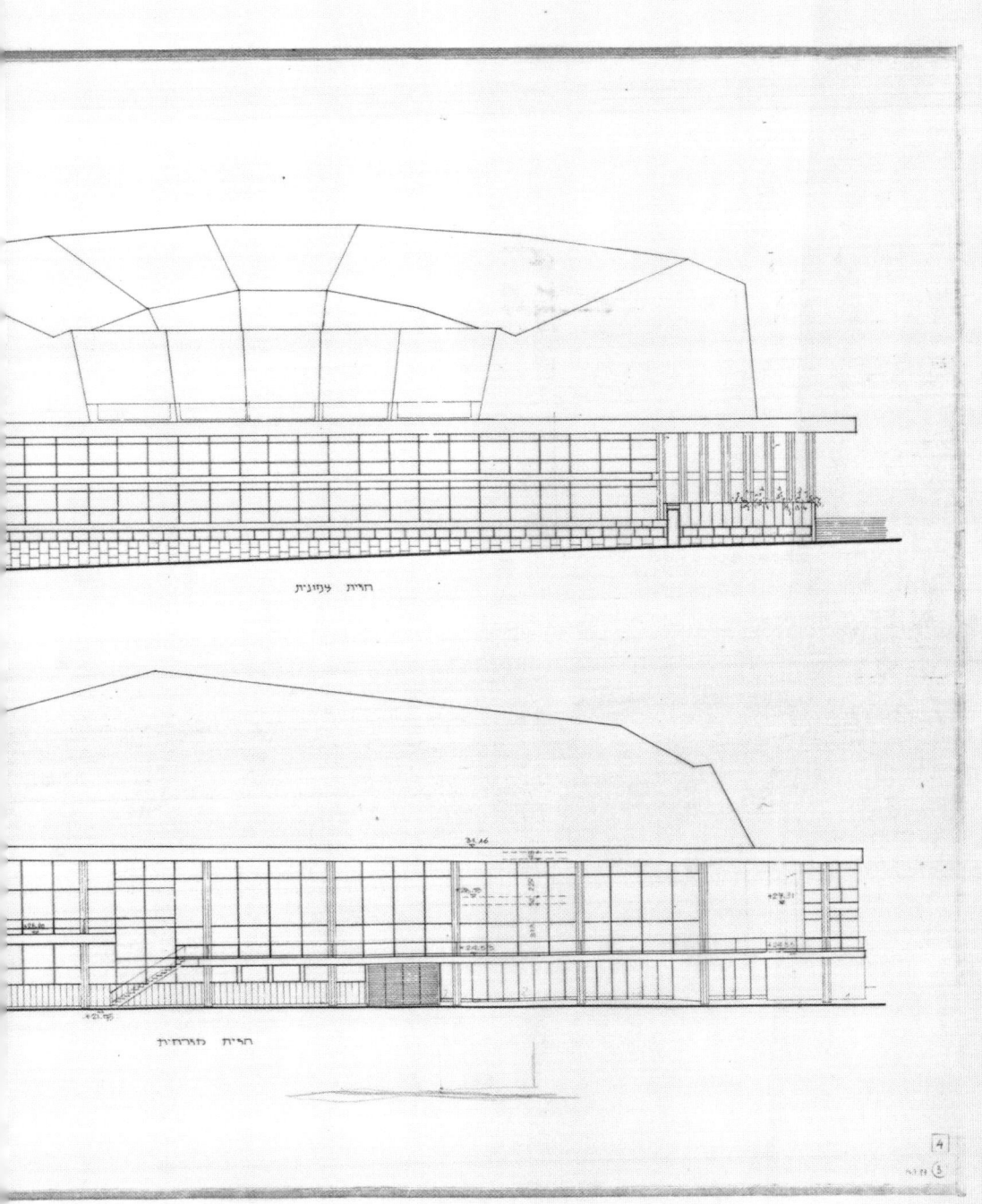

חזית צפונית

חזית מזרחית

Figure 5.16 | Rechter-Zarhi-Peri Architects in collaboration with Avraham Karavan, Yaakov Garden, Tel Aviv, 1965; garden's second-story view toward concert hall.

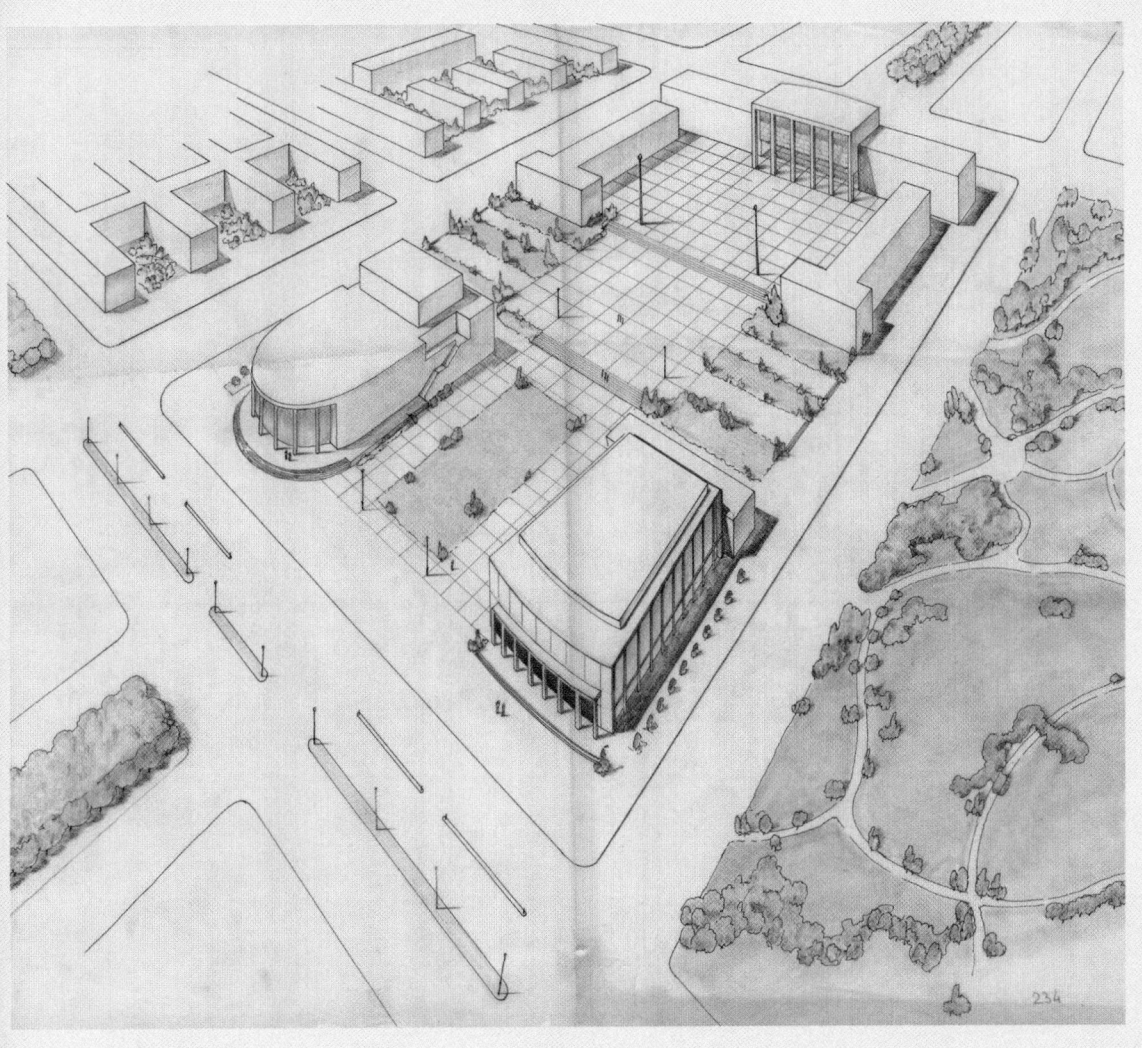

Figure 5.17 | Dov Karmi and Zeev Rechter, Heichal HaTarbut concert hall, Tel Aviv, 1957; perspective.

Figure 5.21 | Rechter-Zarhi-Peri Architects in collaboration with Avraham Karavan, Yaakov Garden, Tel Aviv, 1965; garden's second-story view toward ramp and Chen Boulevard.

Figure 5.22 | Rechter-Zarhi-Peri Architects in collaboration with Avraham Karavan, Yaakov Garden, Tel Aviv, 1965; view west on Tarsat Avenue.

Figure 5.23 | Yaakov Rechter and Avraham Karavan, Yaakov Garden, Tel Aviv, 1965; view south to public square and Rothschild Boulevard.

Figure 5.24 | Yaakov Rechter and Avraham Karavan, Yaakov Garden, Tel Aviv, 1965; garden view toward concert hall.

Figure 5.25 | Dov Karmi and Zeev Rechter, Heichal HaTarbut concert hall, Tel Aviv, 1957; view of the Heichal HaTarbut concert hall and Yaakov Garden from public square.

Stephen Anderson

Of Architecture, Its Artifacts, and the City

Sverre Fehn's Norwegian Pavilion and the Structure of Urbanity

The Norwegian Pavilion for the Brussels Expo '58 was a project that its designer, Sverre Fehn (1924–2009), included in his own public accounts of his architecture but strangely one that has not garnered much attention in the years since its construction, even by those who have taken a particular interest in Fehn's broader work. **Figure 6.1** Some of that oversight can be attributed to the relative fame of the project's slightly younger, more striking, and still-standing brother, Fehn's Nordic Pavilion for the Venice Biennale in 1961. There are also archival difficulties—images of the constructed project are scarce and often of poor quality. A third reason, more subtle than these two, will become apparent in the themes I explore below.

Figure 6.1 | Sverre Fehn, Norwegian Pavilion for Expo '58, Brussels, 1958; entry.

The Norwegian Pavilion, I will show, is an essentially urban work of architecture. This characteristic has rendered it marginal in two senses. First, the depth of Fehn's attention to urban configurations has not yet been generally understood, making the pavilion difficult to fit within prevailing narratives of his work;[1] and second, pavilions for expos are more typically designed as autonomous structures than as participants in urban settings, and so are not common candidates for advancing understanding of a building's urban engagements. Nevertheless, the Norwegian Pavilion is instructive on both counts. Close examination reveals a concern for urban settings that Fehn would develop in his architecture over the ensuing five decades, and more importantly, that examination yields several lessons regarding architecture and the structure of urbanity. Dalibor Vesely wrote that all architecture is directly or indirectly conditioned by urban culture, and that "the city is a framework and measure for what architecture can or should be in order to play its proper and expected role in culture."[2] Because framework indicates receptivity, and measure indicates a datum that is given, a reciprocal relationship between city and architecture is proposed. While Vesely did not proceed to develop this point, implicit in that formulation is its inverse, that all urban culture is directly or indirectly conditioned by architecture, and that architecture, in reciprocity with the city, delineates conditions within which urban culture can be enacted. If so, architecture's engagement of urban conditions will prove to be not only a wellspring for architectural creativity (and, perhaps, renewed purpose), but also essential to the sustenance of urban culture. Fehn's Norwegian Pavilion will help us better understand these relationships.

I want to consider two ways in which Fehn's pavilion design can be understood as belonging to a discussion of urban configurations, each a variant on the idea of the urban setting. **Figure 6.2** The first and the most familiar has to do with the project's setting within its wider circumstances. While not a city *per se*, the plan for the Brussels exposition featured several city-like characteristics. Pedestrian streets were varied in scale, ranging from grand avenues to footpaths, with the main intersections typically punctuated with some nodal installation, such as a fountain, statue, or small plaza. The largest of these streets was defined by densely arranged pavilions and despite prohibitions on vehicular traffic included tree-lined sidewalks and curbs. In contrast were the expo's several parks, the most extensive of which, Parc D'Osseghem, was forested and organized around an elongated lake—not in a pattern of streets and blocks—and featured an amphitheater built into a low hillside. The expo's infrastructure was equivalent to that of a small city, with the electricity, water, sewage, and food service necessary for the health, comfort, safety, and sustenance of its huge number of visitors. In addition to more obvious provisions like food dispensaries and gift shops, one could also find a cobbler and a pharmacist. More than 41 million people would visit Expo '58 over its six-month course. That last factor was perhaps

Figure 6.2 | Sverre Fehn, Norwegian Pavilion for Expo '58, Brussels, 1958; Avenue of Nations, looking west (Norwegian Pavilion, middle right).

1 Addressing this lacuna in Fehn's work was one of the goals of my forthcoming book. Anderson, Stephen, *Sverre Fehn and the City: Rethinking Architecture's Urban Premises*, London: Routledge, 2023.
2 Vesely, Dalibor, "Between Architecture and the City," *Phenomenologies of the City*, H. Steiner and M. Sternberg eds., New York: Routledge, 2015, pp. 154–5.

the greatest contributor to the expo's city-like character: there were multitudes of diverse people there who spent entire days navigating the vast grounds.

The site for the Norwegian Pavilion was nested between one of the venue's larger streets—the Avenue des Nations—and the Parc D'Osseghem. **Figure 6.3 (see p. 162)** Fehn's design engaged both conditions. The project presents a long, low facade parallel to the street. At least in part to negotiate a six-meter variation in the site's topography, the pavilion's floor level was set one meter above the street so that stairs were required on its south side. Instead of being confined to specific points of access, those stairs were configured as broad landings spanning the project's entire facade, suitable for occupation as well as navigation, and setting the building 25 meters from the sidewalk. Similarly, at the top of the steps a cantilevered roof defined a portico or porch running the building's length, casting the lower portions of this south-facing elevation in shadow. Although the portico-porch accommodated entry and afforded some protection from the weather, it was not designed to emphasize the point at which one entered the project's interior. That work was done by a simple white partition—an extension of an interior wall—that projected into the space of the porch at a right angle. The hybrid type at the front negotiated between the life of the street on one side and the building's interior on the other in several ways. There is, for instance, the simple provision of shade in the Belgian summer, or the space to await others approaching from the street, or to collect oneself before entry. More elaborate uses were also provided for: the pavilion included a small café for which tables were set toward the portico-porch's east side, sheltered but well positioned for street viewing. In what amounts to an urban-scaled attenuation of the threshold, the building's facade borrows from the life of the street and in turn contributes to the activities it structures back to the streetscape.

On the whole, characterizing the general appearance of the facade requires some care. As mentioned, the building's profile was horizontal and low. Relative to most of the expo's 150 or so other pavilions, Fehn's design was remarkably restrained as seen from the street. Compare it, for example, to Le Corbusier and Xenakis's Philips Pavilion, two blocks to the south, which is neither low nor horizontal, nor, for that matter, orthogonal in its layout, as were both Fehn's pavilion and the streets and walks. But then neither was the Norwegian Pavilion mute in its setting—as if the only alternative to subordinance is autonomy, Fehn's design alternately pursued a measure of each.

Among the materials that Fehn submitted for his competition entry was a facade drawing that located the building between street and park. **Figure 6.4 (see p. 161)** Fehn would make adjustments to the design after winning the competition, but the role of the 26-meter laminated timber beam that crowns the portico is as unignorable in the drawing as in its constructed form. In fact, the drawing emphasizes the component's presence, locating it directly in the middle of the image like a quotient line between street and tree canopy. In a building unusually spare in its signage, the long expanse of varnished wood catching the south light cannot have aimed at silence. Note that the beam is not strictly load-bearing—remember that the roof and soffit assembly over the portico-porch is cantilevered—and may be best described as a barge-rafter or fascia, which is to say that while it does some work as a stabilizing band-beam, its role in the project exceeds the purview of structural economy. To assert that the beam's role was ornamental would invite misunderstanding, or at least require revisiting definitions. And yet the beam was the most insistent of a set of elements in the project that advanced horizontality as a theme and as an organizing principle.

Expressions above are echoed by those below. Consider the details of the terrace-like steps connecting the project to the street. The treads stopped short of each adjoining riser, leaving gaps that accommodated an entirely improbable garden. As specified in an early drawing labeled "Garden Plan" (also shown in construction drawings), these slots were filled with topsoil and densely planted with grasses. **Figure 6.5** Photographs show that the detail created a green, shadowy, and irregular lower-limit for the risers, lending the treads planarity and independence, as if the stone terraces were moored, just as the long beam above and its associated ceiling plane were tethered. A sense emerges of planes levitating between sky and earth, light and soil, so much so that "floor" seems a less apt descriptor than "platform." I will return to the possible significance of this emphasis on horizontality and platform in consideration of urban settings.

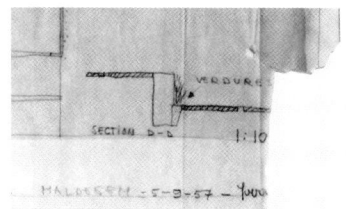

Figure 6.5 | Sverre Fehn, Norwegian Pavilion for Expo '58, Brussels, 1958; detail of garden plan showing step with planted gap.

Embodied in the design of the entry, and preparatory to similar expressions found further inside the building, is an odd confluence of familiar architectural tropes. The insistent planarity recalls the reductive abstraction pursued in De Stijl works and in the pavilion and pavilion-like designs of Mies van der Rohe. Fehn's representations of the Norwegian Pavilion's interiors are surely reminiscent of the latter.[3] But in a departure from the examples of Van der Rohe and, say, Gerrit Rietveld, Fehn's planes are endowed with details and surface-work that render those planes—how should I say it?—less hermetic. If the entry terraces' detailing suggests planarity, their liberation from the ground is decidedly partial. The steps' "gardens" and coarse slab-edges assure that. As we'll see, Fehn's free planes are everywhere endowed with expressions of mass, materiality, luminosity, and earthen-ness. To the degree that free planarity can be typically understood as emphasizing the distinction between universal and local senses of order, Fehn's seems aimed at emphasizing their interrelation.

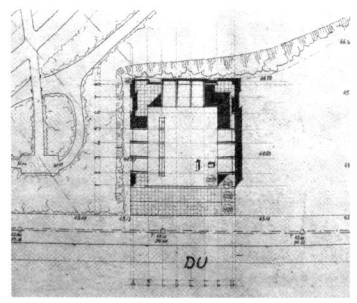

Figure 6.6 | Sverre Fehn, Norwegian Pavilion for Expo '58, Brussels, 1958; site plan.

3 Fehn made at least a half-dozen drawings of the project's interior that were a hybrid of line drawings and montage, and where, as with Mies van der Rohe's compositions, there was a pronounced contrast between the abstraction of the proposed building and the specificity of both the interior objects and the framed circumstantial landscape. See, for example, Figure 6.18.

The project's address to the verdant side of the site was no less premeditated and demonstrates a similar calibration between receptivity to what is given and assertion of what is not. Consider the project's relationship to the site's existing topography. **Figure 6.6** The project was nested into the side of a wooded slope that rose six meters from the site's front edge along the Avenue des Nations to a high point at the site's north west corner. The windowless perimeter walls at the building's west, north, and east sides eclipse the site's middle-ground while allowing the crowns of the surrounding trees to figure in the experience of the courtyard areas at the rear of the pavilion, admitting some aspects of the project's surrounds while foreclosing others. Fehn would later comment that the trees effectively served as tall green walls at the back of the project.[4] The section drawings show those perimeter panels doubling as retaining walls along the project's west and north edges, negating the slope in order to achieve a level floor surface. The walls also negated the existing slope in another sense: while the trees' presence was maintained, the given topography was effectively removed from the experience of the pavilion. Or would have been, except that Fehn's original drawings show that he intended to reintroduce an abstracted form of the existing slope within the project's interior, designing terrace-like low steps that cut diagonally across the entire plan. The purpose of these steps is not obvious. They were not responsive to any of the pavilion's programmatic demands and meandered through the plan irrespective of its structural grid and partition layout. As if lines on a topography map had been constructed, the steps rehearsed, in an abstract way and at a reduced scale, the original topography that the building's construction had eliminated. With regard to both flora and topography, Fehn seems in search of a proper ratio between effacement of and engagement with what is given. As with the project's emphasis of planarity, exploring the urban significance of this address to the landscape first requires positing a more elaborate set of connections—admittedly tentative ones.

Figure 6.7 (see p. 161), Figure 6.8

Figure 6.8 | Sverre Fehn, Norwegian Pavilion for Expo '58, Brussels, 1958; northeast corner of perimeter glazing with Plexiglas columns (architecture critic Theo Crosby in foreground).

Figure 6.9 | Sverre Fehn, Norwegian Pavilion for Expo '58, Brussels, 1958; site during construction (Reima Pietilä's Finnish Pavilion seen in background to the right).

It is understandable that the Norwegian Pavilion has been primarily regarded as a tour de force in structural innovation, prefabrication, and material experimentation. Fehn began the design not long after his two-year tenure in the atelier of Jean Prouvé, a period in which that office was developing variations of the Demountable House, the Villejuif Temporary School, and kit-of-parts projects with an eye toward environmental modulation and inventive explorations of industrial fabrication. Fehn's pavilion deployed load-bearing Plexiglas columns, experimental proprietary roofing, 37-meter laminated beams, and prefabricated light-aggregate composite concrete panels. **Figure 6.9** After Fehn abandoned preliminary explorations in translucent concrete (early results were promising but there was not sufficient time to pursue the design), he arranged for the panels to be fabricated in Germany and shipped to Brussels owing to difficulties in locally securing the desired degree of precision at feasible prices.[5] Once the components were on site, the project's structural frame was designed to be assembled with merely 48 bolts—a fact that Fehn often mentioned in his later accounts of the project, even if that tended to obfuscate the amount of preparatory site work the design had demanded.

[4] Fehn, Sverre, "Pavilion in Brussels," *Byggekunst*, no. 4, 1958, pp. 85–94.
[5] The most complete account of the building's construction is in Fjeld, Per Olaf, *Sverre Fehn: The Pattern of Thoughts*, New York: Monacelli Press, 2009, pp. 46–8.

Collectively, the project entailed an impressive[6] array of experiments in structure, construction, enclosure, and lighting.

Considering, then, the pavilion's careful attention to both site and technological possibility, the design exhibited a fusion of the architectural pursuits of autochthony and universality that some authorities seemed unable to parse. For all its inventiveness and experimentation, the project's involvement in its surroundings apparently provoked the ire of the expo's organizers who found its modern credentials lacking—too regional (presumably referring to its use of clear-finished wood beams) and not sufficiently autonomous. According to Emiel de Kooning, longtime critic and historian of the Brussels Expo, "On the tree-lined streets of Laeken Park [Parc D'Osseghem], several of the pavilions in the foreign section did not live up to the expectations of the organizing committee for whom modernist architecture, by definition, had to be detached from any context."[7] In other words, for the expo's organizers, the project's supposed failure to detach itself from its setting negated the ostensibly modern (positive) qualities of its innovative structure and materiality. At the same time, the organizing committee in Norway was also dissatisfied with Fehn's pavilion, though tellingly, for different reasons. After someone had nominated the project for the award of best pavilion at the conclusion of the expo, Norwegian authorities voided the nomination. No formal explanation for the refusal was offered, but Fehn suggested that the committee was displeased with the project's failure to feature imagery and details readily identifiable as Norwegian, and that its technological explorations resulted in too many complications.[8] If Modernism is understood as being abstract and technologically advanced, then this building was too modern.

That Fehn's design could provoke such incongruous critiques betrayed a tension that permeated the entire enterprise of Expo '58. This was the first world expo to be staged in the aftermath of the Second World War. The Cold War was well underway and there were open debates about the consequences of unchecked modernization, the presumed tenets of Modernism, and the ethical and potentially existential dilemmas presented by emergent technologies.[9] The organizing committee's position in those debates was not so subtly represented in the expo's monumental set-piece, the Atomium, a 102-meter model of an iron crystal featuring suspended 18-meter polished chrome spheres that housed exhibits and a restaurant, all connected by entubed escalators.[10] **Figure 6.10** The expo's motto elided any perception of tension between the pursuit of technological possibility and the realization of "a more humane world." But if "*bilan du monde, pour un monde plus humain*" was meant to defuse those tensions, the tenor of the expo itself, with its emphasis on the promotion of consumerism, its troubling tacit endorsement of an anachronistic colonialism, and its blurring of regional and corporate cultures, largely served to exacerbate them. No surprise, then, that its organizers, with the Atomium before them, would look askance at Fehn's pavilion; and no surprise

---

6. Impressive, and to a certain extent daunting—Fehn recounted the difficulties of co-ordinating all the risks he had undertaken, especially as a relatively young architect working with hardened contractors and officials. See Fjeld, *Sverre Fehn: The Pattern of Thoughts*, pp. 46-8.
7. De Kooning, Emiel, "Architecture and Graphics at Expo 58," *Expo 58: Between Utopia and Reality*, Gonzague Pluvinage ed., Brussels: Editions Racine, 2008, pp. 147, 149. The criticism extended also to the Norwegian Pavilion's Finnish neighbor.
8. Fjeld, *Sverre Fehn: The Pattern of Thoughts*, p. 47.
9. For a broad historical reading on this theme, see Jamison, Andrew, "Science and Technology in Postwar Europe," *The Oxford Handbook of Postwar European History*, Dan Stone ed., Oxford: Oxford University Press, 2012. See also, Winner, Langdon, *Autonomous Technology: Technics Out of Control as a Theme in Political Thought*, Cambridge MA: MIT Press, 1977; Edgerton, David, *Shock of the Old: Technology and Global History Since 1900*, London: Profile Books, 2019; and Mumford, Lewis, "Authoritarian and Democratic Technics," *Technology and Culture*, vol. 5, winter, 1964, pp. 1–8. For an analysis of the deeper historical roots of the problem in European modernity, see Gadamer, Hans Georg, "Citizens of Two Worlds," *H.G. Gadamer on Education, Poetry, and History: Applied Hermeneutics*, Dieter Misgeld ed., New York: SUNY Press, 1992, pp. 209–20. For an introduction to those themes within the discipline of architecture, see Smithson, Alison, "Team 10 Primer 1953–1962," *Architectural Design*, December 1962, pp. 559–602; Banham, Reyner, *The New Brutalism: Ethic or Aesthetic?*, New York: Reinhold, 1966; Newman, Oscar, *CIAM '59 in Otterlo*, Stuttgart: Krämer, 1961. On that last set, note that Fehn was friends with Alison and Peter Smithson, and also with several other of the key figures Banham collected in his book, including Giancarlo di Carlo and Aldo van Eyck; Fehn was active from 1950 in PAGON, the Scandinavian branch of CIAM.
10. I cannot look at that structure without thinking of Ribart's elephant for Louis XV.

Figure 6.10 | Expo '58, Brussels, 1958; the Atomium rises in background.

that Norwegian socialist authorities would distrust the project's technological exuberance. Fehn was well aware of these tensions, his writings and lectures consistently reflected a concern for the effects of hyper-modernization on cultural depth and continuity, even while he consistently took technological invention to be one of his primary architectural tasks. As with many of his projects that would follow in the ensuing decades, the Norwegian Pavilion suggests that for Fehn, the apparent opposition constituted a misunderstanding of the relationships between site, invention, and use, and the purposes that subordinated those relationships. An examination of the interior will help me develop these points.

The pavilion's plan was roughly square, with a perimeter zone between a glazed interior wall and an opaque outer one. At the former, floor-to-ceiling glass panels were fixed between the previously mentioned structural Plexiglas columns or fins. Between the central square roof and the undulating perimeter walls, Fehn designed sets of translucent tarps (the text on his competition drawings described these as sails), made from an experimental nylon-resin composite called "Co-coon," that could be spanned between the eaves of the dominant flat roof and the pre-cast composite panels. **Figure 6.11 (see p. 164)** The ceiling beneath the main roof was fitted with translucent sheets too, though of a different proprietary material, "Marolux," that concealed fluorescent light fixtures positioned between the beams. "The ceiling," Fehn said, "functions in the evening like one great lamp."[11] Introducing ideas that in the coming decades would inform various parts of the Nordic Pavilion (Venice, 1961), the Fotohuset camera shop (Oslo, 1960), and the Hedmark Museum (Hamar, 1970), the Brussels project is especially conversant with Fehn's pavilion for the Museum of Architecture (Oslo, 2008), sharing with that project concentric zones with garden-like perimeters, luminous mantles meant to stage the encounter of displayed objects, and relatively darker cores. The unusual range in qualities of light orchestrated by the pavilion's ceiling reflected Fehn's belief that the display of different artifacts benefited from the design of object-specific lighting conditions, writing that "an effort has been made to satisfy the displayed objects' varied need for light."[12] **Figure 6.12 (see p. 165)**

One of the drawings included with Fehn's competition documents builds on that idea, but in an unexpected way. At first glance, the drawing appears to be a graphic representation of the varied lighting conditions described above, the sub-spaces with which each is associated, and their overlaps. But while the figures loosely correspond with specific decisions about lighting, the shaded zones are darkened at those overlaps. The accompanying text offers some clarification: the drawing is titled *rytme* (rhythm). The diagram is not an idea about light, or, more precisely, not only about light: rhythm implies movement. But there is nothing in the drawing or its text that describes sequence or procession. Close inspection reveals that each zone in the diagram was marked with its own shading pattern. The "rhythms" here suggest different qualities for

[11] Fehn, "Pavilion in Brussels," pp. 85–94.
[12] Fehn, "Pavilion in Brussels," p. 86.

different spaces within the overall order, like an ambience or mood, each associated with a different mode of display and occupation, where the rhythms of the spaces prefigure the rhythms of bodily movement and orientation. Here rhythm seems not so much a matter of pattern and repetition, but varied intervals between distinct atmospheres. Fehn wrote, "The pavilion as a whole gave an option of light. The corners were open to the sky, as the borders from one country to another overlapped in the freedom of light and air."[13] We cannot know exactly what Fehn meant here by "country," but the analogy corresponds with the diagram's suggestion that the plan accommodated territories with distinct characteristics and, in this case, open borders. Fehn understood that it was not the mood of the light alone that tailored each ambience, but a correspondence between the light, the artifact, the manner of its display, the bodily posture implied for the occupant, and the physical properties of the bounding conditions.

It was the artifacts at the Norwegian Pavilion that were the progenitors of those sets of relationships and the ambiences—"rooms," Fehn would say—that they structured. A full account of Fehn's extensive and varied use of the terms "room" and "shadow" is not feasible here; but it may suffice to note that "room" most often suggested something akin to atmosphere, ambience, or a spatial mood, and that "shadow" suggested an object's contribution to, and participation in, that setting. "Every object," Fehn wrote, "led to a story of the use of related subjects ... The play from one material to the other was the bond for every object displayed."[14] Fehn sought to structure a relationship between the artifacts, the material architecture, and the mood or ambience of the pavilion's different "countries."

Fehn's work at Brussels cannot properly be understood as the design of a series of stage-sets; and if there is such a thing as using architecture to script behavior, Fehn's career would prove him to be, on the contrary, dedicated to the possibility of architecture's structure of social improvisation. But, as we've seen, Fehn *was* using variegated qualities of lighting to help effect particular moods. And he did, as the previous quote attests, seek to contribute to a story of each artifact and its "related subjects." There was something decidedly theatrical in his design of the devices meant to exhibit the artifacts at the Norwegian Pavilion, an idea to which I will return. All of which is consistent with the career that would unfold in the decades after the Brussels Expo. The whole of Fehn's work can generally be understood—and may be best understood—as an opus preoccupied with the exploration and embodiment of the interrelation of architecture and artifact. Here is the aforementioned second sense of urban setting that Fehn obtains at the Norwegian Pavilion. The two subcategories share some attributes. Both involve architecture's engagement with given conditions—no less than sites are a place's artifacts the creation of the designer. And to the degree that sites *are* invented through operations like framing, bracketing, excavating, and other

Figure 6.13 | Sverre Fehn, Villa Norrköping, Sweden, 1964; corner cabinet from garden.

13 Sverre Fehn, in Fjeld, Per Olaf, *Sverre Fehn: The Thought of Construction*, New York: Rizzoli, 1983, p. 106.
14 Fjeld, *Sverre Fehn: The Thought of Construction*, pp. 106-7.

Figure 6.14 | Sverre Fehn, Villa Norrköping, Sweden, 1964; looking through corner cabinet into kitchen.

Figure 6.15 | Sverre Fehn, Villa Norrköping, Sweden, 1964; corner cabinet from dining room.

15 Fehn presented that idea in the essay "The Order of Display." Presenting a mythology about the origins of civilization, he concluded, "All of this evolved from the bowl. The bowl is the root of all objects." See, Fjeld, *Sverre Fehn: The Thought of Construction*, p. 94.
16 Fjeld, *Sverre Fehn: The Pattern of Thoughts*, p. 48.

forms of representation, so too does architecture invent modes of engagement with given artifacts. The architectural engagement of the circumstantial site contributes to the prospects for urban living by strengthening opportunities for inhabitants to behold and participate in what is underway around them. An amplified prospect for understanding, participation, and sociation with others through engagement and reinvention of what is already underway in a place is a promising start to a definition of urbanity. Fehn shows us that opportunities for such engagement exist not only in outward reach toward a circumstantial horizon, but also in the architectural engagement of what is indoor and nearby.

Fehn's Hedmark Museum provides the clearest illustration of that principle. He designed manifold devices given to the presentation of archaeological artifacts in ways meant to provoke imaginative and direct dialogue between artifact and occupant. Fehn's concern for this capacity of architecture was not reserved for the design of museums, as it can also be found in his design of more mundane architectural types, even residences. **Figures 6.13, 6.14, and 6.15** At Villa Norrköping (Norrköping, Sweden, 1964), Fehn repeatedly created opportunities to frame, light, or otherwise offer to attention, various artifacts of daily life, interfusing quotidian concerns with representational ones: the bowl is just a bowl—I need it for my meal and it is convenient to reside where I am cooking—but the bowl is also curiously presented, as if offered for speculation, perhaps pertaining to its relationship, for instance, to the setting of the adjacent table or to the garden beyond, or perhaps to more ephemeral ideas about "bowl" as anthropological artifact.[15] **Figure 6.16 (see p. 166)**

I asserted earlier that while Fehn was not crafting a series of stage sets, this slippage between the opacity of "the everyday" and its enframement had a theatrical air to it. At the Norwegian Pavilion, the presentation of the artifacts assumed a character oscillating between the theatrical and quotidian. One of the most dramatic, and consequently most photographed, were two display cases constructed of glass and supported, slightly higher than one might expect, on glass fins extended from the adjacent glass walls. Of course, glass display cases were not uncommon in exhibits, and no doubt many visitors walked past this one without giving it a second thought. But because the case was constructed without secondary connecting materials, and because the bottom of the case was also made of glass, instead of the rectangular shadow of the case, the shadows of the artifacts themselves were projected onto the pavilion's floor, effectively extending their participation in the space, extending their reach. As Per Olaf Fjeld put it, "The shadows cast on the floors and walls themselves became objects in the display."[16] **Figure 6.17 (see p. 167)**

Less spectacular but no less designed were a series of tablelike displays in the northern portion of the pavilion. These were all unusually low, but set at slightly different heights, and were positioned to overlap in places, lending the ensemble a topographical cast—perhaps Fehn was interested in recovering the allusion to topography that had been lost when the interior steps discussed above were edited from the project. Also unusual were sunken planters incorporated into the center of each table so that flora would inhabit the same plane as the presented artifacts. As always with Fehn, these installations were not an afterthought: construction drawings show the tables' concrete bases to be monolithic with the concrete floor slab—they were to be poured at the same time—so that the soil in the planters was continuous with the soil beneath the slab, assuring a waterproof condition and good drainage. At roughly knee-height, a quickly passing visitor would look down at the artifacts on those tables from above, someone more curious might stoop or kneel. The arrangement is oddly domestic, casual, like a coffee table beset with trinkets and a vase of flowers.

The description "oddly domestic" implies a tension: the domesticity is familiar, but, in this context, strange. In neither instance—glass cases or low tables—did the presentation of the artifacts conform with expectations for a typical exhibition. If the intent of the exhibit designs, then, could rightly be described as provocative, what was it that Fehn sought to provoke? Fjeld wrote that the artifacts at the Norwegian Pavilion "were experienced in a new light and a new vulnerability,"[17] suggesting that at least part of the displays' intent was to establish conditions wherein the artifacts would be rendered more available to the viewer. I think Fjeld was on to something here. The goal seems not to have been the presentation of artifacts per se, but the interjection of artifacts into the lives of the visitors and their relationships with each other. That assertion, I know, could be dismissed as a truism. But throughout his career Fehn was critical of the museum as a type, and the crux of his argument was based on the detachment of the displayed artifact from the richness of its making and subsequent stories of its uses. Fehn's complaint was not one about historical inaccuracy, but about the diminishment of an artifact's potential to continue informing the present. At the Norwegian Pavilion, Fehn was evidently already concerned with those themes. In an essay titled "The Order of Display," which served as a preamble for an explication of the Norwegian Pavilion, Fehn wrote:

> The key to the art of display resides in the architect imagining himself as an object. If the dialogue between the curator and his possession can be visualized through the architect's projection, the object will demand an interaction with the viewer. In this situation, the viewer becomes involved in the "place" of the object.[18]

The sentences denote several relationships implicit in an artifact's display—curator-artifact, architect-curator, architect-artifact, artifact-"projection," viewer-curator, viewer-artifact, place-artifact, viewer-place—and emphasize a comingling of "the 'place' of the object" and the place of its display. I take Fehn's "projection"

[17] Fjeld, *Sverre Fehn: The Pattern of Thoughts*, p. 48.
[18] Fjeld, *Sverre Fehn: The Thought of Construction*, p. 97.

to allude to the designed device that reframes the artifact, and presumably Fehn set the word "place" in quotation marks because he meant something more extensive than its common meaning. Restated, the artifact is displayed in a manner to elicit dialogue that involves the place of the artifact with the place of the viewer, where place indicates something like horizon or circumstance. A multiplication is implied, of complexity and, I think, of possibility. Perhaps that is the promise of all dialogue. What is clear is that, at least for Fehn, the display of an artifact only succeeds when this imaginative and productive comingling is made possible. This, I believe, is what Fehn intended to provoke: dialogue between the place of the artifact and the place of its beholder. Dialogue is not only a sign of urbanity but one of its preconditions.

For those who might complain that inanimate objects do not participate in dialogue, I need only remind them that every time they read a book, they are part of a dialogue that interjects one place, distant in geography and time, into another that is nearby and present. Or, at least, that is possible if the ambient conditions are right. As we've seen, Fehn's concern for structuring ambient conditions exceeded an interest in the way various qualities of light, materiality, surface treatment, and posture, for example, played their parts in his "rooms" or "countries." Add to that the condition of silence. Fehn remarked that the fiber-resin composite used as translucent roofing in parts of the pavilion conferred that quality: it dampened sound. He noted how the resultant quietness, in contrast to the din of the fronting street, supported the ambience of those spaces, effecting a calmness conducive to attention or meditation. "The project had silence. It worked with sound as a vital part of the space [...] The Japanese sat right down and stroked the silence."[19]

The last part of that recollection from Fehn connects the project's silences to notions of pause or rest. It is an idea that pervaded the project. Years later Fehn would write that "idleness is the secret of any large city." He continued:

> At the same time the city is a waiting situation, in which the soldier waited for his order, and the merchant waited for his ship to arrive. The writer waited for his chance to publish, the artist for his first show, and the prisoner for his freedom. This labyrinth gave birth to the whore, the dancer, the actor and acrobat, the comedian, the speaker, the clown and the student. A sense of rest was also present in the objects. The conveyance of merchandise, the secret of the package, the moment of surprise when a parcel in one place appears in another, all these are urban impulses[20]

As with much of Fehn's writing, the passage veers toward poetry, and one is left wondering what to take from it. The kind of idleness he has in mind seems not indifferent but poised or charged. There is a sense of things in a state of becoming, of objects yielding surprising delights. Rest, pause, seem critical here to reaping what

[19] Sverre Fehn, in Fjeld, *Sverre Fehn: The Pattern of Thoughts*, p. 47.
[20] Fjeld, *Sverre Fehn: The Thought of Construction*, p. 142.

Of Architecture, Its Artifacts, and the City

Figure 6.19 | Sverre Fehn, Norwegian Pavilion for Expo '58, Brussels, 1958; seated in sculpture garden, with small pond immediately below the artwork on the wall to the left.

Figure 6.20 | Sverre Fehn, Norwegian Pavilion for Expo '58, Brussels, 1958; drawing of entry portico, with bench, looking west.

the room, building, street, square, or city might offer. In the context of the expo, with its 41 million visitors and long lines streaming like pilgrims in and out of the pavilions, beneath its cable-lifts and in the shadow of the Atomium, Fehn's design invited visitors to meander and linger in relative quiet. If the logistics of herding large numbers of visitors through the park tended to isolate and propel, Fehn's design offered connectedness and pause. Once one passed the pavilion's clearly, if somewhat quietly, delineated entrance, the preferred route forward became increasingly unprescribed, with sliding doors to outdoor seating and large open areas that permitted visitors to chart their own courses. Reconsider now the project's emphasis of platform and horizontality and its select address of its circumstance: might the project, in its risk-taking structure, its form, and materiality offer conditions wherein the occupant, no longer a visitor in a line, is afforded an opportunity to become, like the objects' shadows, a participant in the setting? If so, that participation unfolded not only along the occupant's own route, but also at their own pace. If the artifacts' displays were designed to provoke dialogue, the project seemed content to let that conversation unfold when the time was right. Objects displayed in the exterior display-gardens at the pavilion's corners were positioned not in their court's center, but more peripherally, and in arrangements that lacked clear hierarchy. **Figure 6.18** (see p. 168) Tiny ponds and gardens were incorporated into those spaces, and long benches were integrated into the undulating retaining walls. The resulting ambience was less like a gallery than a place to wander and wonder, rest or linger, alone or with others. While many of the photographs of the project show visitors closely inspecting the exhibits, pointing to the play of shadows, or marveling at the pavilion's translucent structure, there are at least as many images that show people not in dialogue with the exhibit's objects, but with each other, casually occupying a corner in the garden, a bench in the shade, a table on the porch. **Figure 6.19** Many of Fehn's earliest drawings of the project advanced this idea—artifacts and strangers occupying the project's spaces as peers in a larger ensemble. The images of the inhabited project, then, seem not so different from Fehn's vision of the city, diverse people in various states of waiting and fulfillment, fueled and guided by their attentions to the lives of others, by opportunities beheld in dialogue with those present, and with the artifacts, who stand in for those who are not. If, as I've suggested, the structure of such dialogue is a marker of urbanity, Fehn's work at the Norwegian Pavilion was a study of how architecture could establish conditions that rendered such dialogue fuller and more likely. **Figure 6.20**

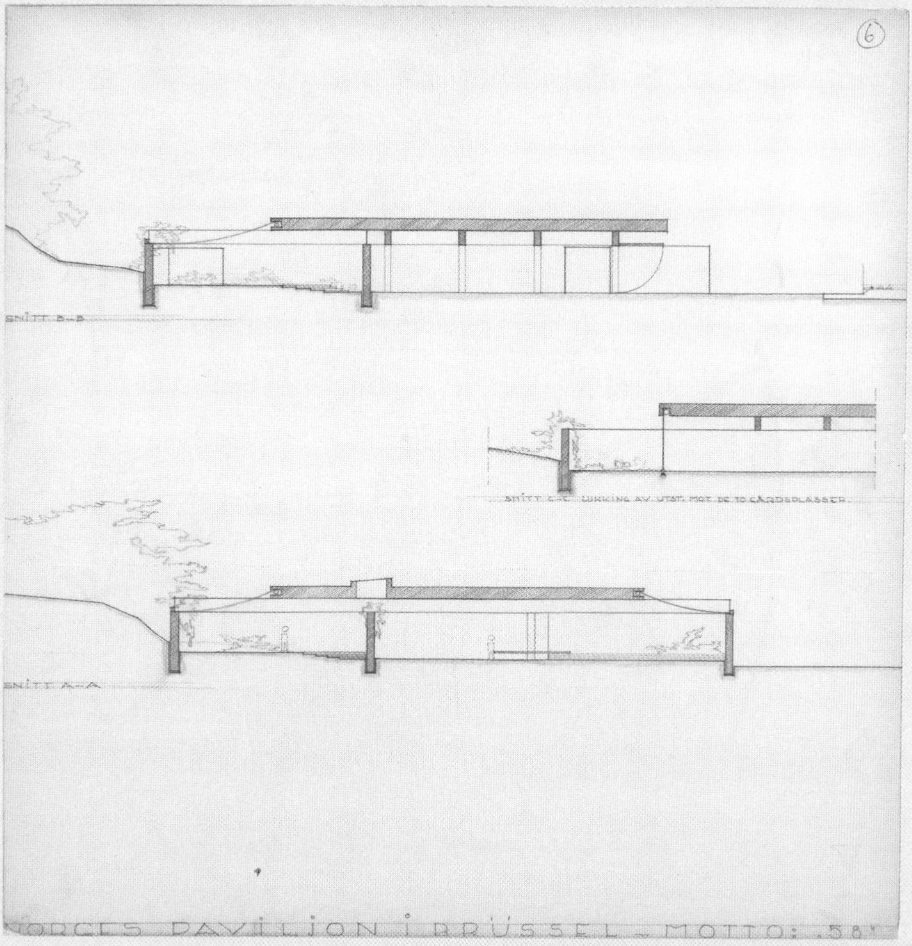

Figure 6.4 | Sverre Fehn, Norwegian Pavilion for Expo '58, Brussels, 1958; perspective drawing of street facade.

Figure 6.7 | Sverre Fehn, Norwegian Pavilion for Expo '58, Brussels, 1958; section drawings from competition entry.

Figure 6.3 | Sverre Fehn, Norwegian Pavilion for Expo '58, Brussels, 1958; view from street.

Figure 6.11 | Sverre Fehn, Norwegian Pavilion for Expo '58, Brussels, 1958; north portion of gallery, looking northeast.

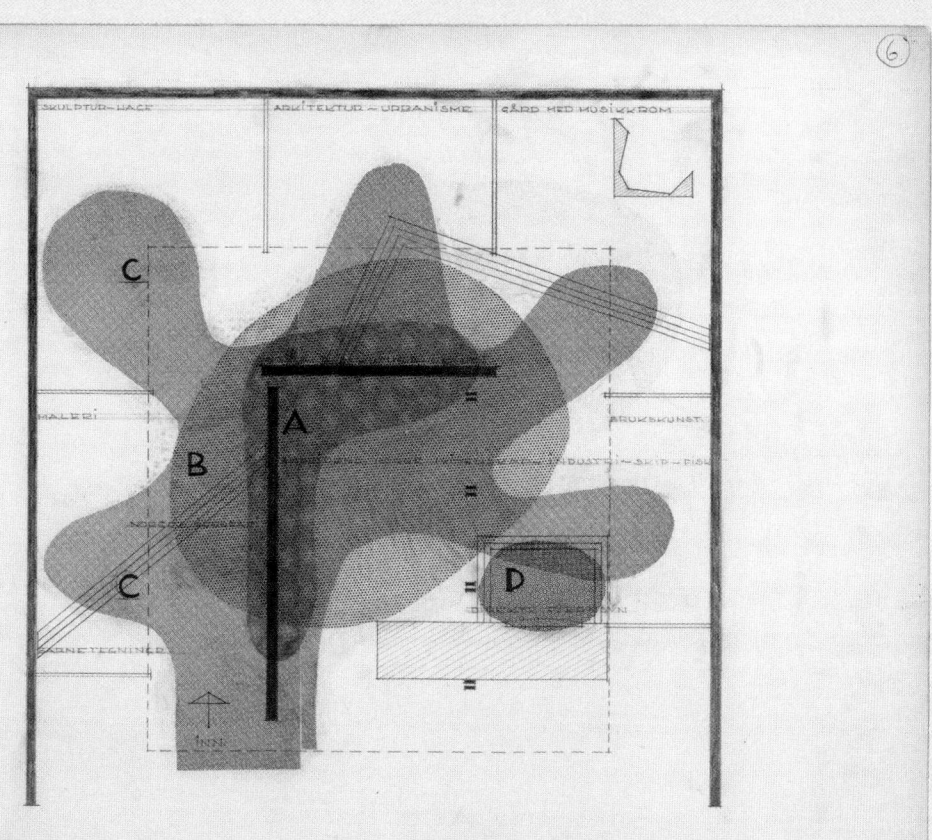

Figure 6.12 | Sverre Fehn, Norwegian Pavilion for Expo '58, Brussels, 1958; diagram from competition drawings indicating zones of display.

Figure 6.16 | Sverre Fehn, Norwegian Pavilion for Expo '58, Brussels, 1958; view from interior toward northwest sculpture garden, with glass display in foreground.

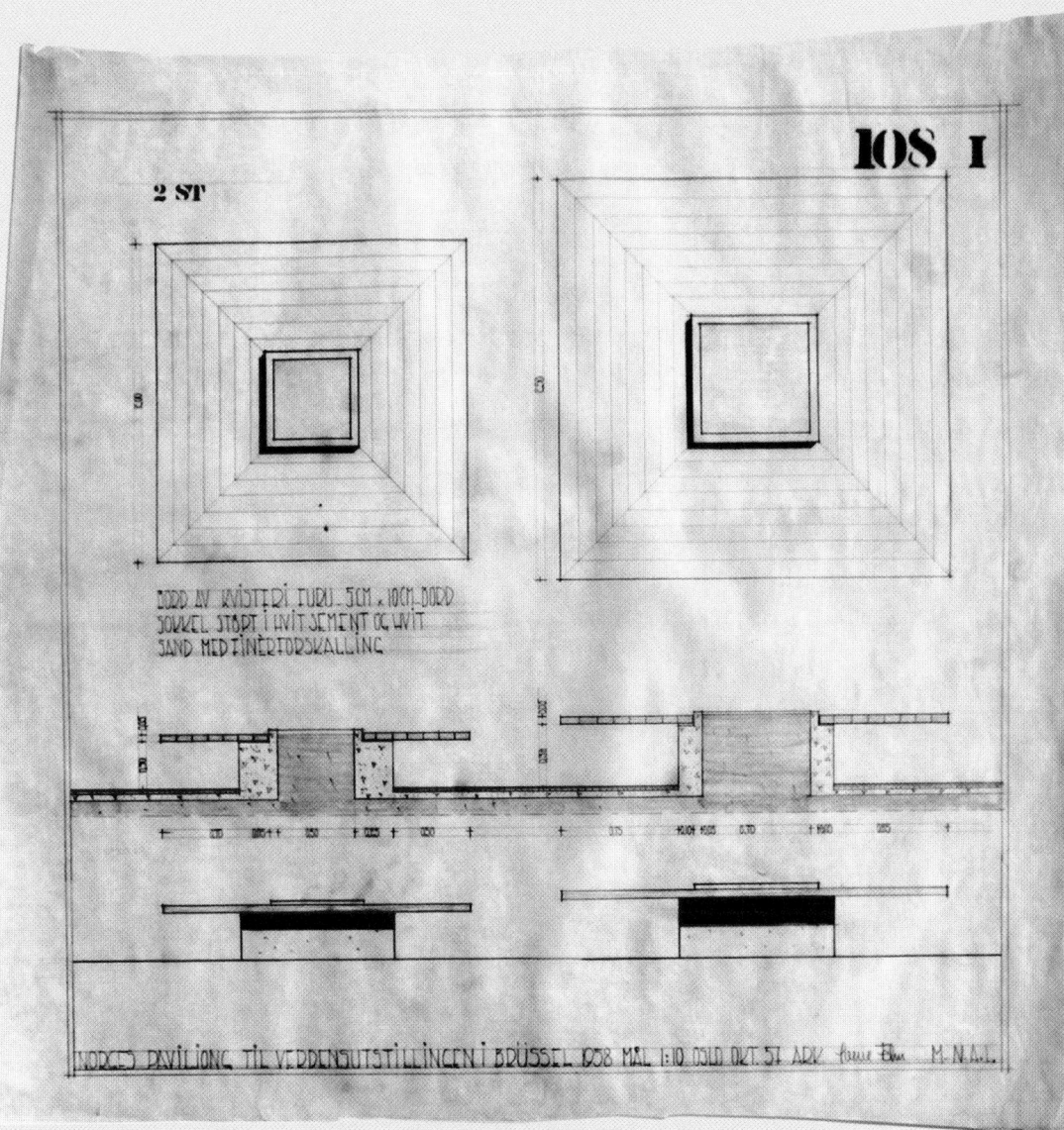

Figure 6.17 | Sverre Fehn, Norwegian Pavilion for Expo '58, Brussels, 1958; display tables, construction details.

Figure 6.18 | Sverre Fehn, Norwegian Pavilion for Expo '58, Brussels, 1958; conceptual perspective collage of gallery.

7

Jin Baek

The Terrain of Urban Institutions

H-Sang Seung's Gudeok Presbyterian Church

Gudeok Presbyterian Church (2008) in Busan, South Korea, designed by leading Korean architect H-Sang Seung, is composed of a church, a seven-story tower, and a courtyard between the two. Curiously, the complex has prayer rooms for small groups and individuals on the top floor of the tower. The oddity is that this intensely private activity is located in a space more visible than any other. The orientation and location of these rooms mark a stark contrast with the internalized church, no less oddly placed, closer to the ground but above street level. What is strange is that the institution's most public practices are housed in depths that are typically thought to be particularly private. In the subdued, cave-like interior of the church, the landscape of everyday life seems entirely remote, at least temporarily. Yet that same landscape enters the prayer rooms with dramatic immediacy, thanks to inescapable views toward stadia and their light towers, apartment complexes, commercial and office buildings, and distant mountains.

Figure 7.11 | H-Sang Seung, Gudeok Presbyterian Church, Busan, South Korea, 2008; interior.

These arrangements raise obvious questions. Why are the prayer rooms vertically distanced from the church, positioned on such a high plateau, and inclined towards the prosaic cityscape? Similarly, why does the church, equipped with personal and interpersonal spaces, remove itself from the street? What is the role of the courtyard in this unlikely distribution of parts? Though it will take me some time to develop answers to these questions, one thing seems plain at the outset: improbable positioning and unlikely stratification are factors that structure the orientations and atmospheres that define the status of the church both as an institution in itself and how it is situated within its urban terrain.

To answer these questions, a number of topics must be considered: terrain, levels or platforms, different atmospheres or climates, and institutions. The role of terrain in architectural design is often framed from the perspective of its physical aspects, such as slope, shape, area, features of weather, and so forth. It is apparent, however, that the significance of a given terrain is not only physical but also social and cultural, as it is often historically embedded in the stories of human life and operates as a stage for those stories to unfold. Accordingly, the combination of physical and cultural dimensions not only affect the experience and meaning of buildings, but also their design. This is true whether the location is rural, suburban, or urban. In this regard, securing a platform, or the stage of the stories of human life, is probably the architect's first or most basic task, one initiated by the social and cultural dimension of a given terrain, as well as its natural condition.

A building without a platform (or platforms variously stratified) is indeed nonsensical, for interpersonal human life necessarily presupposes a built horizontal plane that can be shared because it is widely open, stable, and (comparatively) permanent. The construction of a platform out of a given natural topography, which is rugged, sandy, undulated, muddy and so forth, indicates the fact that what is natural has to be cultivated, if cultural and social situations are to establish themselves. What cultivation is to agriculture, construction is to architecture—planted fields are like inhabited platforms. Climate plays a key role here. Within given terrain, platforms and their enclosed spaces work with and against climatic conditions, modulating the forces of dryness and wetness, unsettled and still air, and day and night as they vary seasonally and through diurnal cycles. Only in this way can they perform properly for the different situations and institutions of human gathering.

Accordingly, there is a necessary connection between platforms and human institutions. As a matter of fact, the platform's social and cultural dimension finds its origin in the typical forms of the human gathering, the very raison d'être of institutions. Indeed, a building that embodies a series of platforms must be understood as a particular articulation of a given institution. Louis I. Kahn once wrote, "Every building that I do, I know, must answer some institution of man."[1] From this thought it follows that a building is not just an individualized, isolated, or singular entity; rather, it

[1] Kahn, Louis I., "Address to Naturalized Citizens," *Louis Kahn: Essential Texts*, New York: W.W. Norton, 2003, p. 264.

is one among others that are similar in kind, having been formed in the history of a given institution, and must "answer," Kahn insists, to the status of that historical-cultural pattern or form. If the terrain's influence on the building and its transformation into a platform, in support of the social or communal dimension, is to be self-evident, and if we are to understand the building as a particular instance of an institution, the terrain must then be seen as a way of qualifying, even transforming the institution. As institutions develop historically, both natural and human time affect their formation, with accumulations and adjustments animating their traditions. Newness refreshes. As they retain and renew pre-existing practices and performances, buildings measure the history and prospects of institutions.

To explain further the inter-relationships between terrain, platforms, climates, and institutions, I would like to interweave topics addressed by David Leatherbarrow, Tetsuro Watsuji, Louis I. Kahn, and Peter Carl. These studies clarify concepts and vocabulary that will help us understand the Gudeok church.

Terrain, Human Relationships, and Institutions
In "Building In and Out of Place," Leatherbarrow differentiates production from project making. The former is non-territorial, instrumental, and self-generating. It operates on an enclosed system of rules, not acknowledging any necessity to modify itself in reference to conditions outside the system or field in which it operates. In contrast, project making carries out a tangible form of creativity, which is "an engaged and involved way of working in which the play with possibilities is constrained by existing conditions."[2] If the first seeks, borrowing Dalibor Vesely's terminology, pure possibility, the latter, real possibility. Similarly, if the first is an example of a degraded version of *techne*, the latter represents *poiesis*, involving mediational and interpretive moments between different layers of reality. Engagement with a given terrain and the conditions it presents is an essential way of defining a task as a project rather than a production.

Leatherbarrow explores various layers of meaning of the term landscape: the scenic or aesthetic sense, the territorial sense, and, lastly, the communal sense, as it signifies a domain for civic life. While the first layer is often something designers and architects concern themselves with, the second and last layers are equally important in apprehending the full spectrum of meanings conveyed by the term. These constructive and thus humane dimensions are also verified by studies into cognate terms, such as "scape" and "scope," as well as *schaft*, which means ship, and *schaffen*, which means to build or create. Ship and shape are related, as the township is "a body of politics formed under law as well as the territorial domain shaped by those citizens."[3] "A given stretch of territory would be called 'land,'" writes Leatherbarrow, "because of its legal system or style of governance as much as by its physical characteristics—and when those were considered, climate was as

[2] Leatherbarrow, David, "Building In and Out of Place," *Architectural Design*, March 2015, p. 27.
[3] Leatherbarrow, "Building In and Out of Place", p. 27.

important as ground area."⁴ Pieter Bruegel the Elder's *Netherlandish Proverbs* (1559) shows a spectrum of inter-related conditions, from the natural land patterns, the styles and manners of a people's ways of living, and to the political system of governance. There is also a reverse case that narrows the spectrum by eliminating the prosaic activities of daily life, presenting a kind of 'pure nature,' set in opposition to the village, city, or town. *Landscape with Spruce Tree* (c. 1522) by Albrecht Altdorfer illustrates this stance, as does the fact that he is often acknowledged as "the first modern landscape painter because many of his scenes omit all indications of local custom and life, as they do religious themes, concentrating instead on water, soil, vegetation, and sky."⁵

Another thinker who reflected on the reciprocity between the features and forces of a given landscape and the way people live together is Tetsuro Watsuji, a pre-eminent thinker in the intellectual history of modern East Asia. Watsuji's *Fudo* (1935), which was translated into *A Climate: A Philosophical Study* (1961), elucidates the intertwined reciprocity between natural conditions and interpersonal human relationships. His reflection upon this mutuality led him to publish a related key text, *Ethics* (1937), which addressed more narrowly interpersonal dynamics. While one habitually deals with nature and interpersonal relationship as two separate domains, Watsuji theorized the intertwined relationship between the two.

The initial idea for *Fudo* was developed while he traveled across the Indian Ocean, the Arabian Sea, and the Mediterranean on his way to Berlin to study with Martin Heidegger in 1927. *Fudo* signifies climate but extends its scope to indicate land in a wide-ranging and inclusive sense, its topography, scenic features, soil characteristics, fauna and flora, influence on the way people live, and so on. The distinctiveness of Watsuji's notion of *fudo*, however, consists in his original insights into what it means for the human way of living and the human mind. First, Watsuji saw *fudo* as an agent for discovering "who I am" (the self) and "who we are." *Fudo* is "the agent by which human life is objectified, and it is here that man comprehends himself; there is self-discovery" in it.⁶ It is for this reason that "the climatic character is the character of subjective human existence."⁷ His examples included *sabaku*, the Japanese term for desert—one example being the Arabian Desert around Aden, which Watsuji himself experienced, and another being the Gobi Desert that spans from northern and north western China to southern Mongolia. The term *sabaku* is a combination of sand (*sa*) and bleakness (*baku*) to signify one single reality. For Watsuji, this coinage indicates that *sabaku* is not solely a physical expanse of sand, but a phenomenon of the human heart—aridity, bleakness, and loneliness—creating unity between man and the sandy landscape.⁸ "Who we are"—aridity, bleakness, and loneliness—is objectified in the landscape, with the latter operating as the mirror of the former.

Fudo's embracing, atmospheric effect is another distinctive aspect of Watsuji's theory of climate. A person's relationship with

4 Leatherbarrow, "Building In and Out of Place," p. 28.
5 Leatherbarrow, "Building In and Out of Place," p. 28.
6 Watsuji, Tetsuro, *A Climate: A Philosophical Study*, Geoffrey Bownas trans., Ministry of Education Printing Bureau, 1961, p. 14.
7 Watsuji, *A Climate: A Philosophical Study*, p. 16.
8 Watsuji, *A Climate: A Philosophical Study*, pp. 39–40.

a climatic condition does not mean that they decide whether or not to feel it, but that before they decide, the climate's effect is already unfolding within them. Put differently, it is not that there is first an ambient condition and then an experience, but that there is an experience first, and then its preconditions can be objectified. As a climatic condition defines an area, I, you, he, and she are all embraced by the same climatic phenomenon and filled with its effects. At that moment, I, you, he, and she turn into "different 'I's'" despite their particularities. The coupling between sameness, or the typical sensation, and particularities form the very basis for the articulation of social relationships. On a cold morning, a father may say to his son without hesitation, "Why don't you put on more clothes? It is quite chilly this morning." The interconnection between what is natural and what is interpersonal is actualized through *fudo* or climate.

A concrete example of the common sensation and the articulation of the human relationship would be the dramatic openness that characterizes traditional Japanese residential architecture. Unimpeded connectivity was interpreted by many critics as a realization of the ideals of modernism, such as functional flexibility and beautiful spatiality, based upon diagonal visual axes. However, this view is superficial. Openness in this case must be understood primarily in reference to the *fudo* of Japan.

The Japanese summer is very hot and made even more difficult when combined with high humidity. Heat alone would be tolerable, but when combined with humidity it is commonly felt to be suffocating. Cross-ventilation is thus essential. The critical point is that in order for cross-ventilation to occur there must be an interconnection of spaces, not merely through windows, but whole sections of walling, as with sliding doors between rooms. The co-ordination of doors means that in Japanese domestic living there is a unique sense of privacy, when compared to alternative understandings, represented by fixed walls and doors leading to corridors.

In consideration of sliding doors, Kon Wajiro's (1888-1973) recording of the pattern of daily traffic in a Japanese house is immensely helpful, for it demonstrates direct room-to-room transits between family members (without corridors), testifying to the intimacy that prevails through the whole house. The dramatic openness of the Japanese house thus embodies a spatial embodiment of intimacy. Cross-ventilation comes into being on account not of the natural movement of air but of the human relationship, or at the very least, becomes fully effective only when its operation is combined with the tuning of interpersonal relationships. Watsuji himself characterizes such openness as the basis for cross-ventilation "selfless openness."[9] The terrain here appears as forces—hotness combined with humidity—and it articulates human relationships, collective tuning, and sharing a benefit.

Next, I would like to reflect upon the relationship between the interpersonal dynamic and the nature of institutions. One figure who raised the issue is Louis I. Kahn. A case in point is his fictive

[9] Watsuji, *A Climate: A Philosophical Study*, p. 145.

story of the school's origin, an institution that emerged from the human relationship of "a man who did not know he was a teacher talking to children who did not know they were pupils."[10] On the basis of the school that is understood in this way he coined the term "human agreement," the nature of which is not legal or contractual but instinctual. Kahn's call to transform the institution—a call which was probably prompted by America's social turmoil during the 1960s and 1970s—was intended to refresh the inspiration that gave rise to the institution which he thought had fallen to oblivion.

His search for "volume zero," however, left something to be desired. Kahn's discussion of the human relationship as the basis for the institution confined itself to the sort of harmony that could be achieved through typical forms of interpersonal relationships—parental, filial, pedagogical, friendly, erotic, and so forth. He failed to clarify the potential for a higher dimension, on which the human relationship might give rise to conflictual moments, tensions that may emerge between the parental and the erotic, for example.

A more recent thinker who addressed institutions, Peter Carl, extended the significance of the institution to address conflicts between the typical forms of the human relationship. The story of Orestes, who was torn between two forces, having to kill his mother in accordance with the oracle of Apollo, and the other, saving her life to follow a filial duty, is a good example, particularly the civility of the resolution. The transforming of antagonism into *agon*—differences negotiated and resolved through rhetoric in the Aristotelian sense—is precisely the role of the institution. In this context, Carl characterized both the Athenian law court and its tragic drama as great institutions. In particular, the law court transformed violent antagonism into a public matter of rational litigation, cutting the vicious chain of vendetta. Justice of reciprocity was enacted as the most important value in the sustenance of a city.[11]

I would like to argue that when terrain is embedded with forces and qualities that articulate human relationships, it acts as an agent of the transformation of institutions, as long as it is an institution of human relationships. While Kahn's call for the transformation of an institution did not interpret terrain as an agent, terrain embedded with the ethical dimension of the human relationship can be, I think, acknowledged as another positive and active source for an institutional transformation. But I'd like to stress once again that terrain thus understood is not merely physical but also ethical. Here, ethical conditions and consideration have historical dimensions, as stories about the dynamics of people living together unfold over time, according to a plot animated by the interplay of opposing forces.

H-Sang Seung's Gudeok Presbyterian Church

Gudeok Presbyterian Church by Seung, who was born in 1952, amid the Korean War, leads us to reflect concretely upon two

[10] Kahn "Address to Naturalized Citizens," p. 263.
[11] Carl, Peter, "*Convivimus Ergo Sums*," *Phenomenologies of the City*, Henriette Steiner and Maximilian Sterberg eds., Farnham, Surrey: Ashgate, 2015, pp. 11-32.

senses of terrain: 1) embedded with an ethical dimension; and 2) as an agent for the transformation of an institution.

The area around Gudeok mountain was originally one of the places where refugees from North Korea settled during the war. Seung's parents were themselves refugees and also devout Christians. An intense sense of community emerged among the refugees, based on the common loss of home and town, and the shared fate of beginning a new life from nothing in a foreign land. The first Gudeok Presbyterian Church was consecrated in 1953, and the second in 1961. Seung's residence was very close to the second church, facing its side wall and separated only through an extremely narrow alley that two adults could barely pass through. Apart from on Sundays, Seung spent most of his time after school in the church. The *madang*, a small ground-level open space with a fig tree on one side, became his playground, and an attic in the bell tower, his study nook. Seung left his hometown in the early 1970s to study architecture at Seoul National University. He then worked for a leading Korean architect before opening his own firm in the early 1990s. In the meantime, the third church was built on the same site in a crude gothic style around 1980.

In 2008, Seung won a competition to build yet another new church on the same site. Demolition would, of course, be required. The new church was supposed to accommodate 1,200 people, marking a significant increase from the previous church's capacity, which accommodated 300 to 400 people. Not surprisingly, the area of the site was found to be too small. Seung suggested incorporating adjacent small lots, including the one where his family house once stood. Thus, the site's boundary lines became irregular. The overall shape was long and narrow, also sloped. Incorporating a couple of tiny lots into the original site was helpful, but only to a minimal degree. Building a church that would accommodate 1,200 people was a truly demanding challenge. **Figure 7.1 (see p. 185)**

While coping with the practical challenge of housing a congregation whose size was expected to grow exponentially, Seung pursued a couple of themes that would interact with the physical, cultural, and ethical dimensions of the given terrain and eventually transform the church's institutional status. The two themes are: first, molding a series of platforms out of the given irregular and sloped terrain; and second, the site and building's vertical stratification.

Molding a Platform
The most critical task of Seung's early design was locating a platform at an easily accessible level from the street. As noted above, that task had both physical and ethical dimensions, for Seung understood the platform as the first premise of human gathering. In this case, a sloped terrain was cut and leveled so that the new platform would operate as the community's practical and symbolic center. Leveling the terrain to set a flat open courtyard—a *madang*—in the middle meant that the whole complex would be

divided into two bodies: a seven-story tower; and the main church building. Both share and stand on the courtyard platform.

The configuration of spaces at the platform level is significant. Its program included communal spaces, such as a café, dining hall, lobby, and so forth. The entrances to these spaces were located in such a way that direct access from the courtyard would be possible. Windows also promote visual connections between the courtyard and the surrounding spaces. In particular, the café is set between two orientations: one towards the street, and the other on to the platform, or *madang*. Towards the street, the café is raised above the ground, as if it were hovering in the air. Towards the courtyard, the continuity of the floor of the café with the platform on the outside is emphasized. **Figures 7.2, 7.3, 7.4 (see p. 186), and 7.5 (see p. 186)**

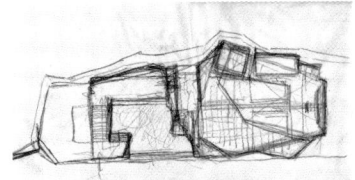

Figure 7.2 | H-Sang Seung, Gudeok Presbyterian Church, Busan, South Korea, 2008; plan sketch for the church.

Figure 7.3 | H-Sang Seung, Gudeok Presbyterian Church, Busan, South Korea, 2008; exterior sketch for the church.

The bridge that connects the two separate bodies of the complex operates as an awning-like cover to enhance the connectivity, as it provides shade and offers protection when it rains. The corridor that runs along the dining hall turns at a right angle a couple of times and joins together, on one side, the platform, and on the other, an extremely narrow alley—this is the alley Seung himself strolled during the 1970s. This spatial configuration, composed of a spacious courtyard, an interior corridor, and an alley of the 1970s is, in a way, a representation of Seung's childhood daily sequence. Thanks to this arrangement of parts, including the bold division between the tower and the church, the programmatic distribution, the articulation of the elements such as the awning-like bridge that enhances "occupiability," and the representation of the daily routes, the courtyard operates as the center of communal activities, open to one another and to the neighborhood. The courtyard, thus, is anything but a device for solitude; more than anything else, it accommodates and represents the interpersonal dimension of gathering by opening a common ground for people's daily activities.

A comparison with Sujoldang, a residential work by Seung completed in the middle of the 1990s, clarifies the distinctively communal nature of the platform at Gudeok Presbyterian Church. The platform in this work is different from that of Gudeok Presbyterian Church in terms of performance. It is a very intimate courtyard bounded with a wall traditionally patterned, the blank backside of the house in front, and a wing of the house itself. The positioning of the tree and objects on the platform is skillfully composed: a skinny persimmon tree stands at the center, a terracotta lamp to the left, a lonely chair to the right, and so forth. Like a picture, the whole setting is fabricated for a visual appreciation from inside the living room. The platform is not so much a place for daily chores—what would a house be without them?—than a place composed to give perceptual pleasure, picture-like I've said, though three-dimensional. Its atmosphere is melancholic, too: loneliness prevails. The configuration of the plan further confirms the pictorial nature of the platform. One who has just entered the gate is met with the

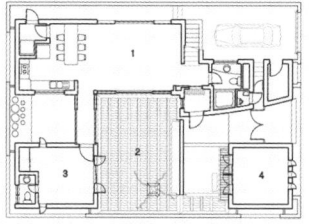

Figure 7.6 | H-Sang Seung, Sujoldang, Seoul, South Korea, 1992; plan.

Figure 7.7 | H-Sang Seung, Sujoldang, Seoul, South Korea, 1992; view toward the *madang* (courtyard) from the living room.

Figure 7.8 | H-Sang Seung, Sujoldang, Seoul, South Korea, 1992; original setting of the *madang*.

traditionally patterned wall that blocks the path. He then has to enter the house to discover from the living room the platform to the outside. This is a unique sequence, as houses in traditional Korean architecture must go through a courtyard first before one is led to the interior. **Figures 7.6 and 7.7**

The visual appropriation of the traditional courtyard and the alienation of the platform away from daily activities reflect Korean modernity during the Post-War period. In the aftermath of the Korean War, clumsy modernization, undertaken by culturally unprepared military dictatorships, transformed Seoul into a bleak metropolis full of bulldozed construction sites for buildings and infrastructure, such as boulevards, subways, and exposed highways. Tradition was left as a collection of isolated fragments in an urban fabric dominated by homogeneous capitalistic urban sprawl and a few free-standing museum artifacts. For some intellectuals, including Seung, Seoul was a bleak metropolis as a living environment and in terms of its politics. The highly intimate and even melancholic nature of the platform of Sujoldang should be understood in this cultural context. Somewhat paradoxically, inward focus led to widely external reference, far beyond Korea. According to Seung, Samuel Beckett's play *Waiting for Godot* provided a model for the setting. While its occupancy was sporadic, the courtyard symbolized the distance between what people desired to possess in a nostalgic manner—a piece of tradition—and the style of life that had already moved far from tradition. The strong sense of protected interiority of the house operates as an antidote to the chaotic metropolis, and its attendant sense of being lost amid the masses. **Figure 7.8**

Here, one might be reminded of Watsuji's discussion of the contrast between the city and the house. At the time, Tokyo was busy attaining (modern) civilization. The civilizing process was, however, paradoxically primitive, too, with its destructive constructions, unchecked speed, crudeness, abrasive noise, and so forth. The house fenced off with high walls, and its intimate, complete openness was an antidote to the Japanese modernity. A disproportionate relationship between the city and the house reinforces the latter's role as an oasis—selfless complete openness— where one could be relieved from the harsh, hectic, and dangerous public reality of the outside world. One would also be reminded of Georg Simmel's discussion of the intellectual who builds up an inner intellectual refugee camp or a fortress in confrontation with the incessant concatenation of schizophrenic stimulations. In comparison with Sujoldang's platform, the platform at Gudeok Presbyterian Church wasn't designed to promote nostalgic and melancholic pictorial appreciation, but for practical occupation, that is to say the daily life of the congregation and the neighbors. It was, I've said, the center of communal activities.

Securing an open platform in the middle of the site gave rise to intriguing and difficult moments in the process of design. First, as the body of the church dedicated to service was put to the side, the whole complex appears as if it did not have a proper face. Thereby the church lost an opportunity to acquire a monumental front, to be perceived in perspective. Equally undesirable was the risk that its distance from the street would marginalize its urban presence. As realized, however, the church embodies a sort of balance between non-presence and presence. While appearing in a non-imposing manner, the front of the church engages the people who come into the courtyard below by tilting its outermost layers forward, and by articulating them with different materials. The preparation of the path that leads one to the church is atypical, too, an extended labyrinthine passageway. First, as one enters the platform, the tilted front of the church above is discovered. **Figure 7.9 (see p. 187)** Direct and convenient access to the church is denied, however, as a turn is required to find the flights of steps. Next, a bridge takes one to the narthex. The axis along which she or he has walked, however, does not coincide with the central axis of the church interior. The path to the main entrance is diagonal. The narthex is where the shifting axes are gathered and negotiated. **Figures 7.4 (see p. 186) and 7.5 (see p. 186)** A series of shifts of axes is thus implemented, analogizing the experience of going through an alley that once existed on the site, and that is still observable partially in the immediate vicinity of the complex.

The cross inside the church appears to the right and is set high. A battle between linear axiality and diagonal shifts is observed here, too. In the interior of the church, the central axis is clearly present. However, the church itself is an ensemble of different program elements and orientations. The choir is accessed from the level below, through a narrow alley-like passage and a stairway. The enclosed service room for those accompanied by toddlers and children is particularly interesting. The spot where the room is designed was where Seung's family house once stood before it was incorporated into the site. The room is accessed from the narthex in a way that again reminds one of the alleyways that existed on the site. The unusual vertical proportion of the church could also be seen as the side effect of the effort to secure the open central platform. As noted above, the church was intended to accommodate 1,200 people, a large-sized congregation compared to the very tight size of the site. The task of accommodating the congregation became still more difficult, however, because the architect sought an open platform in the very middle of the complex. The placement of communal functions on the ground-level platform meant that the church itself had to be placed above. The result is a church that is vertically extended to an unusual degree—even if great heights are common in Christian churches. What modulates the extended vertical proportion is, first, the cubic free-standing, exposed concrete structure that houses audio-visual equipment, and second, the high cross that is enveloped by light coming from a source that is still higher. **Figures 7.10 (see p. 188) and 7.11 (see p. 170)** The exaggerated verticality of the church caused complaints from the church members. For instance, the replacement of a broken bulb on the ceiling required the installation of a crane, raising the overall cost of the project to an unexpected level.

Vertical Stratification

Another aspect of Gudeok Presbyterian Church I would like to discuss in reference to the creation of the platform is vertical stratification. First of all, the tectonic articulation of the church reinforces its programmatic articulation; both unfold vertically. Rough-finished concrete sets the lower horizon, wrapping the platform, or *madang*, with punctuations to allow entrances and windows to the surrounding rooms, such as the dining hall, café, and lobby. The cladding of the second story and above with basalt panels coincides with the beginning of a higher horizon. The tectonic articulation shapes a recognizable basis out of which one may emerge to another platform above the bridge. On this platform, one perceives an extended horizon marked eventually by the peaks of distant mountains via high-rise apartment buildings recently constructed. Elevated positions also look down to the main platform below. The immersion in a semi-enclosed platform at the lower level and the emergence into a higher horizon above, where the full extent of the city can be discovered, reminds one of Le Corbusier's (1887–1965) mapping of the Acropolis, which conflated profiles that were near and far; namely, the edge of the temple platform and limit of the distant sea, comparable, he thought, because each line was implacable and silent, despite the rugged, rough, and variously elevated terrain between.

The cladding pattern is repeated in the interior of the church, but the material changes from gray basalt to birch wood panels. **Figure 7.12 (see p. 190)** In the division of the panels, on both the exterior and interior, uprightness is strongly emphasized. Such uprightness resonates with both the uprightness of the free-standing concrete structure to the side of the altar and that of the cross. What is extremely interesting is the fact that uprightness was also emphasized in the design of the pews, with backs set at 90 degrees to seats. Seung rejected an earlier version of the pews, which he found to be slack. In other words, the uprightness of the pews is not merely about keeping a compositional consistency characterized by verticality. The whole space is filled with the ethos of being alert: verticality from the cross and the free-standing structure, to the panel divisions, and then to the furniture implements practically and symbolizes alertness.

In terms of program, vertical stratification is significant once again, suggesting a complementarity between tectonics and types of events. All spaces related to small-group communal activities such as the café, dining hall, and meeting rooms are located on the ground level. They are set around the *madang*. While the structural system is post and lintel, these spaces are finished with exposed concrete walls whose surfaces have been punctuated dramatically towards the courtyard, rather like cave openings oriented toward the horizon.

At the upper level, the primary element is the church itself, dedicated to service and worship. The church was constructed out of a steel frame sitting on a base concrete structure and is clad with birch wood panels on the interior, as I've said. Within the church is a series of individual platforms with different orientations and at different heights: the gently sloped main sitting area, a choir, stepped balconies, a special room for the parents with toddlers, a raised altar, and so forth. In its highly interiorized setting, the church itself is nevertheless an amalgam of variegated spaces, all of which work together for an intended service—all together, a spectrum of vertical expressions consisting of two groups. First are the places of prosaic daily activities. Second are the sacred spaces. And these types have perceptual, even emotional characteristics. The first are open and lively, the second enclosed and intimate. Likewise, the first is filled with light, the second is subdued, with a highly controlled amount of light. When thought about in section, the vertical stratification positions the ordinary as the basis for the institution, so that the sacred can be a particular ritualistic moment. It is a form of integration: the first operating as the ground and the second operating as an embodiment of a particular expression.

Another interesting moment related to vertical stratification is found in the location of prayer rooms for small groups and individuals. As I noted at the outset, they are positioned at the top floor of the tower facing, first, the stadia with prominent light towers, second, the uncharacteristic and even disordered urban landscape in the middle ground, and lastly, distant mountains. When articulating the elevation, Seung repeated the same motif of the lower strip window on the top floor. This decision may reflect aestheticism, which is to say a desire to present the tower and its facade in a unified manner. Whatever the reason, the orientation and location of the prayer rooms are quite dramatic, as one is given a full view of the cityscape. While the church appears to shut itself off from its surroundings, as if it were masking the outside world, the prayer rooms are where one rediscovers the naked presence of the world. Albeit elevated, they confront the city face to face, without mitigation. The significance of the location could also be apprehended with reference to the main platform on the ground level. The activity of praying in individual rooms on the highest level of the whole complex in an airy atmosphere is contrasted with the prosaic activities such as parties, markets, wedding ceremonies, festivities, and so forth on the lowest earthbound platform.

The presence of Gudeok Presbyterian Church is not confined to the boundary of the site but has far-reaching influence beyond itself. The tower is located on the edge of the street. Its role is practical, as it blocks noise in order to secure a sense of protection for the platform behind and the main church. The tower also operates as a beacon that gives orientation to the surrounding area, which is, I've noted, characterized by irregular topographical conditions, such as a roundabout, multiple roads meeting at different angles, stadia, and so forth. Its presence is also observed from nearby institutions, such as an elementary school. Additionally, while its presence is certainly vertically prominent, the tower assumes a kind of modest posture as it looks down or tilts its "head". Furthermore, it stood originally without a cross at the top, generally expected in Christian architecture in Korea. The ambiguity of the tower in terms of identity later led the church community to install a modest cross at the top, going against the original intention of the architect. Despite this installation, the tower balances a prominent vertical presence and a modest posture, while intentionally suppressing a specific religious identification, rather like a silent yet distinctive worker on a street.

Conclusion
The relationship between terrain, building, and institution has rarely been considered in the discourse of architectural design. Leatherbarrow's illumination of the full spectrum of the significance of terrain leads us to transcend the fictitious conception of pure nature and the habitual focus on the physical aspects of the terrain. Watsuji's theory of climate, an essential part of terrain, allows one to see the fundamental bond between terrain and humanity, or "who we are," and most importantly, the reciprocity between terrain and the interpersonal ethics. The nomadic nature of Watsuji's study, traversing different climatic zones, also opens a view of conjoined terrains. A terrain does not stand on its own. Rather its character is confirmed and crystalized only through a relationship with others. Both Leatherbarrow and Watsuji clarify design as dealing with productive continuity and conflict between a terrain and a building, as they jointly co-ordinate the human relationship. It is also significant to remind oneself that a building is never a single isolated instance, but a case of an institutional project. Kahn understood the significance of a building in this manner. The interplay of terrain, building, and institutions is, I think, the truly decisive issue.

Seung's Gudeok Presbyterian Church acknowledges the physical and cultural dimensions of pre-existing terrain. This location was richly embedded with the stories of a particular refugee community in the historical context of the Korean War. Also, there was an unmet need to secure a base for communal life. Once discovered, it allowed a productive conflict with the practical need to accommodate an exponentially increased size of the congregation on a very small lot. In terms of programmatic distribution, Seung adopted the strategy of vertical stratification, as rooms such as the café, dining hall, and lobby are located on the ground level in an immediate conjunction with the platform, while the church dedicated to religious service is situated above. The terrain was also something that's significance was to be found beyond the boundary, as if engaging with the surroundings was the responsibility of the church. Being within the boundary and engaging with the conditions outside the boundary also form a productive dialectic.

Consequently, the church complex acknowledges the significance of terrain at different levels: 1) the church which is highly interiorized; 2) the platform (*madang*) which accommodates prosaic activities of the Christian community and the neighborhood; 3) the bridge (or deck) above the platform which brings to one's awareness the primary natural reference points of the city, or the distant mountains; and 4) the tower that operates as a modest beacon for the vicinity. In this process, the institutional status of the church is transformed. It is a church with a platform at the center, one that takes as its ground the prosaic communal spaces and events. The central presence of the platform in conjunction with the social spaces is highly unusual in contemporary Korean Christian architecture that targets largely at accommodating big congregations with little emphasis on open outdoor space accessible not only by the church community but also by the neighborhood. The bridge, the narthex, the shifted central axis in the interior of the church, the vertically extended proportion of the church, and the location of the cross all come into being as the result of this transformed nature of Christian architecture. Its non-perspectival presence, compromised frontality, and inclined postural articulation also transformed the nature of Christian architecture.

Seung once criticized Korea's Christian architecture as having forgotten people, while putting too much emphasis on God. Seung called for a renewal of Christian architecture so that it would be built for people, as well as for God. The platform was the key to this ambition. Again, with the platform as the site of prosaic communal activities came the stratifications—horizontal and vertical—the programmatic variation and the series of gestures of modesty, intending a non-imposing presence. As Kahn claimed, "Every building... must answer some institution of man."[12] Gudeok Presbyterian Church is not just an isolated instance of architectural creation. Rather, it transforms an institution—Korean Christian architecture—by urbanizing it, at the level of the spatial configuration and program. Terrain inscribed not only with physical qualities but also with the stories of the refugee community—social, cultural, and ethical—was the beginning point for this process of an institutional transformation.

[12] Kahn, "Address to Naturalized Citizens," p. 264.

Figure 7.1 | H-Sang Seung, Gudeok Presbyterian Church, Busan, South Korea, 2008; exterior.

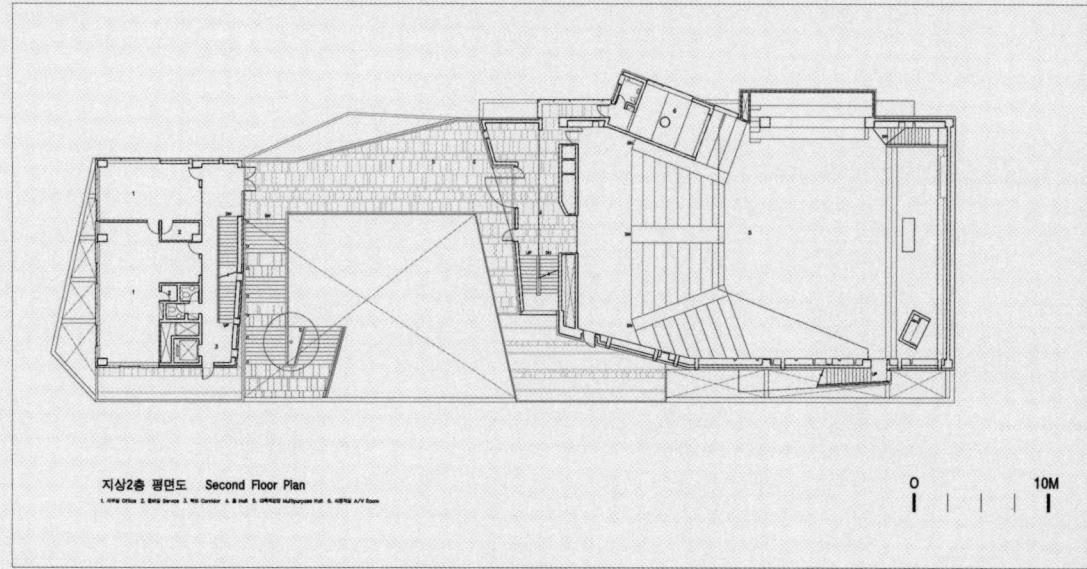

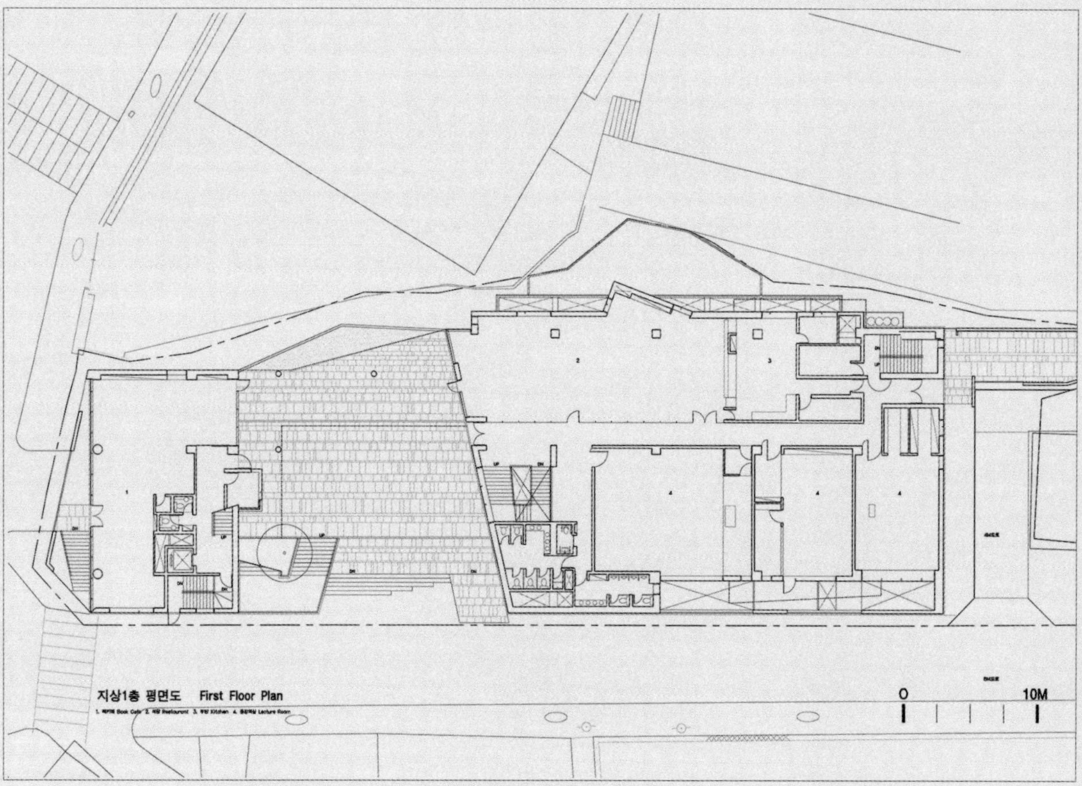

Figures 7.4 and 7.5 | H-Sang Seung, Gudeok Presbyterian Church, Busan, Korea, 2008; (from top) second floor plan, ground level plan.

Figure 7.9 | H-Sang Seung, Gudeok Presbyterian Church, Busan, South Korea, 2008; entrance view.

Figure 7.10 | H-Sang Seung, Gudeok Presbyterian Church, Busan, South Korea, 2008; interior.

Figure 7.12 | H-Sang Seung, Gudeok Presbyterian Church, Busan, South Korea, 2008; interior.

8

David Leatherbarrow

Architectural Depth as Urban Communication

Skirkanich Hall by Tod Williams Billie Tsien Architects

OUT OF THE NEAR
Waterpits,
Graygreen shoveled
Upwards with unawakened hands:

The depth
Gives up its growth, inaudible,
Without resistance.

—Paul Celan, *Threadsuns*.[1]

Figure 8.1 | Tod Williams Billie Tsien Architects (TWBTA), Skirkanich Hall, Philadelphia, 2006; street-front view.

[1] Celan, Paul, "*Threadsuns*," Fadensonnen, first published 1968, Los Angeles, CA: Sun and Moon Press, 2000, p. 89. Celan's original is as follows: *"Aus den Nahen/ Wasserschächten/ mit unerweckten/ Händen heraufgeschaufeltes Graugrün/ die Tiefe/ gibt ihr Gewächs her, unhörbar,/ widerstandslos."*

Figures 8.2, 8.3, and 8.4 | TWBTA, Skirkanich Hall, Philadelphia, 2006; (from top) front facade detail, sidewalk view, and ramp to rear court and main entrance.

2 Parts of this study were first published in "World Building," *Architectural Theory Review*, vol. 14, no. 1, 2009, pp. 32-54. In that paper I didn't address the urban questions this one considers.

3 This part of his text envisaged work in wax or clay (in ancient Greek, he notes, sculptors were called πλάστης, in Latin *fictores*—terms that indicate *fabricating* in both senses of the word).

Anyone who has spent some time walking through the University of Pennsylvania's campus in Philadelphia will have noticed Skirkanich Hall. Although it is an infill building, one among others that make up the perimeter of a typical urban block, it is impossible to miss.[2] Designed by Tod Williams Billie Tsien Architects and finished in 2006 for the School of Engineering, the building's appearance on the street is without parallel in the neighborhood. About a third of its bulk overhangs half the sidewalk, while most of its upper part rises head and shoulders over the roofs nearby. Any view up or down 33rd Street, no matter how hurried or glancing, will have noticed it. Unlike the facade projections one finds in traditional architecture, a bay or bow window, for example, this one's means of support is also atypical: the protruding mass doesn't rest on a solid, side-to-side, load-bearing wall; instead, a perpendicular plane recessed within deep shadow—advance above, retreat below. **Figures 8.2, 8.3, and 8.4**

The Renaissance architect Leon Battista Alberti wrote in his book on sculpture that there are two ways of making a plastic work, by increase or subtraction, which is to say, building up or carving out.[3] Both techniques come into play with moldable material, which can be either added, to emphasize or vivify, or cut away, if it conceals the form within, as Michelangelo famously explained. At Skirkanich, molded space above and hollowed space below take the place of what would have been a tree lawn, in order to foreshadow what is to come in the building's several depths. Once you step into the shadow, the hollow unexpectedly bifurcates. Doors to the interior appear on the right, while a ramp on the left begins its gentle rise toward a mid-block courtyard and garden. Because of the darkness, the two entry points remain unapparent until the last steps of a sidewalk approach, despite any intimations of a space-split the recessed wall's blunt edge might have given from the sidewalk or across the street. **Figure 8.1 (see p. 192)**

The pre-existing buildings standing on either side of the loggia darkness align very nicely with one another, obediently conforming to the geometry of the neighborhood's streets, sidewalks, tree lawns, and fronts, neither overstepping nor retreating from the plot line to which they agreed at the time of their inception, regardless of the widths and depths their plans and use-programs have subsequently filled out. Likewise, for the properties around the corner, aligned fronts jointly define perfectly continuous street walls, without the tree lawns in front, however. Those same lines and angles repeat themselves again on the block's other sides, also by common agreement. The urban layout thus formed extends (or concentrates) Philadelphia's inaugural orthogonality and spacing, which by design (a couple of centuries ago) set the limits for the city's regular but relatively small blocks, small when compared to those of New York or Berlin (Friedrichstadt), for example. **Figure 8.5**

Simple though it is, this geometry has impressed visitors, no less than citizens, throughout the city's history. The Austrian

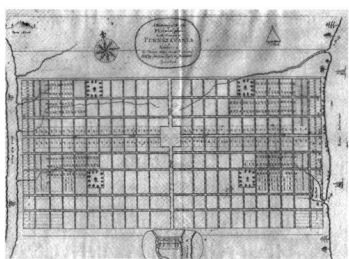

Figure 8.5 | William Penn's plan for Philadelphia, by General Surveyor Thomas Holme, 1683.

Figure 8.6 | A typical alley and urban interior in Philadelphia.

4 Handke, Peter, *Short Letter, Long Farewell*, New York: Farrar Straus Giroux, 1974, pp. 49–50.
5 James, Henry, *The American Scene*, first published 1907, Bloomington, IN: Indiana University Press, 1968.
6 Aristotle's views, together with those of others, are nicely presented in Marquard, Odo, *In Defense of the Accidental: Philosophical Studies*, Oxford: Oxford University Press, 1991.

novelist Peter Handke's notes on Chestnut Street, for example, primarily stressed this point about orthogonality.[4] After commenting on the flatness of the urban terrain, he noted the city's right-angle geometry and the fact that its streets go "straight on." Henry James, three-quarters of a century earlier, made similar observations, but in a more extended and comparative characterization. Attempting to explain the secret of the city's "serenity" (when compared to New York, St. Louis or Chicago, which "bristle"), he turned to the urban layout's proportionality and homogeneity, whose "intensity and ubiquity" accommodated and represented, he thought, a "society" or "town" implicitly governed by a principle of "consanguinity." This last conception is a little mysterious, because common descent and continuous blood lines were not required for the "organic social relations" that made the city so agreeable.[5]

A different pattern—not really a pattern at all—characterizes the city's block interiors, where lanes and alleys widen or intersect. Each of the mid-block passages, courts, or yards in Philadelphia is distinctive, just the opposite of the street and their facades, not because any designer tried to make them interesting or attractive, but as a result of unforeseen and incremental additions or subtractions that have over time accommodated short- or long-term needs. The use of the word "design" to describe how these spaces came into being is probably incorrect, for there are few evidences of self-sameness in conception, and no one seems to have had an overall form or image in mind. But they do not for that reason lack mood, character, or identity. Typical elements can be seen there—fire escapes, bay windows, sheds, and so on—but none acknowledge any sovereign principle that would rule over their conjunction: nothing magnificent, nothing unknown. Rather like the incidents of an episodic plot, the workshops, private gardens, and parking spaces that make up the city's unnoticed urbanity haven't been integrated into a unified scheme, nor was it meant to be read or seen that way, because their several parts were built to serve discrete purposes that had been neglected in the design of the fronts. **Figure 8.6**

Urban interiors in Philadelphia (especially in Center City, on the east side of the Schuylkill River, and University City, on the west side) are thus un-patterned parts of the overall pattern, necessary to the life of the city but accidental to its design and conception, in the sense that each could have been formed otherwise. Accidents, for Aristotle, are those developments that have come about through the unexpected mutual encounter of determining events that were independent of one another, just the opposite of the preconceived and organized unfoldings that follow from the specialized strategic thinking we associate with planning and design.[6] In each of the city's blocks, then, center and periphery sharply contrast in their different beginnings, purposes, identities, and durations: ad hoc versus designed, private against common concerns, local not city-wide orientation, and mutable rather than permanent arrangements. **Figure 8.7 (see p. 203)**

Skirkanich Hall altered this *core form-art form* distinction by reducing the difference and displacing characteristic elements and urban qualities.[7] Walking from 33rd to 34th Street along the new cut through the block interior you get the sense the architects never said farewell to design, even if the way they went about doing things suggests we reconceptualize it. From the sidewalk, through the forecourt shadow, up the ramp, onto the raised rear terrace, past the enclosed garden, and through the opposite-facing building, the urban interior is hardly an interior at all, at least with respect to local (ad hoc) norms, for it resulted from the same kind of thinking that defined the front facade's convexity-concavity: nothing by accident, attending to common not private concerns, proposing interconnectivity not isolation, and built to last. In short, the back is rather like the front, as if street architecture, or some of its attributes, had been displaced to an alley, in order to institute a new type of space, even if this was no less improbable with respect to precedent than the frontside overreach. Like that one, this innovation is entirely persuasive now that it has settled into the local urban culture.

Let's consider the front a little more closely. As it holds itself above the shaded forecourt, the building's big broad chest splices together two surfaces that could hardly be more opposed to one another: on the right, a squared-off, multi-story skin of enclosing brickwork, no less flat than the pavement its shadow darkens, and on the left, a ribcage relief of glass sheets, shingle-like but slip-stacked, with each three-part pane alternately shielding and yielding to the sun, while inhaling all the light, air, and prospect it can reasonably hold. The breastplate on the right excludes the surrounding environment, while the lungs on the left welcome its offerings. Enclosure is the obvious responsibility of the first, outward orientation the desire of the second. **Figure 8.8**

Figure 8.8 | TWBTA, Skirkanich Hall, Philadelphia, 2006; front facade detail.

Why this duplicity or conjunction of opposites? Might the bifold articulation have something to say about the students and teachers who work there, their study habits and research, the in- and outward focus of a professional school, especially one that trains engineers? Could the basic design premise have been that learning has two sides, sheltered study and outward orientation, the first flourishing within protective confines, and the second sizing up the city as its field of operations?

An essay in polite contextualism the building is not. Whatever was intended, the hoisted hulk seems at first glance rather ill-mannered, no less than the sidewalk incursion seemed at first, as was also the case with the improbably elegant block interior. No one who sees it thinks otherwise, at least initially. Tokens of conformity are nowhere to be found: the line of the street wall, reaffirmed by fronts all around this block and the others in the vicinity, has been ignored; so, too, the prevailing cornice line; likewise, local materials and colors (especially the pock-marked glazed-green brick, when compared to the standard, ruddy, and unglazed examples to the right and left). The same affront to commonplaces can be seen in the

---

7 The *kernform-kunstform* distinctions introduced by Karl Bötticher described single architectural elements. The same separation-dependency can be found at other scales, even that of an urban block.

attitude toward the typical ratio between solids and voids; instead of patterned balance—50 percent aperture, 50 percent wall—there is uninterrupted planarity, with each side canted outward from the flanking walls, about 30 degrees, angling toward a vertical center built as a negative joint, hiding the connection in shadow.

Thus selected, shaped, and finished, the construction materials accomplish both practical and figurative purposes, alternately breathing and shielding, while associating themselves with the sky and soil. By sky, I mean the work's atmospheric horizon, by soil its material premise, no less *horizonal* than the vault above. Though the architects never suggested the comparison, an equivalent coincidence of opposites was proposed by Le Corbusier in his account of the sun being both a friend and an enemy. Apollo and Medusa, images of celestial and chthonic powers, appear on the Skirkanich facade as lines of light and scars on baked clay. The epigraph from Celan cited above catches the right half of the pair very economically. "Waterpits/ Graygreen shoveled/ upwards..." Doubly but distantly engaged, the building's apparent indifference to what soldiers up on either side seems to have resulted from a greater interest in remote horizons, reaching outward and above but never freeing itself from the grip of what's below, two environmental powers that were at play long before the urban grid was cut into the land between the city's two rivers. **Figure 8.9**

Figure 8.9 | Le Corbusier, drawing of "The Sun, a friend and enemy."

But maybe not.

Maybe more local engagements also play their parts in the project's urbanity, just less obviously. Proximal extensions were, in fact, required in the building's program of uses and the client's vision of the institution. From the beginning, the new building was to join ranks with the others that formed the university's School of Engineering. When inserted into its site, therefore, it had to develop linkages with neighboring premises, the Towne Building (1906) on the left (to the south) and Moore Building (1912/26) on the right (to the north). Articulating these linkages was not simple, however, for the decision to hoist the bulk of the building over the pre-existing plot line strained neighborly relationships from the start. **Figures 8.10 and 8.11**

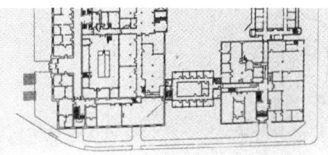

Figure 8.10 | Towne Building, the new link building, and Moore Building; plan.

Figure 8.11 | Geddes, Brecher and Cunningham Architects, Harold Pender Laboratory, Philadelphia, 1958, linking Towne and Moore buildings; demolished in 2003.

Adding to that difficulty was the fact that the space between the buildings on either side impeded connection, because of the way the block was initially laid out and had been recently cluttered. The Moore Building, from the time it was first built faced on to a small, mid-block lane, Chancellor Street, which passed from 33rd to 34th Street. For a connection with the Towne Building to be made, this small street would have to be closed. In fact, that had happened even before Skirkanich Hall was built. Chancellor Street had been blocked by a small-sized insert that attempted to hinge the two buildings together. No one would call the design for that connecting bit particularly inspired, only serviceable: approximately symmetrical overall, set back from the sidewalk, with a rhythmic pattern of structural elements and ribbon windows. Making matters still worse was the fact that the

Architectural Depth as Urban Communication

Figures 8.13, 8.14, and 8.15 | TWBTA, Skirkanich Hall, Philadelphia, 2006; (from top) central stairway, rear court bifold walls, and bifold wall under central stair.

adjoining properties on the two sides had different floor heights, structural systems, and materials. **Figure 8.12 (see p. 204)**

The pre-existing urban and architectural separation required of Skirkanich a rather acrobatic counter-positioning and several difficult moves: enlarged landings, split stairways, extended galleries, cantilevered balconies, and clerestory glazing, all sized and shaped to effect spatial interconnection and lateral continuity between the three parts of the single school. Parts were understood as counter parts to those within the new building and at its margins. Enabling the engagements was a fixed reference point, rather like a stake in the ground that took the form of a very big vertical rectangle rising through the center of the entire section. Maybe a better image is of a wide spinal column that supported the lateral extensions I've listed: from this broad backbone, through its shoulders and arms, then wrists, palms, and fingers to adjoining slabs and spaces that had been until then wholly self-centered. **Figure 8.13**

When this backbone is viewed from either side (imagine yourself leaving either Moore or Towne, on any of their three levels) it can be seen to separate Skirkanich's front and back spaces. The lower floors of its frontside appear as stacked trays of mezzanine-like levels facing the street. Above are the teaching rooms and labs. On the lower floors of its back side, several types of meeting space face the rear court and garden. More locally, the front and back sides support vertical and horizontal movement: flights of steps at the rear and side-to-side passage at the front.

Similar uprights bifurcate other parts of the building: the two runs of back stair, for example, or the divide between doors to the rear seminar room (on the left) and the open-air terrace (on the right). **Figures 8.14 and 8.16 (see p. 205)** The most prominent instances of spine-split, bifold space are of course the conjunctions we've seen on the facade: the carved one within the threshold shadow and the molded one above, where a negative joint cleaves the stacked sheets of glass from the slab of brickwork. **Figures 8.15**

These examples suggest that a single principle of spatial configuration was used to organize key relationships throughout the building: inflexible uprights, acting as vertebral columns, both anchor outward counter-positioning and reach into and extend beyond the several settings at the work's proper borders, as if those borders weren't even there. Here's the thesis: urban continuity constructed through oppositional dialogue matters as much in architecture as a work's internal definition. Spinal bifolds in Skirkanich have the remarkable ability of staking out stable situations whose outward-reaching elements won't restrain themselves from engaging with the varied opportunities beyond their assigned limits. The dynamism of these figures is what I'd like to stress, even though their fixity gives the building and the block its stable form. **Figure 8.17**

Of course, the spaces between these uprights are filled by inhabitable settings that attract a student's or teacher's local interests (lab work, listening to lectures, and so on), more than

Figure 8.17 | TWBTA, Skirkanich Hall, Philadelphia, 2006; rear terrace and garden.

Figure 8.19 | TWBTA, Skirkanich Hall, Philadelphia, 2006; garden fountain.

8 Equivalent to what chemists call elemental, anthropologists structural, linguists grammatical, or philosophers ontological.

the building's tacit (though constituent) elements. That's okay, for the easy and elegant ways of occupying the building's several settings preserve a productive, sense-giving tension between its primary figures and their practical or cultural grounds. Primary here means neither prior nor chiefly significant, but principle, in the sense of a rule or statute internal to the work that governs the associations of parts and counterparts.[8] And what occurs in section can also be discovered on the ground plan, for there, too, parts and counterparts foster alliances with properties outside the building's ostensible concerns. **Figure 8.18 (see p. 206)**

The urbanity that is evident in the main volume's lateral connections also characterizes the rear courtyard, which I've already said is unexpectedly public, as if a typical Philadelphia block had been turned inside out or been reconceived as a setting defined by the characteristics of another type: designed to be shared, interconnected, and long-lasting. Instead of workshop, well, and vegetable patch (some of the ingredients of a traditional and typical yard or court) there is a terrace, a pool and fountain, and a green retreat. It is both more and less than an open-air room: a crossing of routes, a co-ordination of levels, a vantage for multiple prospects, and a garden with a watery receptacle. Taken all together, its elements encourage the kind of surprising intimacy that good public spaces allow.

More architectonically, a three- to four-story light well, together with the wall that backs it up and the stair that climbs it, stands perpendicular to the lines of movement that were initiated by the facade and entry. While the aim and result might seem to be centering, the opposite is also true: these elements spread the building laterally, proposing levels and lines of movement that interconnect the neighboring buildings that house other parts of the same school, together with a newly added classroom building on the opposite side (Levine Hall). The new sequence through the block is as follows: up the ramp that departed from the left half of the shadowed loggia on 33rd Street, onto the lower of the two terraces behind Skirkanich, alongside the fountain and enclosed garden, in the light of the three-story lightwell, through the doorways in Levine Hall, that link up with a walk connecting its front to 34th Street. All in all, it is a set of orthogonally arranged passages that imply a diagonal through the block, replacing the former alley-like passage (Chancellor Street), with the added benefit of a marvelous garden in between. The birch rising from behind its walls make the space equally airy and earthed, also hushed. More than a route but less than a destination, the rear court resembles the forecourt in the way it makes space for lingering at the margins of passage. **Figure 8.19**

Along the route there's another spine-split, bifold element: the pool. Not only does its basic configuration correspond to the primary order of the front facade, it doubles the points of reference in the court. On its calm side at the edge of the lower, uncovered terrace, cloud reflections tremble only slightly when passing breezes disturb the thin sheet of water. After its fall, on the secret side of the split, the water's now agitated surface and dark tones make it more akin to surrounding soil. Here, at the building's most concentrated, co-operative, and communicative center we see once again emblems of remote territories.

Richard Neutra once wrote that good buildings take account of several rings of distance surrounding them.[9] He hinted at but didn't explain relationships with conditions that are: 1) at the immediate margins of the building plot; 2) within the block or the building's immediate vicinity; and 3) the wider territory of the town—at hand, within reach, and remote. The general point this suggests with respect to Skirkanich Hall is that the sorts of figures and settings that can be called architectural are those that palpably and visibly attest to a building's engagement with each of these distances, from the fountain, into the campus neighborhood, and across the grid.

With this thesis in mind, let's consider one last time the front entry, set back from the sidewalk, within the bifold loggia, and shadowed by the split-face facade. **Figure 8.20** (see p. 208) At a rather wide distance from the front door, beyond the limit of the dark paving, and more than half the way forward from the threshold to the street edge, a line of stainless-steel posts cuts the width of the widened walk into two parts, annexing into the building's holdings the sweep that would have extended the public terrain still farther into the area that had once been the tree lawn between existing facades and the sidewalk, maintained at the sides of Skirkanich, we've seen, by common agreement. The result of the building's outlandish claim, exercised through rather modest means, is a space that is at once a footpath and a forecourt, under the sun or in the shade according to solar rhythms of days and seasons. Insofar as it is covered—of the two pavements, the deeper one permanently inscribes a shadow—this newly found space, *in antis*, also works proleptically, gathering or assembling the opportunities clustered in shadow, without losing sight of the aligned walls, sidewalk, and street, which, I've observed, extend still more widely, thanks to the principle of repetition in block formation. Nor should the facade's great height be ignored when considering the integrative (urbanizing) accomplishments of the entry, for it scales itself to the dimension of the block.

What has been discovered at the building's front and back—coupling or intermeshing with salient aspects of the ambient surround along a route—can also be seen in a fascinating but much smaller interior setting that reaches into the street: a stairway seat within the facade's lower right half. **Figure 8.21** One's first impression is of a landing behind a picture window. That's not untrue, just partial. It is a landing that is somewhat improbably filled with a bench that invites but doesn't exactly accommodate gathering, as if its purpose were to show the possibility of assembly, while not exactly fostering it. A comparable, though much, much grander instance of counter-intuitive room-making is the famous

Figure 8.21 | TWBTA, Skirkanich Hall, Philadelphia, 2006; bay window landing.

[9] Neutra, Richard, *Survival Through Design*, Oxford: Oxford University Press, 1954, pp. 168-70.

Vestibule of the Laurentian Library, where Michelangelo made a wonderful room and then proceeded to fill it up with the means of going elsewhere. Here, a reverse strategy is at play: at the top of the stairway's first run, passage is invited but delays its progress. And there's more. Thanks to the rather big sheet of glass, sitting down means both taking a rest and putting oneself on display. Is the oversized bay a place for putting students on show, like fish in a bowl, a box seat for student-spectators who want to enjoy what unfolds on the street stage? Or is it simply one of the ways of conjoining a sidewalk on the outside with a stairway within?

Unlike the image and sense conveyed by the facade's upper part, this encaved setting shows rather directly how the building is occupied, and by whom. Although the bench fills a little too much of the space, its slim horizontal seat is barely apparent from the street. It rests in front of the stair that rises to the mezzanine level, which is, in turn, limited at the rear by the wall that rises and descends with the light well, central spine, and bifold circulation space I've described. The size and extent of that wall, like the dimensions of the glass cube in the foreground, make the front bench seem undersized. But this is not the impression one gets on the landing, nor of the entire setting (bench, window wall, colored glass) when it is seen from the street. Instead, the window-wall bay could be described as a crystal in a cave that puts on show—rather like a shop window—an under- and over-sized emblem of assembly. **Figure 8.22 (see p. 209)**

I've come to understand the entire facade of Skirkanich Hall—including this little bay window—as a split-face portrait of an institution that concentrates crossovers between ambient conditions (of the city and university, the sky and soil) with its interior situations, for individual study, shared discussion, laboratory research, and so on, all stabilized by several space-splitting uprights. These elements and operations come into vivid focus at the center of the building's front: four quadrants and four depths. At the top left, the labs reach toward the afternoon light. Viewed from behind, the stacked sky-blue sheets open toward the stadium, the river, and the town. At the top right, by contrast, work and display spaces within the labs are harbored by a cupped hand whose back side is as firm as the soil on which the building stands. The surface we see is not without richness—thumb-press pock marks in vegetal green—but requires much closer distance to be sensed than what's required of the shingled sky-catchers to the left. Intermediate distances are opened by the two lower quadrants. The darker entry, at the lower left, is secondary for the building but primary for the urban ensemble; it leads directly to the rear court, and from there through another building to the next numbered street. Thus, its reach, like the glazing above, is extensive, but through the block only (the urban middle distance). The quadrant at the lower right offers entry into the school, but the bay window just above the building's name puts the institution's communicative *ethos* on display. All together, these depths and the distances they structure allow much of the building's content to appear, but also the urban conditions under which those appearances make sense.

The division between the routes that appears at the facade's base was anticipated from the distance, for the great bulk of the front is also and insistently bi-fold. Put differently, the elevation and the site plan have the same two-part structure: one side local to Skirkanich, the other side to the natural world, opening to the sky above and to the buildings all around below. The elements that constitute the break and thereby allow for the coupling are, nevertheless, entirely opposite: a gap between molded planes above and the blunt edge of splice-wall in the carved space below, the first a slim shadow within the depth of the facade and the second a thin line with the depth of the forecourt.

Why would a building adopt this integrative, communicative, or co-operative stance? And why would it do so with such insistence and display? From an institutional point of view, the intention, figuration, and story strike me as clear: the building accommodates and represents the border-crossing interdisciplinarity that is aimed at, perhaps required by research today: movement across academic territories, intending synthetic understanding. But, at a larger scale, the university interweaving with the surrounding non-academic conditions is also key, for the professional schools that ring the university's academic core have the task of mediating academic and practical knowledge. This second mediation widens the frame of reference beyond the urban block and seeks to indicate the role of the university in the town, or of scholarship in society. Here, too, insularity is overcome, or mutuality proposed.

But these social and cultural relationships can only be imagined because the building's materials, spaces, and elements demonstrate the possibilities and benefits of working co-operatively with ambient conditions existing within the block, the town, and the environment. While the world it creates has very clear limits—its stake-in-the-ground stance is vividly distinct—Skirkanich Hall also has very far reach, into a network of relationships that is, in the end, what matters above all else.

Figure 8.7 | TWBTA, Skirkanich Hall, Philadelphia, 2006; rear court and facade.

Architectural Depth as Urban Communication

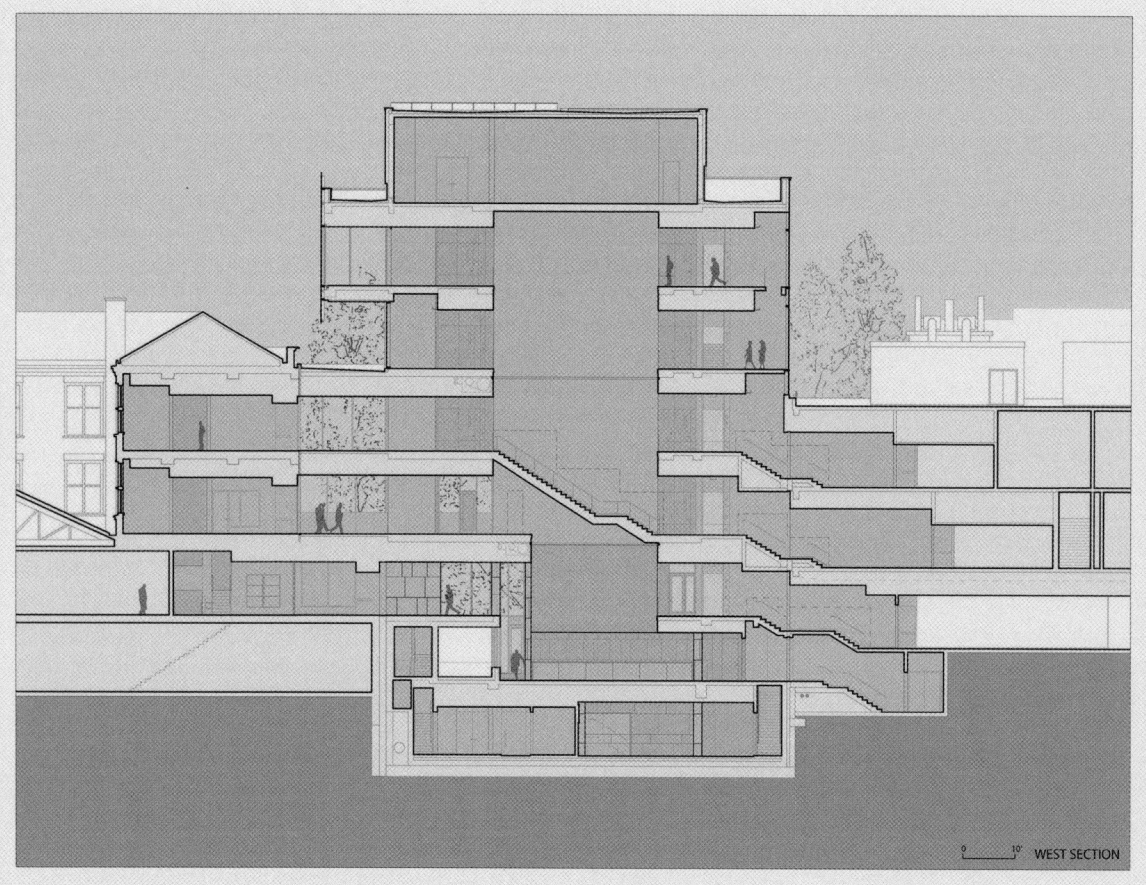

Figure 8.12 | TWBTA, Skirkanich Hall, Philadelphia, 2006; cross-section.

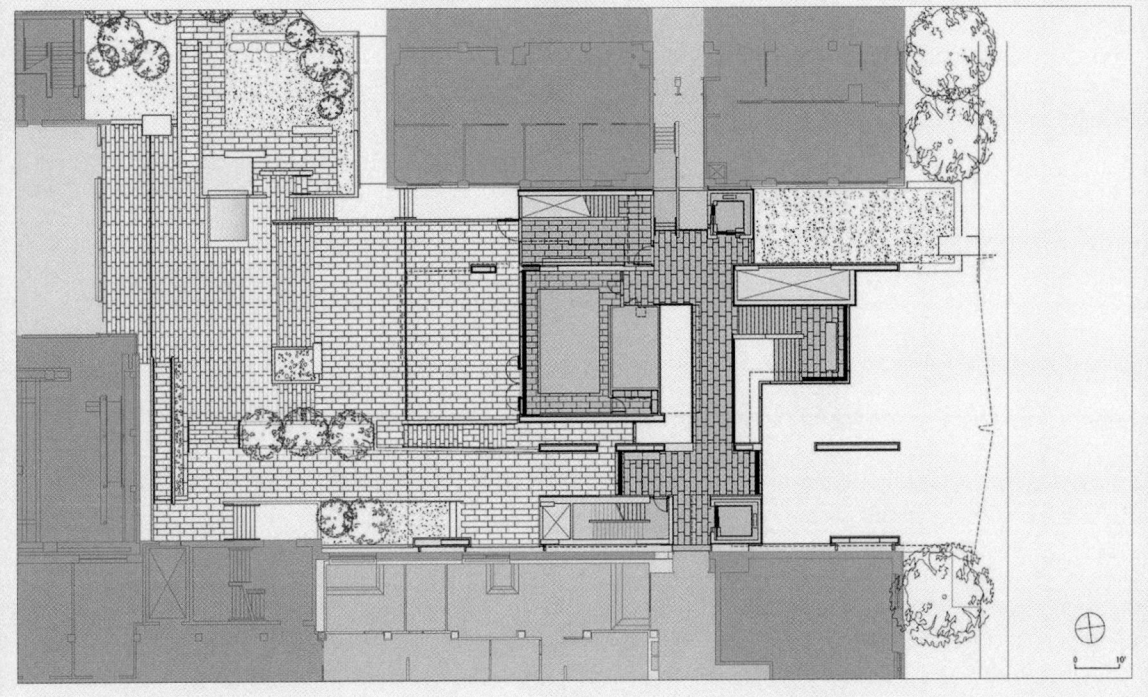

Figure 8.16 | TWBTA, Skirkanich Hall, Philadelphia, 2006; ground plan.

Architectural Depth as Urban Communication

Figure 8.18 | TWBTA, Skirkanich Hall, Philadelphia, 2006; courtyard.

Figure 8.20 | TWBTA, Skirkanich Hall, Philadelphia, 2006; east facade detail.

Figure 8.22 | TWBTA, Skirkanich Hall, Philadelphia, 2006; bay window landing in the lower right quadrant.

Joseph Rykwert

Conclusion

Projecting Urbanity

The group of studies of very different buildings—or groups of them—which you have just examined have this in common: they considered each of the buildings as an urban proposition, working out what remains of the building in your consciousness once you have shut the door behind you and while you may be physically absent from its immediate environment. For all that the building remains lodged in your memory, certainly in your visual memory, as does its physical context into which you step, once you have passed the threshold and closed the door behind you.

Such a building, or even a group of them, inevitably becomes a factor in your mental landscape, which therefore challenges interpretation, as does any statement directly or indirectly presented to you. Such an interpretation will have to take account of the structure and organization of the buildings and their grouping (if they are several) but also of the context, the way it fits in with or contrasts with its environment.

Inevitably, such an interpretation assumes that a building has something in its nature analogous to an utterance, that it can be "read" and even parsed like a verbal construct and so become a part of the world of communication; such an assumption may now be taken for granted in some contexts, yet it may have once—even quite recently—seemed quite alien to any discourse connected with building.

The great variety of the work and the locations of the buildings that have been discussed in this book, from the 1930s offices of a combative trade union in Mexico City to a more recent church in Korea or university building in Philadelphia, suggests that what the authors of these studies do have in common is their analogous approach to how a building might be "read" or even "construed".

This inevitably involves some account of how the formal properties of the building being examined might relate, whether consciously and intentionally or yet instinctively to the way the building may be used; and, if time has passed since they were designed and realized, how they have been adapted to accommodate these changes and how whatever vegetation surrounds them has modified their use and appearance.

Time is therefore an essential dimension to these readings, and in this, too, these essays make a claim on your attention as offering a specific response, which the passage of time demands.

Taken together these ways of reading and understanding buildings as meaningful constructs offer an approach with no exact precedent, and which demands or requires an adjustment of any previous theoretical position of their architects or of any earlier of their students, which it will certainly enrich.

Figure 9.1 | Herbert Bayer, *Lonely Metropolitan*, 1932; photomontage.

Biographies

David Leatherbarrow is Emeritus Professor of Architecture, University of Pennsylvania and Foreign Dean, Southeast University, China. Born in 1953 in the United States and educated in the US and England, he has lectured throughout the world and held guest professorships in Britain, Denmark, and China. Questions of how architecture appears, is perceived, and shapes topography direct his research. Among his books are *Building Time: Architecture, Event, and Experience* (2020), *Three Cultural Ecologies*, with Richard Wesley (2018), *Architecture Oriented Otherwise* (2009), *Topographical Stories* (2004), *Uncommon Ground* (2000), and two books co-authored with Mohsen Mostafavi, *Surface Architecture* (2002) and *On Weathering* (1993). In 2020, he was awarded the Topaz Medallion, the highest award given by the AIA and ASCA for excellence in architectural education.

Tonkao Panin is an architect and Professor at the Faculty of Architecture, Silpakorn University, Thailand. She has advanced and professional degrees from the University of Pennsylvania, University of Houston, and Silpakorn University. She is also the founder of Research Studio Panin, an architectural design and research practice. Her scholarly research and publications focus on 19th-century architectural theory in relation to cross-cultural practices from the early 20th century until today.

Esra Şahin Burat received her BArch from the Middle East Technical University, MArch from Virginia Polytechnic Institute and State University, and MS and PhD from the University of Pennsylvania. Her research interests include theories of nature, materials, orientation, and representation in architecture, with particular focus on the relationship between buildings and the natural/cultural environment. She previously taught at Mersin University, participated in design projects in urban archaeological sites, conducted interdisciplinary research on shelter design in extreme climates, and served as the vice president of Mersin Chamber of Architects. She is currently an Associate Professor at Southeast University School of Architecture.

Juan Manuel Heredia is an Associate Professor of Architecture at Portland State University. He studied at Universidad Iberoamericana and received an MS and PhD from the University of Pennsylvania. He has taught in Mexico, the United States, Colombia, and England. His work has been widely published. He co-organized the Second International Architecture and Phenomenology Conference in Kyoto (2009) and The Place of Theory in Contemporary Architectural Practice and Education conference in Bangkok (2013). His research focuses on Latin American modern architecture. He is author of *The First Modern Building in Mexico*, and co-author, with Miquel Adrià, of *Juan Sordo*

Madaleno (1916–1985), both published bilingually by Arquine. He is also co-editor, with Nicholas Temple and Andrzej Piotrowski, of the *Routledge Handbook on the Reception of Classical Architecture*.

Daphna Half is an architect and an architectural historian and theorist. Her work focuses on typology, public space, craft, and topography, as these issues were manifest in approaches to design in Palestine-Israel during the British Mandate and the first decades of statehood. Her work examines how these disciplinary themes reflected a broader search for a new national style undertaken by local architects since the 1920s. She holds a PhD from the University of Pennsylvania, an MA from Tel Aviv University School of Philosophy, and a BArch from Tel Aviv University School of Architecture. She was a research fellow at the Azrieli Architectural Archive Scholars Program at the Tel Aviv Museum of Art, and a postdoctoral fellow at the Technion, Israel Institute of Technology. She established her architectural practice in Tel Aviv in 2017.

Stephen Anderson is a licensed architect and architectural educator in Philadelphia, where he serves as Associate Professor of Instruction in graduate and undergraduate architectural history, theory, and studio courses at the Tyler School of Art and Architecture at Temple University. His main areas of interest are the ethical and civic dimensions of architecture; the intersection of cities, nature, and architecture; and the natural tensions and potentials that arise between architectural theatricality and the practices and institutions of everyday life. His recent book, *Sverre Fehn and the City: Rethinking Architecture's Urban Premises* (Routledge, 2023), explores the embodiment of urbanity in the architectural works of the Norwegian Pritzker Prize laureate.

Jin Baek is a Professor at the Department of Architecture and Architectural Engineering, Seoul National University. He acquired his BS from Seoul National University, MArch from Yale University, and completed his PhD in the history and theory of architecture at the University of Pennsylvania. His research focuses on phenomenology-based design theory and environmental ethics. He is the author of *Nothingness: Tadao Ando's Christian Sacred Space* (Routledge, 2009) and *Architecture as the Ethics of Climate* (Routledge, 2016). His articles have been published in various journals, such as the *Architectural Research Quarterly*, *Journal of Architectural Education*, *Architectural Theory Review*, and *Center*.

Joseph Rykwert (born 1926) is Paul Philippe Cret Professor Emeritus of Architecture at the University of Pennsylvania, and one of the foremost architectural historians and critics of his generation. He is the author of many influential works on architecture, including *The Idea of a Town* (1963), *On Adam's House in Paradise* (1972), *The Dancing Column* (1996) and *The Seduction of Place* (2000). All his books have been translated into several languages, and he is the 2014 recipient of the RIBA Gold Medal.

Projecting Urbanity

List of illustrations

		1	**Introduction**

6	Figure 1.1	Robert Rauschenberg, *Watermark*, 1973. Courtesy of the Robert Rauschenberg Foundation.
11	Figure 1.2	North Broad, Philadelphia, c. 2010. Photo David Leatherbarrow.
11	Figure 1.3	Ambrogio Lorenzetti, *Effects of Good Government in the City* (left) and *Effects of Good Government in the Country* (right), Siena, 1338-9; detail.
25	Figure 1.4	Doorstep, from Aldo van Eyck, "The In-between Realm." Photo Aldo van Eyck Archive.
12	Figure 1.5	Hand doorknocker, Tavira, Portugal, nd. Photo Creative Commons.
12	Figure 1.6	Cave of Altamira Give, Santillana del Mar, Cantabria, Spain, 34,000 BC. Photo Creative Commons.
26	Figure 1.7	James Tissot, *Shop Girl*, c. 1885. Courtesy of Art Gallery of Ontario.
27	Figure 1.8	Streetside bar, Philadelphia, 2019. Photo David Leatherbarrow.
14	Figure 1.9	Window onto the Campo, Siena, c. 1980. Photo David Leatherbarrow.
28	Figure 1.10	O'Donnell+Tuomey, Lyric Theater, Belfast, 2011; entry threshold. Photo O'Donnell+Tuomey.
17	Figure 1.11	Uncontrolled burning, Detroit, nd. Photo Creative Commons.
17	Figure 1.12	Controlled burning, Kansas, nd. Photo Creative Commons.
19	Figure 1.13	Abandoned house within cleared lots, Detroit, nd. Photo Creative Commons.
30	Figure 1.14	Italian market, Philadelphia, 2009. Photo David Leatherbarrow.
23	Figure 1.15	Dov Karmi and Zeev Rechter, Tel Aviv Culture Complex, Tel Aviv, 1951. Photo David Leatherbarrow.

		2	**Within and Beyond Architectural Boundaries**

47	Figure 2.1	Vienna map, 1848; Cartographer: W.B. Clarke, Engraver: J. Henshall. London: Charles Knight.
48	Figure 2.2	The Ringstrasse development, Vienna, 1860; plan. Courtesy of Österreichische Nationalbibliothek.
37	Figure 2.3	Gottfried Semper and Carl von Hasenauer, Kaiserforum, Vienna, 1869; plan. Courtesy of Österreichische Nationalbibliothek.
40	Figure 2.4	Otto Wagner, Hietzing Station, Vienna, 1894; elevation, drawn by Joseph Maria Olbrich. Wagner, Otto, *Einige Skizzen, Projekte und ausgeführte Bauwerke*, Vienna: Anton Schroll & Co, 1889, 1897, 1906, 1922, vol. II, pl. 61.
50	Figure 2.5	Otto Wagner, Hietzing Station, Vienna, 1894; plan. Wagner, Otto, *Einige Skizzen, Projekte und ausgeführte Bauwerke*, Vienna: Anton Schroll & Co, 1889, 1897, 1906, 1922.
51	Figure 2.6	Otto Wagner, Unt-Döbling Station, Vienna, 1895-6; elevation. Wagner, Otto, *Einige Skizzen, Projekte und ausgeführte Bauwerke*, Vienna: Anton Schroll & Co, 1889, 1897, 1906, 1922, vol. II, pl. 21.

List of illustrations

40	Figure 2.7	Otto Wagner, Währinger Strasse viaduct, Vienna, 1895-6; elevation and plan. Wagner, Otto, *Einige Skizzen, Projekte und ausgeführte Bauwerke*, Vienna: Anton Schroll & Co, 1889, 1897, 1906, 1922, vol. II, pl. 21.
41	Figure 2.8	Otto Wagner, Karlsplatz, Vienna, 1898-9; masterplan around the area of Karlsplatz and Naschmarkt. Wagner, Otto, *Einige Skizzen, Projekte und ausgeführte Bauwerke*, Vienna: Anton Schroll & Co, 1889, 1897, 1906, 1922, vol. II, pl. 46.
52	Figure 2.9	Otto Wagner, Karlsplatz, Vienna, 1898-9, first design against the backdrop of the Technische Hochschule; plan. Wagner, Otto, *Einige Skizzen, Projekte und ausgeführte Bauwerke*, Vienna: Anton Schroll & Co, 1889, 1897, 1906, 1922, vol. III, pl. 2.
52	Figure 2.10	Otto Wagner, Karlsplatz, Vienna, 1898-9; final design, plan and elevation. Wagner, Otto, *Einige Skizzen, Projekte und ausgeführte Bauwerke*, Vienna: Anton Schroll & Co, 1889, 1897, 1906, 1922, vol. III, pl. 3.
53	Figure 2.11	Otto Wagner, Karlsplatz, Vienna, 1898-9; frontal view. Wagner, Otto, *Einige Skizzen, Projekte und ausgeführte Bauwerke*, Vienna: Anton Schroll & Co, 1889, 1897, 1906, 1922, vol. III, pl. 3.
54	Figure 2.12	Kaiser Franz Josef-Stadtmuseum, Vienna, 1901-2; competition entries. Sitte, Camillo, *Die Ergebnisse der Vorconcurrenz zu dem Baue des Kaiser Franz Joseph Museums der Stadt Wien*, Vienna: Waldheim, 1902 and *Allgemeine Bauzeitung*, LXVII, 1902, pp. 61-6.
43	Figure 2.13	Max Fabiani, Kaiser Franz Josef-Stadtmuseum, Vienna, 1902. Sitte, Camillo, *Die Ergebnisse der Vorconcurrenz zu dem Baue des Kaiser Franz Joseph Museums der Stadt Wien*, Vienna: Waldheim, 1902 and *Allgemeine Bauzeitung*, LXVII, 1902, pp. 61-6.
55	Figure 2.14	Otto Wagner, Kaiser Franz Josef-Stadtmuseum, Vienna, 1903. Wagner, Otto, *Einige Skizzen, Projekte und ausgeführte Bauwerke*, Vienna: Anton Schroll & Co, 1889, 1897, 1906, 1922, vol. III, pl. 33.
56	Figure 2.15	Otto Wagner, Karlsplatz, Vienna, 1909; bird's-eye view. Wagner, Otto, *Einige Skizzen, Projekte und ausgeführte Bauwerke*, Vienna: Anton Schroll & Co, 1889, 1897, 1906, 1922, vol. III, pl. 32a.
58	Figure 2.16	Otto Wagner, Kaiser Franz Josef-Stadtmuseum, Vienna, 1909; perspective showing enclosed Karlsplatz with the Kaiser Franz Josef-Stadtmuseum, Karlskirche and Technische Hochschule. Wagner, Otto, *Einige Skizzen, Projekte und ausgeführte Bauwerke*, Vienna: Anton Schroll & Co, 1889, 1897, 1906, 1922, vol. III, pl. 32.
43	Figure 2.17	Otto Wagner, Kaiser Franz Josef-Stadtmuseum, Vienna, 1909; front facade. Wagner, Otto, *Einige Skizzen, Projekte und ausgeführte Bauwerke*, Vienna: Anton Schroll & Co, 1889, 1897, 1906, 1922, vol. III, pl. 28.
32	Figure 2.18	Otto Wagner, Kaiser Franz Josef-Stadtmuseum, Vienna, 1910; scale model of two bays of Kaiser Franz Josef-Stadtmuseum on Karlsplatz. Courtesy of Historisches Museum der Stadt Wien.
44	Figure 2.19	Otto Wagner, Länderbank, Vienna, 1883-4; plan. Geretsegger, Heinz and Max Peintner, *Otto Wagner 1841-1918, The Expanding City, The Beginning of Modern Architecture*, London: Pall Mall Press, 1970, p. 147.
45	Figure 2.20	Camillo Sitte, Votive Church area, Vienna, 1889; plan. Sitte, Camillo, *Der Städtebau nach seinen künstlerischen Grundsätzen*, Vienna: Prachner, 1972, p. 163.

	3	**City as Compass and Calendar**	
78	Figure 3.1	Le Corbusier, A Contemporary City for Three Million Inhabitants, 1922, published without color and captioned in *The City of Tomorrow*, Cambridge, MA: MIT Press, 1971, pp. 246–7. © FLC/ADAGP, Paris–SACK, Seoul, 2022.	
65	Figure 3.2	Le Corbusier, sketch of "man, the medium," *La Ville radieuse*, Boulogne: Éditions de l'Architecture d'Aujourd'hui, 1935, p. 83. © FLC/ADAGP, Paris–SACK, Seoul, 2022.	
80	Figure 3.3	Promotional brochure of the Société Immobilière de Paris-Parc des Princes, Paris, early 1930s; site plan showing the means of transportation to the city center. © FLC/ADAGP, Paris–SACK, Seoul, 2022.	
60	Figure 3.4	Le Corbusier and Pierre Jeanneret, 24NC, Paris, 1931–4; east facade, as seen from rue Nungesser et Coli. Photo Albin Salaün. © FLC/ADAGP, Paris–SACK, Seoul, 2022.	
67	Figure 3.5	Le Corbusier and Pierre Jeanneret, 24NC, Paris, 1931–4, west facade, as seen from rue de la Tourelle. Photo James Frazer Stirling. James Stirling/Michael Wilford fonds. Canadian Centre for Architecture.	
81	Figure 3.6	Le Corbusier and Pierre Jeanneret, 24NC, Paris, 1931–4; plan drawing of the basement, dated October 12, 1931 (corrected February 26, 1932). © FLC/ADAGP, Paris–SACK, Seoul, 2022.	
67	Figure 3.7	Le Corbusier and Pierre Jeanneret, 24NC, Paris, 1931–4, "a fragment of the facade and the entry porch," Le Corbusier and Pierre Jeanneret, *Œuvre complète volume 2 1929–34*, Basel, Boston, Berlin: Birkhäuser, 2006, p. 147. © FLC/ADAGP, Paris–SACK, Seoul, 2022.	
68	Figure 3.8	Le Corbusier and Pierre Jeanneret, 24NC, Paris, 1931–4; living room of the first-floor apartment, Le Corbusier and Pierre Jeanneret, *Œuvre complète volume 2 1929–34*, Basel, Boston, Berlin: Birkhäuser, 2006, p. 153. © FLC/ADAGP, Paris–SACK, Seoul, 2022.	
68	Figure 3.9	Le Corbusier and Pierre Jeanneret, 24NC, Paris, 1931–4; dining area of the second-floor apartment, Le Corbusier and Pierre Jeanneret, *Œuvre complète volume 2 1929–34*, Basel, Boston, Berlin: Birkhäuser, 2006, p. 153. © FLC/ADAGP, Paris–SACK, Seoul, 2022.	
82	Figure 3.10	Le Corbusier and Pierre Jeanneret, 24NC, Paris, 1931–4; plan of the seventh floor. © FLC/ADAGP, Paris–SACK, Seoul, 2022.	
84	Figure 3.11	Le Corbusier, photo collage panel titled *Habitation*, exhibited at the Pavillon des Temps Nouveaux, Paris International Exposition, 1937. Photograph of the 1:2 scale reconstruction realized by Arthur Rüegg and Publigraph, exhibited at Musée des beaux-arts La Chaux-de-Fonds, 2012. Photo Aline Henchoz. Courtesy of Musée des beaux-arts La Chaux-de-Fonds.	
77	Figure 3.12	Le Corbusier and Pierre Jeanneret, 24NC, Paris, 1931–4; Le Corbusier in the roof garden, 1952. Photo Lucien Hervé. Getty Research Institute, Los Angeles (2002.R.41). © J. Paul Getty Trust.	
88	Figure 3.13	Le Corbusier and Pierre Jeanneret, 24NC, Paris, 1931–4; longitudinal section drawing of the seventh and the eighth floors. © FLC/ADAGP, Paris–SACK, Seoul, 2022.	
86	Figure 3.14	Le Corbusier and Pierre Jeanneret, 24NC, Paris, 1931–4; view of the roof terrace. Photo Joël Plasse Le Caisne. © FLC/ADAGP, Paris–SACK, Seoul, 2022.	

List of illustrations

89	Figure 3.15	A house with a courtyard; sketch by Le Corbusier, captioned "Eyoub 1911." © FLC/ADAGP, Paris–SACK, Seoul, 2022.
86	Figure 3.16	A cemetery, Istanbul, 1911; photograph by Le Corbusier, inscribed "Constantinopel, Cemetery Eyüp." © FLC/ADAGP, Paris–SACK, Seoul, 2022.
87	Figure 3.17	Le Corbusier and Pierre Jeanneret, 24NC, Paris, 1931–4; detail from an early section drawing of the living room and the roof garden, dated July 7, 1932. © FLC/ADAGP, Paris–SACK, Seoul, 2022.
86	Figure 3.18	Le Corbusier and Pierre Jeanneret, 24NC, Paris, 1931–4; Le Corbusier in his living room, 1946. Photo Nina Leen. The LIFE Picture Collection © Time Inc.
90	Figure 3.19	Le Corbusier and Pierre Jeanneret, 24NC, Paris, 1931–4; Le Corbusier in his living room, 1954. Photo Ida Kar. National Portrait Gallery, London.
91	Figure 3.20	A café, Istanbul, 1911; sketch by Le Corbusier, captioned "Le café de Mahmoud Pasha." © FLC/ADAGP, Paris–SACK, Seoul, 2022.
	4	**Urban Topography and the Workers' City**
92	Figure 4.1	Juan O'Gorman, Mexican Cinema Workers Union building, Mexico City, 1936–7; exterior. From *Arquitectura y Decoración*, no. 3, 1937.
108	Figure 4.2	Calla Orozco y Berra, Colonia Guerrero, Mexico City, December 12, 1939. Courtesy of Museo Archivo de la Fotografía.
109	Figure 4.3	Calla Orozco y Berra, Colonia Guerrero, Mexico City, November 1, 1937. Courtesy of Museo Archivo de la Fotografía.
110	Figure 4.4	Juan O'Gorman, Mexican Cinema Workers Union building, 1936–7; perspective. Courtesy of Universidad Autónoma Metropolitana, Azcapotzalco–Fondo Especial de la Coordinación de Servicios de Información.
111	Figure 4.5	Juan O'Gorman, Mexican Cinema Workers Union building; floor plans. From *Arquitectura y Decoración*, no. 3, 1937.
112	Figure 4.6	Members of the union, c. 1923. From Eco Cinematografista.
99	Figure 4.7	Juan O'Gorman, Mexican Cinema Workers Union building, Mexico City, 1936–7; facade. From *Arquitectura y Decoración*, no. 3, 1937.
100	Figure 4.8	The union's band and dancers occupying the street and seen from the balcony, 1954. Courtesy of the archive of José Mondragón Robles.
101	Figure 4.9	The union building artificially lit and decorated for the union's 21st anniversary celebrations, 1954. Courtesy of the archive of José Mondragón Robles.
102	Figure 4.10	Casa de los Mascarones, Mexico City, late 18th century.
102	Figure 4.11	Juan O'Gorman, Frances Toor House, Mexico City, 1935. © Esther Born Estate/Center for Creative Photography, University of Arizona.
114	Figure 4.12	Aerial view of Colonia Guerrero, Church of San Fernando (bottom center), SMC building (bottom right), and Monument to the Revolution (center right), c. 1945. Courtesy of Fundación ICA.
103	Figure 4.13	Jerónimo de Balbás, Church of San Fernando, Mexico City, 1736–55.
103	Figure 4.14	Juan O'Gorman, *Retable of Independence*, Museo Nacional de Historia, Mexico City, 1960–1; detail.
113	Figure 4.15	Juan O'Gorman, Mexican Cinema Workers Union building, Mexico City, 1936–7. Courtesy of the archive of José Mondragón Robles.

105	Figure 4.16	Raising the strike flag, early 1970s. From Eco Cinematografista.
106	Figure 4.17	Detail of Figures 4.2 and 4.4.
116	Figure 4.18	Juan O'Gorman, Project for the National Union of Telephone Workers building, Mexico City, c. 1937; perspective. Courtesy of Universidad Autónoma Metropolitana, Azcapotzalco – Fondo Especial de la Coordinación de Servicios de Información.
117	Figure 4.19	Juan O'Gorman, Project for the CTM headquarters, Mexico City, c. 1937. Courtesy of Universidad Autónoma Metropolitana, Azcapotzalco – Fondo Especial de la Coordinación de Servicios de Información.
	5	**Assembling Differences**
131	Figure 5.1	Dov Karmi and Zeev Rechter, Heichal HaTarbut concert hall, Tel Aviv, 1957; view from Yaakov Garden. Photo David Leatherbarrow.
132	Figure 5.2	Dov Karmi and Zeev Rechter, Heichal HaTarbut concert hall, Tel Aviv, 1957; survey plan. Courtesy of Dov Karmi archive, Tel Aviv.
133	Figure 5.3	Dov Karmi and Zeev Rechter, Heichal HaTarbut concert hall, Tel Aviv, 1957; perspective. Courtesy of Dov Karmi archive, Tel Aviv.
133	Figure 5.4	Zeev Rechter and Yaakov Rechter, the Helena Rubinstein Art Pavilion, Tel Aviv, 1959; north elevation. Photo Yaron Mirlin. Courtesy of Rechter Center for Architecture Archive, Tel Aviv.
134	Figure 5.5	Rechter-Zarhi-Peri Architects in collaboration with Avraham Karavan, Yaakov Garden, Tel Aviv, 1965; perspective looking south. Courtesy of Rechter Center for Architecture Archive, Tel Aviv.
122	Figure 5.6	Dov Karmi and Zeev Rechter, Heichal HaTarbut concert hall, Tel Aviv, 1957; bird's-eye view of concert hall and Yaakov Garden. Photo Isaac Percal. Courtesy of Rechter Center for Architecture Archive, Tel Aviv.
122	Figure 5.7	Dov Karmi and Zeev Rechter, Heichal HaTarbut concert hall, Tel Aviv, 1957; site plan. Courtesy of Rechter Center for Architecture Archive, Tel Aviv.
123	Figure 5.8	Rechter-Zarhi-Peri Architects in collaboration with Avraham Karavan, Yaakov Garden, Tel Aviv, 1965; model. Photo Isaac Percal. Courtesy of Rechter Center for Architecture Archive, Tel Aviv.
123	Figure 5.9	Rechter-Zarhi-Peri Architects in collaboration with Avraham Karavan, Yaakov Garden, Tel Aviv, 1965; garden's second story. Photo Isaac Percal. Courtesy of Rechter Center for Architecture Archive, Tel Aviv.
118	Figure 5.10	Rechter-Zarhi-Peri Architects in collaboration with Avraham Karavan, Yaakov Garden, Tel Aviv, 1965; garden's second-story view toward concert hall. Photo Isaac Percal. Courtesy of Rechter Center for Architecture Archive, Tel Aviv.
136	Figure 5.11	Dov Karmi and Zeev Rechter, Heichal HaTarbut concert hall, Tel Aviv, 1957; interior view of concert hall. Photo Itzhak Kalter. Courtesy of Rechter Center for Architecture Archive, Tel Aviv.
137	Figure 5.12	Dov Karmi and Zeev Rechter, Heichal HaTarbut concert hall, Tel Aviv, 1957; interior view of foyer. Photo Itzhak Kalter. Courtesy of Rechter Center for Architecture Archive, Tel Aviv.
123	Figure 5.13	Dov Karmi and Zeev Rechter, Heichal HaTarbut concert hall, Tel Aviv, 1957; interior views of foyer and concert hall. Photo Itzhak Kalter. Courtesy of Rechter Center for Architecture Archive, Tel Aviv.

138	Figure 5.14	Dov Karmi and Zeev Rechter, Heichal HaTarbut concert hall, Tel Aviv, 1957; elevations. Courtesy of Rechter Center for Architecture Archive, Tel Aviv.
123	Figure 5.15	Dov Karmi and Zeev Rechter, Heichal HaTarbut concert hall, Tel Aviv, 1957; south and east elevations. Photo Itzhak Kalter. Courtesy of Rechter Center for Architecture Archive, Tel Aviv.
140	Figure 5.16	Rechter-Zarhi-Peri Architects in collaboration with Avraham Karavan, Yaakov Garden, Tel Aviv, 1965; garden's second-story view toward concert hall. Photo Studio Keren Or. Courtesy of Rechter Center for Architecture Archive, Tel Aviv.
141	Figure 5.17	Dov Karmi and Zeev Rechter, Heichal HaTarbut concert hall, Tel Aviv, 1957; perspective. Courtesy of Rechter Center for Architecture Archive, Tel Aviv.
125	Figure 5.18	Dov Karmi and Zeev Rechter, Heichal HaTarbut concert hall, Tel Aviv, 1957; site plan. Courtesy of Rechter Center for Architecture Archive, Tel Aviv.
125	Figure 5.19	Dov Karmi and Zeev Rechter, Heichal HaTarbut concert hall, Tel Aviv, 1957; perspective. Courtesy of Rechter Center for Architecture Archive, Tel Aviv.
125	Figure 5.20	Dov Karmi and Zeev Rechter, Heichal HaTarbut concert hall, Tel Aviv, 1957; perspective. Courtesy of Rechter Center for Architecture Archive, Tel Aviv.
142	Figure 5.21	Rechter-Zarhi-Peri Architects in collaboration with Avraham Karavan, Yaakov Garden, Tel Aviv, 1965; garden's second-story view toward ramp and Chen Boulevard. Photo Studio Keren Or. Courtesy of Rechter Center for Architecture Archive, Tel Aviv.
143	Figure 5.22	Rechter-Zarhi-Peri Architects in collaboration with Avraham Karavan, Yaakov Garden, Tel Aviv, 1965; view west on Tarsat Avenue. Photo Studio Keren Or. Courtesy of Rechter Center for Architecture Archive, Tel Aviv.
144	Figure 5.23	Yaakov Rechter and Avraham Karavan, Yaakov Garden, Tel Aviv, 1965; view south to public square and Rothschild Boulevard. Photo Isaac Percal. Courtesy of Rechter Center for Architecture Archive, Tel Aviv.
145	Figure 5.24	Yaakov Rechter and Avraham Karavan, Yaakov Garden, Tel Aviv, 1965; garden view toward concert hall. Photo Studio Keren Or. Courtesy of Rechter Center for Architecture Archive, Tel Aviv.
146	Figure 5.25	Dov Karmi and Zeev Rechter, Heichal HaTarbut concert hall, Tel Aviv, 1957; view of the Heichal HaTarbut concert hall and Yaakov Garden from public square. Photo David Leatherbarrow.
	6	**Of Architecture, Its Artifacts, and the City**
148	Figure 6.1	Sverre Fehn, Norwegian Pavilion for Expo '58, Brussels, 1958; entry. Photo Reginald Hugo de Burgh Galwey/RIBA Collections.
150	Figure 6.2	Sverre Fehn, Norwegian Pavilion for Expo '58, Brussels, 1958; Avenue of Nations, looking west (Norwegian Pavilion, middle right). Courtesy of Department of Architecture and Urban Planning, University of Ghent.

162	Figure 6.3	Sverre Fehn, Norwegian Pavilion for Expo '58, Brussels, 1958; view from street. Photo John Donat/RIBA Collections.
161	Figure 6.4	Sverre Fehn, Norwegian Pavilion for Expo '58, Brussels, 1958; perspective drawing of street facade. Courtesy of Nasjonalmuseet, Oslo.
152	Figure 6.5	Sverre Fehn, Norwegian Pavilion for Expo '58, Brussels, 1958; detail of garden plan showing step with planted gap. Courtesy of Nasjonalmuseet, Oslo.
152	Figure 6.6	Sverre Fehn, Norwegian Pavilion for Expo '58, Brussels, 1958; site plan. Courtesy of Norsk Teknisk Museum, Oslo.
161	Figure 6.7	Sverre Fehn, Norwegian Pavilion for Expo '58, Brussels, 1958; section drawings from competition entry. Courtesy of Norsk Teknisk Museum, Oslo.
153	Figure 6.8	Sverre Fehn, Norwegian Pavilion for Expo '58, Brussels, 1958; northeast corner of perimeter glazing with Plexiglas columns (architecture critic Theo Crosby in foreground). Photo Monica Pidgeon/RIBA Collections.
153	Figure 6.9	Sverre Fehn, Norwegian Pavilion for Expo '58, Brussels, 1958; site during construction (Reima Pietilä's Finnish Pavilion seen in background to the right). Courtesy of Nasjonalmuseet, Oslo.
155	Figure 6.10	Expo '58, Brussels, 1958; the Atomium rises in background. Photo Hans Lachmann.
164	Figure 6.11	Sverre Fehn, Norwegian Pavilion for Expo '58, Brussels, 1958; north portion of gallery, looking northeast. Photo Reginald Hugo de Burgh Galwey/RIBA Collections.
165	Figure 6.12	Sverre Fehn, Norwegian Pavilion for Expo '58, Brussels, 1958; diagram from competition drawings indicating zones of display. Courtesy of Norsk Teknisk Museum, Oslo.
156	Figure 6.13	Sverre Fehn, Villa Norrköping, Sweden, 1964; corner cabinet from garden. Courtesy of Nasjonalmuseet, Oslo.
157	Figure 6.14	Sverre Fehn, Villa Norrköping, Sweden, 1964; looking through corner cabinet into kitchen. Courtesy of Norsk Teknisk Museum, Oslo.
157	Figure 6.15	Sverre Fehn, Villa Norrköping, Sweden, 1964; corner cabinet from dining room. Photo Per Berntsen.
166	Figure 6.16	Sverre Fehn, Norwegian Pavilion for Expo '58, Brussels, 1958; view from interior toward northwest sculpture garden, with glass display in foreground. Courtesy of Nasjonalmuseet, Oslo.
167	Figure 6.17	Sverre Fehn, Norwegian Pavilion for Expo '58, Brussels, 1958; display tables, construction details. Courtesy of Nasjonalmuseet, Oslo.
168	Figure 6.18	Sverre Fehn, Norwegian Pavilion for Expo '58, Brussels, 1958; conceptual perspective collage of gallery. Courtesy of Nasjonalmuseet, Oslo.
160	Figure 6.19	Sverre Fehn, Norwegian Pavilion for Expo '58, Brussels, 1958; seated in sculpture garden, with small pond immediately below the artwork on the wall to the left. Photo Monica Pidgeon/RIBA Collections.
160	Figure 6.20	Sverre Fehn, Norwegian Pavilion for Expo '58, Brussels, 1958; drawing of entry portico, with bench, looking west. Courtesy of Norsk Teknisk Museum, Oslo.

List of illustrations

	7	**The Terrain of Urban Institutions**
185	Figure 7.1	H-Sang Seung, Gudeok Presbyterian Church, Busan, South Korea, 2008; exterior. Photo JongOh Kim. Courtesy of IROJE Architects & Planners.
178	Figure 7.2	H-Sang Seung, Gudeok Presbyterian Church, Busan, South Korea, 2008; plan sketch for the church. Courtesy of IROJE Architects & Planners.
178	Figure 7.3	H-Sang Seung, Gudeok Presbyterian Church, Busan, South Korea, 2008; exterior sketch for the church. Courtesy of IROJE Architects & Planners.
186	Figure 7.4	H-Sang Seung, Gudeok Presbyterian Church, Busan, South Korea, 2008; second level plan. Courtesy of IROJE Architects & Planners.
186	Figure 7.5	H-Sang Seung, Gudeok Presbyterian Church, Busan, South Korea, 2008; ground floor plan. Courtesy of IROJE Architects & Planners.
179	Figure 7.6	H-Sang Seung, Sujoldang, Seoul, South Korea, 1992; plan. Courtesy of IROJE Architects & Planners.
179	Figure 7.7	H-Sang Seung, Sujoldang, Seoul, South Korea, 1992; view toward the *madang* (courtyard) from the living room. Photo Osamu Murai. Courtesy of IROJE Architects & Planners.
179	Figure 7.8	H-Sang Seung, Sujoldang, Seoul, South Korea, 1992; original setting of the *madang*. Photo Osamu Murai. Courtesy of IROJE Architects & Planners.
187	Figure 7.9	H-Sang Seung, Gudeok Presbyterian Church, Busan, South Korea, 2008; entrance view. Photo JongOh Kim. Courtesy of IROJE Architects & Planners.
188	Figure 7.10	H-Sang Seung, Gudeok Presbyterian Church, Busan, South Korea, 2008; interior. Photo JongOh Kim. Courtesy of IROJE Architects & Planners.
170	Figure 7.11	H-Sang Seung, Gudeok Presbyterian Church, Busan, South Korea, 2008; interior. Photo JongOh Kim. Courtesy of IROJE Architects & Planners.
190	Figure 7.12	H-Sang Seung, Gudeok Presbyterian Church, Busan, South Korea, 2008; interior. Photo JongOh Kim. Courtesy of IROJE Architects & Planners.
	8	**Architectural Depth as Urban Communication**
192	Figure 8.1	Tod Williams Billie Tsien Architects (TWBTA), Skirkanich Hall, Philadelphia, 2006; street-front view. Photo David Leatherbarrow.
194	Figure 8.2	TWBTA, Skirkanich Hall, Philadelphia, 2006; front facade detail. Photo David Leatherbarrow.
194	Figure 8.3	TWBTA, Skirkanich Hall, Philadelphia, 2006; sidewalk view. Photo David Leatherbarrow.
194	Figure 8.4	TWBTA, Skirkanich Hall, Philadelphia, 2006; ramp to rear court and main entrance. Photo David Leatherbarrow.
195	Figure 8.5	William Penn's plan for Philadelphia, by General Surveyor Thomas Holme, 1683.

195	Figure 8.6	A typical alley and urban interior in Philadelphia. Photo David Leatherbarrow.
203	Figure 8.7	TWBTA, Skirkanich Hall, Philadelphia, 2006; rear court and facade. Photo Michael Moran.
196	Figure 8.8	TWBTA, Skirkanich Hall, Philadelphia, 2006; front facade detail. Photo David Leatherbarrow.
197	Figure 8.9	Le Corbusier, drawing of "The Sun, a friend and enemy." Le Corbusier and François de Pierrefeu, *La Maison des Hommes*, Paris: Plon, 1942, p. 156.
197	Figure 8.10	Towne Building, the new link building, and Moore Building; plan. Courtesy of University Archives, University of Pennsylvania.
197	Figure 8.11	Geddes, Brecher and Cunningham Architects, Harold Pender Laboratory, Philadelphia, 1958, linking Towne and Moore buildings; demolished in 2003. Courtesy of the Athenaeum, Philadelphia, Pennsylvania.
204	Figure 8.12	TWBTA, Skirkanich Hall, Philadelphia, 2006; cross-section. Courtesy of Tod Williams and Billie Tsien Architects.
198	Figure 8.13	TWBTA, Skirkanich Hall, Philadelphia, 2006; central stairway. Photo David Leatherbarrow.
198	Figure 8.14	TWBTA, Skirkanich Hall, Philadelphia, 2006; rear court bifold walls. Photo David Leatherbarrow.
198	Figure 8.15	TWBTA, Skirkanich Hall, Philadelphia, 2006; bifold wall under central stair. Photo David Leatherbarrow.
205	Figure 8.16	TWBTA, Skirkanich Hall, Philadelphia, 2006; ground plan. Courtesy of Tod Williams and Billie Tsien Architects.
199	Figure 8.17	TWBTA, Skirkanich Hall, Philadelphia, 2006; rear terrace and garden. Photo David Leatherbarrow.
206	Figure 8.18	TWBTA, Skirkanich Hall, Philadelphia, 2006; courtyard. Photo David Leatherbarrow.
199	Figure 8.19	TWBTA, Skirkanich Hall, Philadelphia, 2006; garden fountain. Photo David Leatherbarrow.
208	Figure 8.20	TWBTA, Skirkanich Hall, Philadelphia, 2006; east facade detail. Photo David Leatherbarrow.
200	Figure 8.21	TWBTA, Skirkanich Hall, Philadelphia, 2006; bay window landing. Photo David Leatherbarrow.
209	Figure 8.22	TWBTA, Skirkanich Hall, Philadelphia, 2006; bay window landing in the lower right quadrant. Photo David Leatherbarrow.
	9	**Conclusion**
210	Figure 9.1	Herbert Bayer, *Lonely Metropolitan*, 1932; photomontage. Courtesy of Metropolitan Museum of Art, New York.

David Leatherbarrow

Acknowledgments

The University of Pennsylvania was where most of the authors who have contributed to this book first came to know or know of one another. All would like to acknowledge the formative role that that university and its architecture programs played in their thinking and approach to urban architecture. What's more, if architecture can be seen as a cultural practice, and cultures obtain their most durable and eloquent embodiment in cities, then the City of Philadelphia played no less significant a role in the thinking developed in this book.

The book's chapters were initially developed as lectures in a course on urban architecture at Southeast University (SEU) in Nanjing, Jiangsu province, China. The university subsequently provided financial support for the transformation of those chapters into this publication. All contributors are very grateful for the support.

Thanks are due to the architects who gave permission for the reproduction of drawings and photographs of their work, H-Sang Seung, and the team of Tod Williams and Billie Tsien. Ada Karmi-Melamede is warmly thanked for sharing her knowledge of Heichal HaTarbut and its history, as is Amnon Rechter for granting access to the Rechter Center for Architecture Archive, and its staff, particularly Dana Gordon. Isabelle Godineau from Fondation Le Corbusier kindly provided expert assistance on the collections. José Mondragón Robles generously opened his collection of Eco Cinematografista materials, and kindly provided images of the Cinema Workers Union Building. Silpakorn University in Thailand has our thanks for its support, as do the lending institutions identified in the List of Illustrations.

Lastly, we would like to acknowledge the significant contributions of the team at Artifice Press, Ludovica Bellomaria, Stephen Mitchell, Rachel Pfleger, and, of course, Anna Danby.

© 2023 SJH Group, the architects and authors.

This book is published by Artifice Press Limited, a company registered in England and Wales with company number 11182108. Artifice Press Limited is an imprint within the SJH Group. Copyright is owned by the SJH Group. All rights reserved.

Artifice Press Limited
The Maple Building
39–51 Highgate Road
London NW5 1RT
United Kingdom
—
+44 (0)20 8371 4047
office@artificeonline.com
www.artificeonline.com

Creative direction and design by Rachel Pfleger
Printed in Lithuania by Kopa

ISBN 978-1-911339-50-2

British Library in Cataloguing Data. A CIP record for this book is available from the British Library.

Neither this publication nor any part of it may be reproduced, stored in a retrieval system or transmitted in any form or by any means, electronic, mechanical, photocopying, recording or otherwise, without the prior permission of the SJH Group or the appropriately accredited copyright holder.

All information in this publication is verified to the best of the author's and publisher's ability. However, Artifice Press Limited and the SJH Group do not accept responsibility for any loss arising from reliance on it. Where opinion is expressed, it is that of the author and does not necessarily coincide with the editorial views of the publisher. The publishers have made all reasonable efforts to trace the copyright owners of the images reproduced herein, and to provide an appropriate acknowledgment in the book.

Front cover | Rechter-Zarhi-Peri Architects in collaboration with Avraham Karavan, Yaakov Garden, Tel Aviv, 1965; garden's second-story view toward concert hall. Photo Studio Keren Or. Courtesy of Rechter Center for Architecture Archive, Tel Aviv.